America's Tax Revolution

How It Will Affect You

ABOUT THE AUTHORS

The American Institute of Certified Public Accountants (AICPA) is the premier national professional organization for CPAs, with more than 328,000 members in public practice, industry, government, and education.

Martin A. Sullivan has a B.A. in Economics from Harvard University and a Ph.D. in Economics from Northwestern University. He has served as an economist for the Office of Tax Analysis of the U.S. Treasury Department and for the Staff of the Joint Committee on Taxation of the U.S. Congress. He is now an economic consultant and an Adjunct Scholar at the American Enterprise Institute.

America's Tax Revolution
How It Will Affect You

THE AMERICAN INSTITUTE OF CERTIFIED PUBLIC ACCOUNTANTS

AND

MARTIN A. SULLIVAN, PH.D.

John Wiley & Sons, Inc.
New York • Chichester • Brisbane • Toronto • Singapore

ACKNOWLEDGMENTS

The AICPA Tax Division acknowledges the efforts of the Consumption Taxation Task Force and the Tax Policy and Planning Committee in the preparation of this book.

Consumption Taxation Task Force
Byrle M. Abbin, Chair
Gary Cesnik
Edmund Outslay
Lawrence Zommick
Phillip Tatarowicz

Tax Policy and Planning Committee (1994-95)
Steven J. Leifer, Chair
Victor E. Barton
Lorence L. Bravenec
Stanley E. Heyman
Brent H. Hill
James A. Moore
James E. Power
William L. Raby
Judyth A. Swingen
Donna M. Zerbo

Tax Executive Committee (1994-95)
Deborah Walker, Chair
Harvey L. Coustan
Ira Bergman
Rick G. Betts
Robert L. Holman
William F. Huber
David A. Lifson
Lorin D. Luchs
C. Ellen MacNeil
Michael E. Mares
Dan L. Mendelson
Eileen J. O'Connor
Robert M. Pielech
Jay Starkman
Samuel P. Starr

AICPA Tax Division Staff
Gerald W. Padwe, Vice President-Tax
Edward S. Karl, Director
Carol B. Ferguson, Technical Manager

Special acknowledgment is given to Byrle Abbin, Chair, Consumption Taxation Task Force, for his effort and dedication to this project.

FOREWORD

There is a great debate currently preoccupying the minds of the American people, and that debate is none other than the one about taxes—current taxes, revolutionary taxes, flat taxes, consumption taxes. The discussion has been raging in Congress, in the media, and in America's public and private arenas. But what exactly do all these proposals, projections, potential results, and scenarios mean to the American citizen—and who, in fact, is this American citizen? The variables are extensive and complex: a diversity of proposals, with many nuances and varieties, and a diversity of American citizens, with all of our nuances and varieties. Clearly, there is a maze of possible combinations to be explored.

We don't yet know which of the proposals—or which parts of them—may come into existence; nor exactly how that would affect us. But what we do know is that if fundamental tax reform does become a reality, it will have definite real-life effects and consequences—some good, some bad—on all of us.

In current discussions and publications regarding the proposed reforms, proponents and opponents often project results and ramifications that reflect their own opinions. It is not easy to separate fact from opinion, nor to determine the effect of any or all of the conceivable scenarios on our own lives. How, then, can we come to a reasonable conclusion about the effect of these changes on our future? And consequently, how can we make a difference in the political process that will determine that future?

What we need is an objective presentation of the various tax proposals in discussion, a presentation that states the facts as they are, impartially, and without subjective input, thus allowing us to digest the information and make up our own minds about the consequences.

America's Tax Revolution: How It Will Affect You does precisely that. Authored by the American Institute of Certified Public Accountants (AICPA) and Martin A. Sullivan, Ph.D, this book combines the professional tax and accounting expertise of the AICPA with the economic insight of Dr. Sullivan. It is a clear and direct discussion of the various proposals being debated, while remaining impartial. Not only does this book review and analyze the competing proposals, it also provides us, the American people, with examples of the possible consequences on our finances of each proposal, and how these consequences would vary depending on our economic situations.

This information is essential—to the individual taxpayer, business owners, advisors, and professionals—to gain an unbiased understanding of the issues, to derive a personal assessment of the issues, and to determine exactly how our personal situation, as well as the situation of other Americans, will be changed. The last item is most important, because once that determination is made, Americans will, as always, participate in the political system by making our voices heard—at the ballot box.

—Muriel F. Siebert

Contents

PREFACE

There are major issues involved in completely revising federal tax policy. This is particularly true with regard to the proposals discussed in this book. In reading this book, and in thinking about the revolutionary changes contemplated, the following are some points to ponder, and some pros and cons that let you be the judge.

POINTS TO PONDER

Issues Concerning Households and Individuals

- How should you adjust for financial planning?
- What about estate and gift taxes under the new system?
- Could your returns on existing investments be adversely affected by incomplete transition relief?
- Should some types of investments not favored under the current system (for example, high-dividend stocks, CDs) be given added weight in your personal portfolio?
- What about some types of tax-favored investments (like municipals, whole life insurance)? Should these receive less weight?
- If there's no deduction for charitable giving, should your contributions be accelerated before the effective date?
- Should your charitable giving be reduced over the long term?
- If there's no deduction for state and local income and property taxes, should you reconsider relocation decisions since cost differences between low- and high-tax jurisdictions may increase?

Issues Concerning Businesses

- What about new business recordkeeping and reporting rules?
- How should your business computer software and information be changed?
- Should businesses reconfigure their multinational operations that are currently structured around current rules?
- How are plans for business reorganizations affected by the change to a replacement consumption tax?
- Given that business interest is unlikely to be deductible under these taxes, should businesses be reducing their indebtedness?
- Since fringe benefits probably won't be a deductible business expense, should businesses continue to provide health insurance to their employees?
- Should partnerships and sole proprietorships consider incorporating now that they are subject to the same tax as corporations?
- With all the forms of savings tax favored under a consumption tax, should pension plans be altered?
- Will taxpayers delay capital purchases until the date the new system takes effect to be able to expense their purchases?

Economic Issues

- Will taxpayers defer recognition of capital gains until the effective date?
- What effect will the flat tax or the other consumption taxes have on employment, wages, inflation, and productivity?
- How long will it take for any positive effects of the new tax system take hold?
- What effect will a new tax system have on income distribution?
- What effect will a replacement consumption tax have on federal revenues?
- If there is a shortfall or excess in revenue from the predicted levels, will there be automatic adjustments in tax rates?

- Will preenactment behavioral responses significantly reduce revenues in the early years of the tax?
- What effect will a replacement consumption tax have on real estate values?

Issues Concerning Tax Administration

- Will the Internal Revenue Service administer the new tax?
- What are the additional, if any, administrative costs of transitioning into a new consumption tax?
- What new audit procedures need to be developed?
- How will new audit procedures be coordinated with the states?
- What new forms and instructions need to be produced?
- What new regulations need to be written?

Issues Concerning State and Local Governments

- Would a national sales tax force states to conform to federal rules?
- How would states administer their income taxes in the absence of the federal income tax?
- How would state taxes be figured without reference to the federal return?
- Would states need to increase their income tax audits?
- If a replacement consumption tax reduces property values, what effect will this have on property tax revenue?

Political Issues

- Will possible "losers" under a consumption tax (for example, realtors, insurance companies, unincorporated businesses) be accommodated with special tax relief?
- Is there any room for compromise on the notion of totally replacing the current income tax system?
- Could a new consumption tax be used to reduce income tax rates?
- Could a new consumption tax be used to just eliminate the corporate tax?

xvi   America's Tax Revolution—How It Will Affect You

Some Pros and Cons: You Be the Judge

Issue: The new tax proposals, especially the flat tax, would shift the tax burden.

Commentary: Since the top 5 percent of taxable returns provide nearly 50 percent of federal income taxes, and the top 1 percent contribute almost 30 percent, a system using a flat tax would probably shift a large portion of the tax burden downward.

On the One Hand: The U.S Treasury contends that replacing the current system with a value-added tax could result in a long-term shift in the burden of taxation from high-income taxpayers to middle- and low-income families.

On the Other Hand: The flat tax levies the same percent tax on every income level. Thus, those who earn more money will pay more in taxes and those who earn a lower income will pay less in taxes. Those earning low- or middle-income wages receive the largest reduction in average tax rates because the family allowance involves a large portion of their total income. Some experts have pointed out that, over the last several years, high-income taxpayers have seen their portion of the tax burden steadily rise.

Issue: Under the individual flat tax, the mortgage interest deduction would be eliminated.

Commentary: While personal interest has been eliminated as an itemized deduction, the deduction for mortgage interest has been retained. This deduction has been viewed as a significant incentive for home ownership.

On the One Hand: Eliminating the home mortgage deduction would raise the cost of owning a home and lead to a decline in home values. One study suggests that a flat tax would raise the cost of debt financing and equity financing.

On the Other Hand: Under a flat tax system, interest rates will decline. Thus, what homeowners lose in the interest deduction, they gain in lower interest rates. According to one study, a family earning $50,000 with a mortgage interest deduction of about $3,800 could save nearly $600 in taxes from the deduction. However, a drop in interest rates could more than make up for the loss of that deduction.

Issue: The flat tax proposal would eliminate the charitable contribution deduction.

Commentary: The current tax system is designed to encourage charitable giving.

On the One Hand: Some studies have suggested that lower marginal tax rates and doing away with the charitable deduction would cause charitable giving to decline.

On the Other Hand: Most people give to charities because they want to help others, they believe in the cause, or they feel a sense of social responsibility. Most people don't give to charities solely to reduce their federal taxes.

Issue: Municipal bonds would lose their tax advantage.

Commentary: Under the flat tax, individuals would no longer be taxed on their interest income. This means that while state and local bonds would remain tax exempt, interest on other bonds (for example, U.S. Treasury, corporate) would also become tax exempt.

On the One Hand: The tax advantages provided to state and local bonds under current law permits them to pay lower interest than those that are taxable. The loss of this advantage would force states to seek alternative ways to finance their capital projects.

On the Other Hand: Eliminating the tax advantage would put an end to the unwise practice of using the federal tax system to subsidize spending by state and local governments.

Issue: Employer-provided fringe benefits would not be deductible.

Commentary: Under the current system, wage and salary income is taxed but fringe benefits are not. This would remain the same under the flat tax. However, employers would no longer be able to deduct their costs for these fringe benefits.

On the One Hand: This might be a disincentive for employers to provide certain key fringes. Some experts contend that, in the case of employer-provided health insurance, the loss of the deduction could cause an increase in the price of the insurance.

On the Other Hand: The tax subsidy for such items as employer-provided health insurance is inefficient and unfair because most of the benefits go to people who least need them. The current system encourages wasteful spending on health care and penalizes employers and employees who keep health costs under control.

FURTHER READING

For additional reference, please consult *Changing America's Tax System: A Guide to the Debate*. Also written by the AICPA and Martin A. Sullivan, Ph.D. and published by John Wiley & Sons, Inc., *Changing America's Tax System* specifically addresses accounting and tax professionals.

Introduction

Choosing Sides in the Tax Revolution

Early American patriots fought a revolution in part to overcome the tyranny of taxation without representation. Thanks to their determination and sacrifice, we have representation today. But the taxation battle rages on, and it's becoming more intense. A tax revolution may lie just beyond the next election.

The nation's tax system has emerged as a major issue in this year's presidential campaign, as well as in congressional races. Earlier tax debates—over rate adjustments, special capital gains treatment, or exemption levels—seem trivial by comparison. This year's contest is wide open. It's not just how much to tax. It's whether and what.

Should we have an income tax or not?

Should we have a flat tax?

Should we exempt contributions to savings?

Should we exempt income from savings?

Should we exempt you?

Or should we squeeze you for a bigger contribution?

The stakes have been raised dramatically. Winners will have more money to spend. Losers will have less. Under some proposals, people who live off their investments will be able to live tax-free as long as they stay out of the workforce. Middle-income families living paycheck to paycheck may find themselves paying more under some proposals, less under others.

A family with one child, earning $50,000 from wages, might see their taxes reduced by nearly one-third under a major flat tax proposal. In another case, a family with most of its income from self-employment might see its tax bill rise by 80 percent under an unlimited savings allowance proposal, largely because of a new tax on business income.

The current system, by taxing income, is often criticized for penalizing work and investment—the very values many people think the nation needs more of. The tax system is so precariously laden with layer upon layer of rules that no one knows exactly what it all means. Almost no one defends it. Even accountants, who earn much of their incomes by wading through its murky intricacies, would like a simpler system.

As an alternative, there is the flat tax, along with a slew of other consumption-based tax plans. Consumption taxes could improve on the current income tax by rewarding investment. Unfortunately, they tend to be regressive, putting a heavier burden on those less able to pay and penalizing people too strapped, or too indulgent, to save.

A consumption tax might have much the same effect as repealing the annual contribution limits on individual retirement accounts. You could put as much as you like—or as much as you could afford—into savings and investments. You'd pay no tax on the money you save until it is taken out and spent; and, under some plans, you'd pay no tax on any income those investments produce.

Although a consumption tax could come in many forms, with various modifications to counter its inherent regressiveness, the current hot ticket is the flat tax. The debate over how or whether to switch to some form of flat tax became a major issue in presidential politics this year. One candidate, Steve Forbes, spent the early months of 1996 attempting to gather convention delegates with a campaign centered on replacing the current income tax—whose rates range up to 39.6 percent—with a flat 17 percent tax on the wages of the middle and upper classes.

Forbes never quite caught fire, and both Republican candidate Senator Bob Dole and President Bill Clinton are cool to the idea of massive tax reform, although Dole might favor a flatter tax. Clinton is committed to a graduated income tax.

Still, the idea of swapping out the nation's widely criticized, 83-year-old income tax continues to smolder, fanned by a series of hearings in the House Ways and Means Committee. Chairman Bill Archer vows to make this year the beginning of the end of the income tax as we know it.

Besides the flat tax as proposed by Forbes, Texas Congressman Dick Armey, and others, alternatives to the current income tax include a national retail sales tax, a value-added tax (VAT), and an individual consumption tax, such as the Unlimited Savings Allowance (USA) Tax.

While most industrialized countries have adopted consumption taxes, they typically replaced poorly functioning excise taxes on liquor, tobacco, and other commodities. No major industrialized country has ever repealed its personal or corporate income tax.

And while a major objective in the search for a new system is simplification, simplification is not simple. The transition to a new tax setup will involve enormously complex political, economic, and technical issues—no matter how simple the new system at the end of the tunnel.

The extent of the changes being considered is unprecedented. Even the sweeping tax revisions of the early- to mid-1980s are insignificant when compared to the proposals now being made to restructure the tax system. Every American will be affected by the changes.

HOW THIS BOOK CAN HELP YOU

The primary goal of this book is to give you an insight into the key consumption taxes and how they will affect you. We examine each of the proposals individually and in detail, providing a comparative analysis where relevant. Your job is to look at the proposed systems, look at the numbers, compare them with your own tax situation (present and future), and make an informed assessment about what's fair and appropriate.

If a tax revolution is coming, you need to know which side to take. The next President and the next Congress will decide whether and how to overhaul our tax system. They may represent you, or they may represent someone with other priorities. You have the right to be represented—or you have the right to remain silent.

1

Is There a Better Way?

In an effort to solve some of the stubborn problems that have grown up under the current system, economists and political leaders are proposing stunning, revolutionary changes in how the nation pays and collects taxes. Four important goals are driving the debate:

- Competitiveness: Increase business competitiveness through a build-up of capital resources.

- Simplification: Eliminate the current system's complexity.

- Fairness: Repeal of most of the special tax breaks in the current law.

- Redistribution: Redistribute the tax burden to different groups of taxpayers. Even if this were not a goal itself, it is an inevitable consequence of pursuing the first three goals. It is this point that makes the debate so divisive.

Out of Nowhere

Until now, any type of consumption or flat tax had very little chance at passage. Yet, in less than a decade, the idea rose from obscurity to celebrity. By the early 1990s, Congress began showing significant interest in consumption taxes. In the past, consumption taxes were championed mainly by business leaders interested in capital formation and by economists seeking ways to reduce the deficit or increase international competitiveness. Now, the media have entered the fray, and the general public has taken notice. There is particular interest in the proposed flat tax, with advocates claiming it's so simple that both businesses and individuals could file postcard-sized returns—an idea with enormous appeal to a general public frustrated with the current system's complexity. Adversaries, however, contend that a flat tax would trade complexity for a greater tax burden on lower-income—and possibly middle-income—taxpayers.

One key development is an emerging consensus among certain political groups about how to use consumption tax revenues. In earlier scenarios, consumption taxes were proposed as ways to increase government spending, to reduce the deficit, and even to reduce income and payroll taxes. In all those plans, rates tended to be in the single digits, and the current income tax system would largely remain intact. The old assumption was that any new consumption tax would be an add-on tax. The new model makes consumption taxes a substitute or replacement for the current system. Replacement consumption taxes, including the flat tax, could easily have tax rates exceeding 20 percent.

There is a big difference between the add-on and the replacement consumption taxes. Only a replacement consumption tax has the potential to simultaneously simplify the system and increase private saving. Add-on tax systems would further complicate an already overextended system.

THE CONSUMPTION TAX DIFFERENCE—AND WHY IT'S A PROBLEM

The key difference between an income tax and a consumption tax lies in what is not taxed. With a consumption tax, there is no tax on income you save. By providing greater rewards for saving than an income tax, replacement consumption taxes could increase private saving.

Generally, saving is something the wealthy do more than the poor. As a result, consumption taxes may place a greater overall burden on low-income households than do income taxes. Herein lies one of the major objections to the consumption tax: its potential to shift the tax burden away from high-income taxpayers onto taxpayers at the low end of the income scale, with uncertain effects on those in between. That's because under a progressive rate structure—such as we have in the current tax system—taxpayers at the top of the income scale pay the bulk of the taxes. A proportional, or flat, tax rate structure would impose the same tax rate on all taxpayers, whether high-income or low-income. In a regressive tax system, the tax, as a percentage of income, is greater for low-income households than for high-income households.

Consumption Taxes, Flat and Otherwise

There are four main types of consumption taxes to consider:

- Flat tax
- Individual consumption tax (also known as the Unlimited Savings Allowance, or USA, tax)
- Retail sales tax
- VAT (value-added tax)

The flat tax, despite a widening array of ideas claiming the name, is fundamentally a single-rate tax. Leading alternatives fall only on wages but not on capital gains or other investment income. The tax would be applied across the board to all taxpayers and would replace, not simply augment, the current income tax system.

An individual consumption tax is levied on each individual's annual consumption, measured as the difference between that individual's annual income and saving. An individual consumption tax may or may not be a flat tax.

A retail sales tax is levied on final sales by retail businesses to consumers. Imposed by almost all of the states, it is a tax familiar to most of us.

A value-added tax is levied on the value of a business' gross business receipts that remain after deducting the cost of goods and services acquired from other businesses. The major difference between this and an income tax is that the business deducts only costs paid to other businesses. Wages paid to employees, taxes paid to governments, and certain other costs wouldn't be deductible. The flat tax can be considered a form of VAT that's assessed on individuals as well as businesses.

Pressures on Consumption Taxes

There are several important differences among these types of consumption taxes. Each imposes different compliance costs, not only in terms of total cost, but also in terms of distributing these costs across taxpayer groups. Each of these taxes also imposes different administrative costs on government. Some of the taxes would certainly face vigorous opposition from the states while others probably would not. The taxes also differ in how the public perceives them. Some are highly visible, separately stated, regressive taxes on consumers, while others are considered "hidden taxes" imposed on businesses.

Consumption taxes also vary in how well they can accommodate efforts to give preferential treatment to certain types of products or to certain classes of taxpayers. As a matter of pure tax policy, the broadest consumption tax base would be preferable. Special exceptions that narrow the tax base cut a consumption tax's economic efficiency in three different ways:

1. Exceptions distort both consumption and production as consumers and businesses shift behavior to avoid the tax.

2. Revenue lost to special exceptions has to be made up through higher tax rates.

3. Exceptions make the tax more difficult and expensive to administer.

Still, exceptions may be unavoidable. They're common to all consumption taxes now in existence as well as to our present income tax system. As a matter of political acceptability, a tax that can accommodate special interest provisions ultimately may prove more saleable.

THE FLAT TAX'S SWEEPING BROOM

The issue is bigger than just adopting a consumption or a flat tax. Involved here is the total exchange of one system for another. Out with the income tax; in with the consumption tax. The public is taking a major interest in the flat tax because of the far-reaching pocketbook issues at stake. No taxpayer would go untouched. Like other consumption tax proposals, the flat tax would sweep individual and corporate income taxes into the dustbin of history. Standing in their place would be a new, broad-based consumption tax on both business and individuals.

The flat tax would differ radically from today's income taxes. In broad terms:

• The flat tax would completely revamp the rate structure. A single rate would replace the current progressive tax rate schedule.

• The flat tax would greatly expand the rate base, eliminating numerous credits, exclusions, and deductions (although it would simultaneously create new exemptions for savings).

• The flat tax would, say its proponents, dramatically simplify the tax system. This last feature is a major reason for the flat tax's appeal; most people—experts included—find the current tax law often incomprehensible.

While consumption taxes have the potential to simplify calculations and recordkeeping for many taxpayers, it's less clear whether they would simplify, or further complicate, matters in terms of administration and compliance costs.

COLLAPSING COMPLICATED CONTROVERSIES

Some of the complexity we suffer now is unique to the income tax. Switching to a pure consumption tax would eliminate it. This is particularly true for taxation of business income, as well as income from saving and investment. Look at depreciation, for example. Most consumption tax plans would replace depreciation, now claimed over periods ranging from 3 years to 50 years, with immediate capital-cost write-offs—in effect, universal "expensing." That eliminates often difficult computations and neatly disposes of the constant controversy and dispute over what business development costs to capitalize.

Inventory costs, under most plans, also would be immediately deducted when those costs were incurred, so there would be no need to determine inventory levels from year to year and match costs with the goods actually sold. Gone too, along with corporate income tax, would be the complex corporate alternative minimum tax on accelerated depreciation and other preference items. Then, there are notoriously complex rules dealing with corporate liquidations, reorganizations, and distributions; they too would become almost entirely obsolete.

How About Personal Savings?

Under a consumption tax, most income generated by personal saving (interest, for example) would be effectively exempt from tax. That eliminates the need for the complicated rules and preferences for various categories of saving by individuals. Complex rules on pensions, IRAs, tax-exempt bonds, annuities, and life insurance would no longer exist. They would be irrelevant, because all saving would receive the ultimate tax-favored treatment—no tax at all.

COMPLEXITIES THAT WON'T GO AWAY

Some issues would remain complex even under a consumption tax system. Take, for example, the problem of distinguishing between certain business and personal expenses. Business meals, home-office deductions, and education expenses, for example, would remain as contentious issues under a consumption tax, and all the accompanying rules and regulations would linger.

Some of the complexity relates to special tax breaks and the limitations on those breaks. That's often a by-product of a political system that puts more emphasis on equity than simplicity—not to mention that it finds the tax code a handy way to promote a wide variety of social and economic objectives.

Many consumption tax proposals, especially those of the flat tax variety, include significant base broadening. Under Congressman Dick Armey's proposal, for example, employer-provided benefits, home mortgage interest, charitable contributions, and state and local taxes—all now exempt from the federal income tax—would be added to the tax base.

2

REGRESSION: FINDING AND FIXING THE CONSUMPTION TAX BURDEN

While consumption taxes often are criticized for placing undue burdens on people with low incomes, the hardest hit segment may often extend well into middle-income populations as well. Two features push the tax burden into those segments:

- Consumption as a percentage of annual income is greater for low-income households than for high-income households.
- Consumption taxes generally don't have progressive rates.

A tax system is considered "regressive" if low-income households pay a greater percentage of their income than high-income households. The reverse is true in a "progressive" tax system. A system is considered "proportional" if everybody pays the same percentage of income.

A consumption tax falls heaviest on people who spend, through choice or necessity, most of their income on current consumption. That group includes many individuals and families who wouldn't be considered poor but who are struggling to make ends meet.

Regressivity is a consumption taxation's Achilles' heel. Although the burden on low-income people may be mitigated by government transfer payments and other mechanisms outside the tax system, the tax itself is regressive. No matter how effective any consumption tax might be in increasing saving, improving the trade balance, and reducing complexity, this tax might never become law solely because it is regressive. To be politically viable, the basic structure of any consumption tax may have to be substantially modified or supplemented to wring out its regressiveness. Even that might not be enough for a consumption tax designed to replace the current income tax. To gain acceptance, it might have to be as progressive as current law. Counter-regressivity measures are among the most important design issues in consumption tax systems. A wide variety of options are available. All of them, however, add greatly to administrative and compliance costs.

In addition, efforts to ease the regressive tax burden on low-income people can instead tend to drop the burden in the laps of a hard-pressed middle class. Measures to lift the load from those on the lower rungs of the income ladder can easily deposit most of the load on the next-higher rungs.

REPAIRING REGRESSIVENESS

Since consumption taxes are unlikely to gain much support in their pure state, tax designers have come up with several ways to make them less regressive. Those measures take three general forms:

- Using progressive tax rates
- Exempting necessities
- Providing tax credits and transfer payments

These measures, though, add complexity. Only a personal consumption tax, such as the USA tax, can take advantage of a progressive rate structure. In that case, however, almost any degree of progressivity can be achieved. Large personal exemptions, for example, could render tens of millions of households tax-free. Rates could be slightly or steeply progressive. But figuring the net savings deduction under a personal consumption tax would be a major chore, creating substantial administrative and compliance burdens. This would make it the most complex of all major types of consumption taxes.

Untaxed Necessities

The most common way to counter a regressive consumption tax is by exempting products considered necessities. Most VATs in other countries, as well as most state sales taxes, provide tax relief for food, health care, housing, and other necessities.

But creating preferences for certain types of consumption has a downside in the form of increased complexity and inefficiency. Administrative and compliance costs go up. And consumers may rearrange their buying patterns to avoid tax, thus creating distortions and inefficiencies in the economy.

In addition, given the need to reach certain revenue targets, any exception provided for some items raises the tax on other items. Those higher tax rates further distort consumption and eat into the consumption tax's economic benefits.

Perhaps the most disappointing aspect of exempting necessities is that this type of tax relief doesn't do much to reduce the regressive nature of the tax. Although exempting food may help the poor more than others, a substantial portion, if not most, of the dollar benefit still goes to middle- and upper-income households.

Direct Aid to Low-Income People

Another way to offset a consumption tax's regressiveness is with tax credits or transfer payments to low-income households. Relief could take a variety of forms—expanding the earned income tax credit (EITC), a payroll tax credit, a broad-based refundable tax credit, or transfer payments, for example.

The earned income tax credit, which gives refundable tax credits to low-income working families, is among the more attractive options, since the administrative structure is already in place. Also, since it's refundable, the credit can provide benefits to families who don't pay income tax. The major shortcoming of the credit, as it is currently set up, is that it does nothing to help the nonworking poor.

Another interesting option is to let workers claim payroll taxes as a credit against comsumption taxes (a feature of the Nunn-Domenici proposal, which we'll examine later). Currently, employers and employees split the payroll tax, each paying 7.65 percent on the first $62,700 (1996 level) of wages and 1.45 percent on all wages above that amount. Given this rate structure, and the absence of deductions and exemptions, the payroll tax is highly regressive. A payroll tax credit would apply to more workers than the EITC, broadening its coverage. In addition, the credit can provide relief without refunds for many low-income working families because the payroll tax applies to every dollar of wages while the income tax only applies after personal exemptions and deductions. If the credit is not refundable, it can avoid encountering some of the fraud problems that plague the EITC.

However, a payroll tax credit still doesn't help the poor who are unemployed. Nor would it relieve the burden on certain low-income retirees who depend on small amounts of dividends and interest income. An alternative to a payroll tax credit or an expansion of the EITC would be a new refundable credit for low-income people. Ideally, the credit would be equal or proportional to the consumption tax burden on low-income households. Unfortunately, millions of low-income households, which don't now file tax returns, would be required to file, greatly expanding the administrative and compliance costs.

Or the government could increase transfer payments to low-income households. Actually, some transfer payments, including social security and federal employee retirement benefits, would likely increase automatically. With the imposition of a business consumption tax, consumer price increases would trigger benefit increases in programs that have inflation adjustment mechanisms. If a household gets all its income in the form of indexed transfer payments, the household will be fully insulated from the effects of the tax. A 10 percent rise in the price level due to a 10 percent VAT, for example, will be matched by a 10 percent increase in government support.

Many transfer payments, however, are not indexed for inflation, and many low-income taxpayers bearing the burden of a consumption tax may not be receiving any significant assistance from the government. Unemployment benefits and Aid to Families with Dependent Children (AFDC), for example, are not indexed for inflation. To make up the shortfall, the government could increase nonindexed transfer payments as the new tax is imposed.

ARE CONSUMPTION TAXES TRULY REGRESSIVE?

It's important to recognize that consumption taxes, viewed in a broader perspective, may not be as regressive as they first appear. Even before lawmakers add measures to moderate the tax's regressive tendencies, several other forces already may be at work on the problem:

- While the tax itself may be regressive, that burden may be offset by existing government transfer programs favoring low-income families. The focus on relative tax burdens may be misplaced if the new tax spurs economic growth and makes everybody better off than they were.

- The consumption tax may be closer to the present system than it appears, because the present system may be less progressive than it appears. This conclusion is based on the idea (not shared by all economists) that the corporate income tax actually falls on consumers, in the form of higher prices, rather than on the corporations' shareholders.

- While a consumption tax may be regressive in terms of the tax burden on annual income, it may be much less regressive when it's viewed in terms of lifetime income. The tax you pay during your working years might be offset by freedom from tax in your nonworking years. The result, some economists believe, is that a consumption tax actually is fairer in the long run than an income tax.

The tax system has a major impact on the distribution of income, but so do a wide variety of government programs. Social Security, Medicare, Medicaid, Food Stamps, and Aid to Families with Dependent Children (AFDC) are just some of the federal government's spending programs that collectively amount to a massive redistribution of wealth across income classes and across generations. Some argue that it is misleading and arbitrary to focus attention on the distributional effects of the tax system without looking at the uses of government revenues as well. For example, in analyses of the "fairness" of the tax system, it is common practice to include refundable earned income tax credits (Internal Revenue Code Section 32) in the distributional analysis, but AFDC payments (not in the code)—though in many ways functionally equivalent—are not included. Certainly one's views about the appropriateness of a heavy tax burden on the poor should take into account the use of those revenues. A greater tax burden on low-income households may be more tolerable if those revenues are used to provide food, medical care, and education to the poor. Nevertheless, the notion of including both taxes *and* *transfers* in distributional analyses has received remarkably little attention.

The Growth Factor

Changes in tax law simultaneously may affect the overall *amount* of national income as well as its *distribution*. In its official distributional analyses, the federal government generally holds economic growth constant. (The main reason for this is that there is a great deal of dispute and uncertainty about the impact of taxes on the overall economy.) Thus, government distribution analyses assume tax policy is a zero-sum game.

Despite the difficulties with precise quantification, most economists acknowledge that a replacement consumption tax will increase economic growth—particularly in the long run. Many would consider it especially misleading to assume economic growth will be unaffected in a distributional analysis of a replacement consumption tax. Even if the relative burden of some income classes increases, it may be possible for all income classes to be better off if all incomes rise sufficiently.

The Incidence Factor

It is critical to recognize that the burden or "incidence" of a tax is not always on those writing checks to the government. For example, there is much dispute about whether the burden of the corporate income tax is borne by shareholders of corporations. To some degree, the burden may be shared by the owners of all businesses (because rates of return are driven lower), by business customers (because prices rise), or by employees (because wages fall) as a result of the tax.

For consumption taxes, the general consensus among economists is that the tax is passed forward to consumers in the form of higher prices. There is one important caveat, however; if the Federal Reserve does not "accommodate" the introduction of a consumption tax with an increase in the money supply, it is unlikely prices can rise. In this case, economists believe the burden of the tax would be passed backward to employees in the form of lower wages. If this were to occur, consumption taxes would still be regressive because wages account for a larger percentage of income among low-income households than high-income households. Still, there is an important difference between a consumption tax that increases prices and a consumption tax that would reduce wages: the nonworking poor who did not receive government support indexed to inflation would bear a considerably lower diminished burden under a consumption tax that resulted in lower wages. Thus, there must always be much uncertainty about how the burden would be shared among low-income households because it depends so much on the actions of an independent Federal Reserve.

It is also important to note that the substantial uncertainty about the incidence of the corporate income tax can have a major impact on the consumption tax debate. Almost all major consumption tax proposals call for elimination of the corporate income tax. If the burden of this tax is perceived to be on capital, it is a progressive tax. This is the current view of the Treasury Department. On the other hand, some commentators believe the burden of the corporation is passed along—at least partially—to the consumer in the form of higher prices. The more the corporate income tax is considered progressive, the more difficult it will be for new consumption tax proposals to maintain distributional neutrality to current law.

Redefining Regressiveness

Perhaps the notion that is most damaging to the idea that consumption taxes are regressive is recognition that fairness should not be evaluated by comparing taxes paid as a percentage of annual income. The problem with using annual income as a measure of economic well-being is that many households with low annual incomes are not really poor. Many individuals with significant wealth earn relatively little current income. Sometimes this is due to transitions in and out of the workforce (career switching, child rearing, temporary layoffs). In other cases, relatively well-off individuals may earn low incomes because they have not yet entered the workforce (such as graduate students) or they have retired. Trying to alleviate the burden of these individuals should not receive the same priority as families with similar incomes and no wealth, but this type of distinction is not often made in distribution analyses.

It is sometimes advocated that annual consumption rather than annual income is a better measure of economic well-being. Some argue that each individual should be taxed on consumption rather than on income because income is what one "puts into" the economy while consumption is what one "takes out." The more accepted argument is that wealth or lifetime income are better measures of economic well-being than annual income, and consumption is a good proxy for measuring wealth or lifetime income. Although there is some dissent, the notion that lifetime income is a better approximation of economic well-being has wide acceptance by economists. The major issue is not so much with the concept but with the practical application of the concept. It is much more difficult to measure lifetime income than annual income. Despite considerable uncertainty about the details, there is little doubt that any movement away from annual income and toward lifetime income as a measure of economic well-being will make consumption taxes appear considerably less regressive.

3

FLAT TAX FUNDAMENTALS

Perhaps in part because even its name suggests simplicity and fairness, the flat tax is the most talked-about candidate to replace the complicated, seemingly unfair income tax system we have now. Flat tax plans, along with the Nunn-Domenici USA Tax discussed later in this book, and the retail sales tax are the major consumption tax proposals currently on the table. The leading flat tax plans are those advanced by Congressman Richard Armey and Senator Richard Shelby (the Flat Tax), and by publisher Steve Forbes (Forbes Flat Tax).

Although the flat tax is often assumed to be a flat-rate income tax, it's actually a type of value-added tax collected from both businesses and individuals. Under the Armey-Shelby version of this plan, value added from labor is collected from individuals in the form of a wage tax. All other value added is collected from business using a VAT modified to allow deductions for wages. This tax starts with a 20 percent transition rate but then moves to a flat rate of 17 percent for both individuals and businesses. For individuals, the deductions we're so used to, such as those for mortgage interest, charitable contributions, and state and local taxes, are gone. The child care and other credits are gone, too, at least under the Armey-Shelby plan we're focusing on here.

Other flat tax proposals would keep a few of those popular deductions. The Forbes' plan eliminates the same deductions for interest, charity, and tax payments, but, unlike Armey-Shelby, it keeps the earned income tax credit. The USA Tax also retains some basic personal deductions but uses a progressive, rather than a flat, rate scale.

14

ARMEY-SHELBY PLAN (THE FLAT TAX)

The Armey-Shelby Flat Tax plan is unlike any that has ever been implemented. As a consumption tax, the Flat Tax would eliminate the bias against saving that is so prominent in the current tax system. It also would eliminate dozens of special interest rules. Its advocates point to the Flat Tax as a giant step toward tax simplicity.

What The Flat Tax Would Tax

Under the Flat Tax, individuals would pay at a flat 17 percent rate (20 percent initially). Included in your base would be wages and pensions, but not fringe benefits or income earned abroad. All your capital income, including interest, dividends, and capital gains, also would go untaxed, even if you spend the proceeds on consumer products. If you earn $30,000 from investments, you can celebrate by using it to buy a car without incurring a Flat Tax.

What about your itemized deductions and credits? The answer is very simple. Every itemized deduction and tax credit you're allowed under current tax law would disappear. Besides cutting out deductions for mortgage interest, charity, and state and local taxes, the Flat Tax would eliminate:

- Scholarship and fellowship income exclusion
- Exclusion of employee awards
- Casualty and theft loss deduction
- Child care credit
- Earned income credit
- Credit for elderly and disabled
- Additional standard deduction for blind and elderly

While the dependency deduction would remain, the personal exemption would be dropped: A childless couple wouldn't be entitled to personal exemption deductions found under current law. Standard deductions and dependency deductions would be considerably higher, however, so large numbers of taxpayers may be removed from the tax rolls.

THE FORBES FLAT TAX

Except for keeping the earned income credit, the Forbes Flat Tax would be virtually identical. It would eliminate the same popular deductions and exempt the same investment income. It also would include a similar tax on business income (discussed later), which would eliminate business deductions for most fringe benefits. The major difference between his plan and Armey-Shelby is that Forbes would exempt more income before the tax kicks in and would use a 17 percent rate from the beginning rather starting with a 20 percent phase-in rate.

STANDARD FLAT TAX DEDUCTIONS

The standard deductions (projected for 1996 with indexing for inflation thereafter) for the Armey-Shelby Flat Tax are as follows:

Basic standard deduction	Amount
Married filing jointly	$21,400
Head of household	$14,000
Individual	$10,700
Married filing separately	$10,700

In addition to the basic standard deduction, you'd get a $5,000 additional deduction for each dependent.

The Family of Four

To illustrate how the Flat Tax is figured, let's look at how much the Ryerson family of four would pay in 1996 under the Flat Tax and under the current income tax.

Flat Tax		
Wages		$70,000
Less: Basic standard deduction	$21,400	
Dependency deduction (2 × $5,000)	$10,000	$31,400
Taxable wages		$38,600
Flat tax at 20%		$ 7,720
Income tax under current system		$ 9,655

In this case, the Flat Tax would put an extra $1,935 in the Ryerson's bank account. Their saving would be less dramatic, however, if the Ryersons were able to claim itemized deductions or a child care credit or use other tax-saving provisions in the current system.

Let's jump ahead to 1998, when the 17 percent rate would apply, and look at how the Flat Tax would affect various taxpayers with incomes ranging from $20,000 up to $200,000. (Note that the basic standard deduction and the personal allowance for dependents would be adjusted for inflation.)

Example 1:

Tom Abbott: single

Earnings from wages: $20,000

Pays a Flat Tax of $1,471, figured as follows:

Wages		$20,000
Less: Basic standard deduction	$11,350	
Taxable wages		$ 8,650
Tax (17%)		$ 1,471
Income tax under current system		$ 1,958

Example 2:

Mr. and Mrs. Blair: married

Earnings from wages: $40,000; plus interest from bank account: $500

Pay a Flat Tax of $2,941, figured as follows:

Wages		$40,000
Less: Basic standard deduction	$22,700	
Taxable wages		$17,300
Tax (17%)		$ 2,941
Income tax under current system		$ 4,212

Note that the interest is not included in their Flat Tax computation since it is savings. Also, as in Example 1, no exemption deduction is allowed, since there were no dependents in either situation.

Both Abbott and the Blairs pay less under the Flat Tax than under the current rate structure. The Flat Tax saves Abbott almost $500 and saves the Blairs $1,271.

Example 3:

Mr. and Mrs. Corum: married with one child

Earnings from wages: $50,000

Pay a Flat Tax of $3,740, figured as follows:

Wages		$50,000
Less: Basic standard deduction	$22,700	
Dependency allowance:	$ 5,300	$28,000

Taxable wages	$22,000
Tax (17%)	$ 3,740
Income tax under current system	$ 5,232

Like Abbott and the Blairs, the Corums would pay less under the Flat Tax. In all three examples, the basic Flat Tax deductions and dependency allowances leave more than half their wages untaxed.

Example 4:

Mr. and Mrs. Drake: married with two children

Earnings from wages: $75,000; dividends and interest: $2,500

Other expenses: $3,200 to various charities; $11,500 mortgage interest; $5,500 in property taxes; and $3,000 for state income taxes.

Pay a Flat Tax of $7,089, figured as follows:

Wages		$75,000
Less: Basic standard deduction	$22,700	
Dependency allowance:	$10,600	$33,300
Taxable wages		$41,700
Tax (17%)		$ 7,089
Income tax under current system		$ 6,643

Using the current tax system, itemized deductions would cut the Drakes' tax bill to $6,643. Although the itemized deductions came to more than the basic $22,700 Flat Tax standard deduction, they're no help under that system. Under the Flat Tax, they also lose the benefit of the four personal exemptions, instead getting just two dependency allowances for their children. Note, of course, that the Drakes' income includes their dividends and interest, but the Flat Tax exemption for that income is not enough to offset the loss of other deductions.

Example 5:

Mr. and Mrs. Edwards: married with three children

Earnings from wages: $100,000; dividend and interest income: $1,000

Other expenses: $5,400 to various charities; $14,500 mortgage interest; $7,600 property taxes; and $3,800 for state income taxes.

Pay a Flat Tax of $10,438, figured as follows:

Wages		$100,000
Less: Basic standard deduction	$ 22,700	
Dependency allowance:	$ 15,900	$ 38,600
Taxable wages		$ 61,400
Tax (17%)		$ 10,438
Income tax under current system		$ 9,640

The Edwards would pay less using the current tax system, since they had substantial itemized deductions and are entitled to take five personal and dependency exemptions.

YOU BE THE JUDGE: FIGURE YOUR OWN FLAT TAX

The worksheet that follows is designed to let you plug in your numbers and see how the Flat Tax would affect your own tax bill. While the worksheet uses a 20 percent rate, remember that when the Flat Tax is fully phased in, the rate would be 17 percent, and the personal allowances would be adjusted for inflation.

Flat Tax Worksheet

1. Your wages, salary, and pensions — $_____
2. Your personal allowance:
   a. $21,400 if you are married filing jointly
   b. $10,700 if you are single
   c. $14,000 if you are a head of household — $_____
3. Your dependents (not including your spouse) — _____
4. Your personal allowance for dependents (line 3 multiplied by $5,000) — $_____
5. Your total personal allowances (line 2 plus line 4) — $_____
6. Your taxable wages (line 1 less line 5) — $_____
7. Your tax (20% of line 6) — $_____

Income Tax Worksheet

After you've computed your Flat Tax, you can match it against your latest return, presumably your 1995 personal income tax return, substituting the appropriate 1996 adjusted items (standard deduction, personal exemption, overall limitation on itemized deductions, and rates) that apply in your situation. (We've provided these, as needed, here.)

STEP 1. Take your total income.

STEP 2. Figure adjusted gross income. Note: If you took an IRA deduction, you may have to refigure this amount since the phase-out amounts have been adjusted—$66,250 to $95,250 if you're married, filing jointly; otherwise, these amounts are $43,500 to $58,500.

STEP 3. Take your allowable itemized deductions or the standard deduction, whichever applies in your case.

a. 1996 standard deduction:

If you are married filing jointly, or a surviving spouse	$6,700
If you are a head of household	$5,900
If you are single	$4,000
If you are married, but filing separately	$3,350

Note: The additional standard deduction is $1,000 if you're age 65 or over, or blind and you're single. It is $800 for married persons.

b. If you are itemizing, you may have to take into account the overall limitation. If your adjusted gross income exceeds $117,950 ($58,975 if you are married filing separately), you may have to reduce a portion of your itemized deduction.

STEP 4. Take your personal and dependency exemptions: $2,550.

Note: If your income exceeds the amount listed below for your filing status, you may have to reduce or eliminate your exemptions:

Married filing jointly	$176,950
Head of household	$147,450
Single	$117,950
Married filing separately	$ 88,475

Use the following worksheet:

1. Multiply $2,550 by the number of exemptions you claimed $_____
2. Enter your adjusted gross income $_____
3. Enter the amount previously shown for your filing status _____
4. Subtract line 3 from line 2 $_____

   Note: If line 4 is more than $122,500 (more than $61,250 if you are married filing, separately), you cannot take a deduction for exemptions.

5. Divide line 4 by $2,500 ($1,250 if married filing separately)

   Note: Round off to the next higher whole number. $_____
6. Multiply line 5 by 2% (.02) and enter the result as a decimal amount _____
7. Multiple line 1 by line 6 _____
8. Deduction for exemptions (line 7 from line 1) $_____

STEP 5. Figure your taxable income. Use the appropriate Tax Rate Schedule to compute your 1996 tax.

Note: If you filed a Schedule D, use the Capital Gain Tax Worksheet if you meet the income amounts listed below for your filing status:

If your filing status is:	AND	your taxable income is:
Single		$58,150
Married filing jointly		$96,900
Married filing separately		$48,450
Head of household		$83,050

1. Enter your taxable income $_____
2. Net capital gain $_____
3. Subtract line 2 from line 1 $_____
4. Enter:
   $24,000 if single
   $40,100 if married filing jointly
   $20,050 if married filing separately
   $32,150 if head of household $_____

5. Enter the greater of line 3 or line 4 $_____

6. Subtract line 5 from line 1 $_____

7. Figure tax on amount on line 5
   (use Tax Rate Schedules below) $_____

8. Multiply line 6 by 28% (.28) $_____

9. Add Lines 7 and 8 $_____

10. Figure the tax on the amount on line 1
    (use Tax Rate Schedules on page 33) $_____

11. Take the smaller of line 9 or line 10 $_____

1996 Tax Rate Schedules

Table 1: Married individuals filing joint returns and surviving spouses

If taxable income is:	The tax is:
Not over $40,100	15% of the taxable income
Over $40,100 but not over $96,900	$6,015 plus 28% of the excess over $40,100
Over $96,900 but not over $147,700	$21,919 plus 31% of the excess over $96,900
Over $147,700 but not over $263,750	$37,667 plus 36% of the excess over $147,700
Over $263,750	$79,445 plus 39.6% of the excess over $263,750

Table 2: Heads of households

If taxable income is:	The tax is:
Not over $32,150	15% of the taxable income
Over $32,150 but not over $83,050	$4,822.50 plus 28% of the excess over $32,150
Over $83,050 but not over $134,500	$19,047.50 plus 31% of the excess over $83,050
Over $134,500 but not over $263,750	$35,024 plus 36% of the excess over $134,500
Over $263,750	$81,554 plus 39.6% of the excess over $263,750

Table 3: Unmarried individuals (other than surviving spouses and heads of households)

If taxable income is:	The tax is:
Not over $24,000	15% of the taxable income
Over $24,000 but not over $58,150	$3,600 plus 28% of the excess over $24,000
Over $58,150 but not over $121,300	$13,162 plus 31% of the excess over $58,150
Over $121,300 but not over $263,750	$32,738.50 plus 36% of the excess over $121,300
Over $263,750	$84,020.50 plus 39.6% of the excess over $263,750

Table 4: Married individuals filing separate returns

If taxable income is:	The tax is:
Not over $20,050	15 percent of the taxable income
Over $20,050 but not over $48,450	$3,007.50 plus 28% of the excess over $20,050
Over $48,450 but not over $73,850	$10,959.50 plus 31% of the excess over $48,450
Over $73,850 but not over $131,875	$18,833.50 plus 36% of the excess over $73,850
Over $131,875	$39,722.50 plus 39.6% of the excess over $131,875

STEP 6. Finally, compare the amount of your tax figured under the Flat Tax with the amount figured using the current tax system.

Of course, even if the Flat Tax would cost you money, the lengthy exercise required to prove it may make the Flat Tax look like an improvement.

THE FLAT TAX ON BUSINESS

A special business Flat Tax would be imposed on all corporate and noncorporate businesses. Even "flow-through" entities, such as sole proprietorships, partnerships, and S corporations that are not now subject to an entity level tax, would be subject to the tax along with regular corporations. The business tax base, referred to as "gross active income," starts with gross business receipts and has deductions for:

- Costs of doing business
- Wages and compensation paid, including contributions to pension (but not other fringe benefits)
- Purchase of equipment

No other deductions would be allowed. Credits also would be eliminated, making the business Flat Tax, like the individual Flat Tax, noteworthy for what it excludes. Some of the tax credits eliminated under the Flat Tax are:

- Research tax credit
- Energy tax credits
- Rehabilitation tax credit
- Low-income housing credit
- Tax credit for orphan drug research

The flat tax is on domestic operations. Switching to a flat tax system would change the United States taxation basis to a territorial system from a worldwide system.

The basic operation of the Business Flat Tax is illustrated as follows:

Gross receipts		$100,000
Less: Cost of doing business	$ 20,000	
Capital expenditures	$ 10,000	
Employee compensation	$ 40,000	
Total costs		$ 70,000
Tax base		$ 30,000
Tax (17%)		$ 5,100

Since capital purchases would be expensed, there would no longer be any depreciation deductions. However, you might expect generous transition relief that allows depreciation deductions on capital in place before the enactment date. Transition rules, while making the change more fair, could make it much less simple.

Capital Formation vs. Fairness

Flat Tax advocates point out that since it exempts income from capital, it entirely eliminates the bias against capital formation in general under current law. Others, however, raise the equity issue with regard to allowing capital income to go untaxed under the Flat Tax. Is it fair to tax earnings from someone's labors while exempting the earnings from investments and savings? In any case, to the extent the current system is considered as an impediment to saving and capital formation, the Flat Tax could foster increases in productivity, wages, competitiveness, and economic growth.

The major impediment to enacting the Flat Tax in its current form is the view that this tax, like other consumption taxes, is regressive. Critics contend that the tax burden would be shifted toward low- and middle-income taxpayers, while proponents maintain that this group would receive the largest reduction in average tax rates since their basic allowance would be a large part of their total income.

The Political Outlook

A key attraction of the Flat Tax is its simplicity in comparison to current law. Under the proposal, these would be eliminated:

- Corporate income taxation
- Alternative minimum tax
- Documentation of depreciation, investment income, and charitable contributions

In addition, there would be no taxation of interest, dividends, and capital gains. Proponents claim that under the proposal, both individuals and businesses would file returns the size of a postcard. There can be little doubt that this proposal in its current form is simpler than current law for a large number of taxpayers.

It's unlikely, however, that the tax would be as simple as advocates claim. Here's why:

- Many issues under current law would remain problematic under the Flat Tax. *Case in point:* Under either tax, there is no bright line between business expenses and personal consumption for self-employed persons.
- New issues arise that aren't present under current law. *Case in point:* The value of employee fringe benefits, which businesses cannot deduct under the Flat Tax, must be calculated.

- It's often remarked that it's not really fair to compare a tax system functioning in the real world to an idealized system that has not yet been subjected to the political maneuvering necessary for passage into law. *Case in point:* If history is any indicator, it seems likely that in the name of political expediency, the proposal would rapidly be burdened with special exceptions and adjustments as it moved through the legislative and political processes.

4

AN UNLIMITED SAVINGS PLAN: THE INDIVIDUAL CONSUMPTION TAX

Unlike other consumption taxes, an individual consumption tax is imposed solely on individuals. This tax is also referred to as the "personal consumption tax" or the "expenditures tax." Sometimes, the individual consumption tax component of the Nunn-Domenici proposal is called the Unlimited Saving Allowance tax (USA tax).

Under the individual consumption tax, as with the current income tax, individuals file annual tax returns. But unlike the current system, the new tax would allow an unlimited deduction for net annual additions to saving. To arrive at net additions to saving, additions to savings must be reduced by "dissaving" in the form of additional borrowing or use of savings. Take this simple example to show how the individual consumption tax is figured:

> The Carters have $100 of wage and interest income. Since they have taken out a new car loan of $15 and paid off $10 of mortgage principal, they have $5 of net new debt. This is $5 over and above income available for consumption. On the other hand, the Carters were also able to increase their bank balance by $10. This is $10 of income not used for consumption. Thus, after adding and subtracting from loan and savings balances, the Carters have $95 available for consumption.

Income		$100
Plus: New loan for auto purchase	$ 15	
Minus: Reduction in mortgage principal	$(10)	
Net new debt		$ 5
Less: Start-of-year bank balance	$ 40	
End-of-year bank balance	$(50)	
Increase in saving	$(10)	
Equals consumption tax base		$ 95

PROGRESSIVE RATES POSSIBLE

An individual consumption tax is probably the most complex of all types of consumption taxes. It remains an attractive option, nevertheless, because of its unique ability to address issues of regressivity. Unlike a sales tax, which is levied one transaction at a time, an individual consumption tax is levied on an annual basis. That allows a progressive rate structure. Retail sales taxes and VATs (levied on businesses) can only alleviate regressivity through adjustments to the tax base and/or with administratively complex refundable credits. Preferential treatment of necessities is administratively complex and economically inefficient. In addition, these adjustments to the tax base are not particularly effective in achieving distributional objectives. An individual consumption tax, on the other hand, can achieve almost any desired distribution of after-tax income solely through adjustments to the tax rates.

Thus, at first glance, it appears that an individual consumption tax is the "best of both worlds"; there need not be a trade-off between economic efficiency and equity. An individual consumption tax has all of the economic benefits of a consumption tax base. At the same time, the tax can be made to be just as progressive as the current income tax. But until recently, the individual consumption tax has not received even a small fraction of the attention of that given to other consumption taxes, when significant attention has been focused on the individual consumption tax as one (along with a subtraction-method VAT imposed on business) of the two major components of the legislation proposed by Senators Nunn and Domenici.

THE TRANSITION PROBLEM

The difficulty lies in finding a workable method of figuring the deduction for new saving—the deduction that is at the heart of an individual consumption tax. To better understand the issues involved, it's useful to differentiate "old saving" (that is, the individual net wealth when the tax is enacted) from "new saving" (additions to net wealth after enactment). It's likely that the two would be treated differently under any individual consumption tax.

New Saving: The Easy Part

New saving would be treated like deductible contributions to an IRA that had no limitations on the deduction amount or the timing of withdrawals. You would deduct all amounts you saved, including net additions to bank, mutual fund, and brokerage accounts; all stocks, bonds, and other financial instruments you bought; and all your investments in partnerships and proprietorships. When you withdrew funds from these investments, whether in the form of income or reducing principal, you would be subject to tax on the entire amount of the proceeds. Conversely, you would include in the tax base proceeds from new loans or other forms of indebtedness, while you would deduct payments of both interest and principal.

In computing your deduction for new saving, you would have to know the annual change in the outstanding balance of your investments and indebtedness. Under an individual consumption tax, custodians of each investment and indebtedness account would have to report these amounts to you once a year as they now report interest earned and paid.

Old Saving: The Hard Part

Saving accumulated before the enactment is more problematic than new saving for two reasons. The first is a matter of compliance. The second is a matter of fairness. Once an individual consumption tax takes effect, you would deduct all additions to saving and be taxed on all withdrawals. Shifting funds from one investment to another (for example, depositing a dividend in a bank account) has no tax consequences because receipts (dissaving) are exactly offset by saving. A large revenue loss could result, however, if somehow existing wealth went undetected by tax authorities, and then these funds were deducted when invested in new forms. This could occur if before enactment you drew down your saving and held it in cash. Investing this cash after the enactment date would result in deductions despite lack of additional new saving. To prevent this, it has been noted that it may be necessary to require that outstanding cash balances at the outset be declared (subject to certain *de minimis* rules). It's not clear how such a requirement would be enforced.

The other important transition issue is primarily a matter of policy. Under the standard operating rules of an individual consumption tax, all proceeds from saving are included in gross receipts and subject to tax. The taxation of the entire proceeds, however—not just capital gains, dividends, interest, and other capital income—results in large tax penalties for existing saving. Thus, the standard operating rules of the tax would result in harsh treatment of old saving, and many would consider such tax treatment a retroactive tax increase. This burden would fall primarily on the elderly who draw down their saving during retirement. It's important to recognize that the burdensome taxation of old saving under an individual consumption tax without transition relief is exactly equivalent to what you would experience under a retail sales tax or a VAT.

Special transition relief would be needed to avoid a double burden on the elderly (and others drawing down saving to consume). One method of providing relief would be to treat existing saving like new saving and allow the rest of existing saving to be deducted at the time of enactment. (This deduction of basis equals your selling the asset at the time of enactment and paying income tax on any gain, and then reinvesting and deducting the entire proceeds.) Then, under the regular rules of the individual consumption tax, all proceeds would be included when you sold the assets or you closed out the account. However, here are some potential objections to this type of transition relief:

- The deduction for all existing basis would result in substantial revenue loss (and a tax rate increase to pay for the loss) given the enormous amount of individual wealth outstanding in the United States.

- A large portion of old saving received favorable treatment under the income tax (IRAs, pensions, life insurance, annuities, and tax-exempt bonds). Having never been subject to tax (or having received substantial tax relief), this saving would not be subject to "double taxation" when an individual consumption tax was enacted and inequity would not exist.

- This relief goes against the two major objectives of implementing a consumption tax: increasing savings and simplifying taxation. The tax relief for old saving does nothing to increase incentives for new saving, and the transition rules are very complex. Thus, some have proposed moving to a new system "cold turkey" (that is, without transition relief).

- Some question whether the "retroactive" tax burden imposed on old saving is truly "unfair." They conclude that it's entirely appropriate to impose an additional tax burden on the elderly given the transfer of wealth being exacted by the social security system from the current work force to current retirees. This last view—if it ever gets serious attention in the political arena—will undoubtedly be met with fierce opposition from those savers who would have their after-tax income subject to tax a second time under the consumption tax.

HIGHER, STEEPER TAX RATES

While you must evaluate each individual proposal with its own full array of details, two general observations can be made about tax rates that might prevail under a replacement consumption tax:

- **Observation 1:** In general, because total consumption is less than income, if revenue neutrality is important, it can be expected that a consumption tax will have higher rates than an income tax.

- **Observation 2:** Since upper-income families consume proportionately less of their income than lower-income families, it is generally necessary for a consumption tax to have more steeply graduated rates than under current law to achieve the same degree of progressivity as current law.

5

Unlimited Savings Allowance: The USA Tax

The USA (Unlimited Savings Allowance) Tax, proposed by Senators Sam Nunn and Pete Domenici, eliminates the individual and corporate income taxes and imposes a new consumption tax on individuals and businesses. How does the Nunn-Domenici USA Tax differ from the Armey Flat Tax? Here are the variations under Nunn-Domenici:

- Progressive rate structure for individuals.
- Permits certain itemized deductions, mortgage interest, and charitable deductions.
- Allows personal and dependency exemptions.
- Taxes consumption whether from wages or investment income.
- No wage deduction for business tax.
- All employer and most employee payroll taxes could be credited against the new tax.

The personal exemptions and family allowances (projected for 1996 with indexing for inflation thereafter) under the Nunn-Domenici Individual Tax are as follows:

Personal exemption	$2,250
Family living allowance:	
Married filing jointly	$7,400
Surviving spouse	$7,400
Head of household	$5,400

Individual $4,400

Married filing separately $3,700

Thus, a family of four would not have to pay an individual USA tax unless their gross income exceeded $16,400.

The Nunn-Domenici plan would allow for the following deductions:

- Mortgage interest
- Charitable contributions
- Tuition for education and training
- Additional savings
- Transition basis

The deductions for mortgage interest and charitable contributions would operate under the same rules as apply under the current individual income tax system. The deduction for education expenses would be new; it allows for tuition relating to post-secondary education (limited to $2,000 per year per eligible student with an $8,000 maximum per household annually). As noted, the Nunn-Domenici plan includes a deduction for additional saving that is similar to the deduction allowed for IRA contributions; however, no limitations apply as to the contribution amount, and there are no restrictions on withdrawals.

Except for the transition-basis deduction and the deduction for new saving (these are covered shortly), you would not be allowed other deductions under the new individual USA Tax. In particular, you wouldn't get deductions for state and local taxes, moving expenses, casualty losses, and medical expenses.

STEEPLY SLOPING TAX RATES

The tax rates under the Nunn-Domenici plan are listed in Table 5.1.

With graduated rates and an exemption for saving, you could always lower your taxes by saving instead of spending. Still, the low thresholds for the top brackets mean that a large number of middle-class taxpayers would be taxed on part of their consumption at a 40 percent rate.

TAX CREDITS

As under current law, but unlike the Flat Tax, Nunn-Domenici offers a refundable earned income tax credit. The plan goes beyond the current credit by including an innovative credit for the employee portion

Table 5.1 Individual Tax Rates under the Nunn-Domenici Plan

Taxable Income by Filing Status				Tax Rate in Each Year				
Married Filing Jointly	Head of Household	Unmarried Individual	Married Filing Separately	1996	1997	1998	1999	2000 and after
Up to $5,400	Up to $4,750	Up to $3,200	Up to $2,700	19%	15%	13%	10%	8%
$5,400- $24,000	$4,750-$21,100	$3,200-$14,400	$2,700-$12,000	27%	26%	25%	20%	19%
Over $24,000	Over $21,100	Over $14,400	Over $12,000	40%	40%	40%	40%	40%

of payroll taxes. Under current law, the employee portion of payroll taxes equals 7.65 percent of the first $62,700 (1996 level) of wages and 1.45 percent on all wages above that amount. No other tax credits would be allowed.

To illustrate how the Nunn-Domenici tax is figured, let's see how it affects the Ryerson family we visited earlier:

Wage			$70,000
Less: Personal exemptions (4 x $2,250)		$9,000	
Living allowance		$7,400	
Itemized deductions		$6,500	$22,900
Taxable income			$47,100
Tax liability:			
Tax at 19%	$ 1,026		
Tax at 27%	$ 5,022		
Tax at 40%	$ 9,240		
Total tax	$15,288		
Less: Payroll tax	$ 4,902		
Net tax			$10,386
Tax under current system			$ 9,655
Tax under 20% Flat Tax			$ 7,720

For the Ryersons, who didn't put any money into savings, the USA plan raises their tax bill above either the current system or the Flat Tax.

THE REWARDS FOR SAVING

At the core of the Nunn-Domenici proposal is its treatment of personal savings. There are four main points you should consider:

- You can deduct net additions to savings. Deductible additions to savings include deposits to all types of banks, mutual funds, brokerage, and retirement accounts. You also can deduct any amount used to buy or invest in stock, bonds, certificates of deposits, ownership interests in partnerships and proprietorships, life insurance, and annuities. On the opposite side, withdrawals from these accounts and sales of these assets are included in the tax base. The costs of buying land (whether directly or indirectly) and collectibles are not deductible.

- Money you borrow may be included in taxable income if it exceeds certain generous exemptions. Those exemptions include:

  —Up to $1 million of mortgage debt

  —Up to $25,000 of debt you used to buy a consumer durable (i.e., a car)

  —Credit card charges you paid within the first billing cycle

  —Any other debt up to $10,000

  These exceptions remove most personal debt from consideration.

Comment: It's unclear what in the statute or in practice might prevent anyone from tapping the tax-free borrowing provision and using the loan proceeds for deductible saving. For example, you could take out a second mortgage with a principal of $15,000 and borrow an additional $10,000 secured against a new $10,000 CD. You'd get a $25,000 tax deduction for what appears to be $25,000 in increased saving. This would mean large revenue losses for the government with no net increase in private saving.

- Your withdrawals from accounts and proceeds from your sales are included in taxable income. It wouldn't matter whether the withdrawal came from principal or interest or whether you had a gain or loss on the sale. This could mean major recordkeeping relief—and, possible, a hefty tax increase.

- There are deductions for basis of assets held before January 1, 1997. For investors with less than $50,000 of basis, basis may be deducted ratably over three years. For other investors, basis may only be deducted when there is net dissaving, generally during retirement.

TRANSITION TROUBLE

This cash-flow approach creates serious difficulties during the transition from an income tax to a consumption tax system. What would happen without transition relief? You might be taxed twice on assets bought under the current system and sold under the USA system. From an income tax's perspective, these assets are overtaxed, because basis as well as gain is subject to tax. From the perspective of a consumption tax, the assets are overtaxed because you missed out on the deduction when the original investment was made. In effect, assets whose holding period straddles the effective date are whipsawed between the two systems—subject to more tax than they would be under either system when fully phased-in.

Let's illustrate this with Table 5.2.

- In Panel A, the taxpayer earns $10,000 that is subject to 28 percent, which leaves $7,200 available for investment. At the end of five years, the taxpayer has $9,526.64.

- In Panel B, the taxpayer also earns $10,000, and this entire amount is available for investment under an individual consumption tax where saving is deductible. Over the investment's life (here, five years), the income is not subject to tax. In the last year, however, the investment's entire proceeds ($13,604 + $1,088) are subject to tax, leaving the taxpayer with $10,579.16. Thus, after five years, a taxpayer in the 28 percent bracket who is saving $10,000 of earnings is more than $1,000 richer under a consumption tax than he or she would be under an income tax.

- In Panel C, the taxpayer is caught between an income tax and a consumption tax, getting the worst of both. When the taxpayer makes the initial investment, there is no deduction for saving. However, when the taxpayer liquidates the investment, the entire proceeds are subject to tax. This leaves the taxpayer with only $7,459—a far worse outcome than under the income tax.

To provide relief to "old capital," most proposals for a personal consumption tax provide transition relief for preeffective date assets in the form of deductions for preeffective date basis. Before explaining the particular basis deduction rules under Nunn-Domenici, two points are worth considering:

- **Fairness.** Equitable treatment for both old and new savers is the entire reason for providing transition relief (the fact is that requiring higher tax rates in a revenue-neutral setting is detrimental to growth). It is true that old saving would be unduly penalized without transition rules, but providing relief to existing assets does little to encourage new investment and economic growth.

Table 5.2 Return on an Investment of $10,000

A. Income Tax

	1995	1996	1997	1998	1999
(1) Beginning Basis	7200.00	7614.72	8053.33	8517.20	9007.79
(2) Income	576.00	609.18	644.27	681.38	720.62
(3) Tax	161.28	170.57	180.39	190.79	201.77
(4) Ending Basis (1) + (2) − (3)	7614.77	8053.33	8517.20	9007.79	9526.64

B. Fully Phased-in Consumption Tax

	1995	1996	1997	1998	1999
(1) Beginning Basis	10000.00	10800.00	11664.00	12597.12	13604.89
(2) Income	800.00	864.00	933.12	1007.77	1088.39
(3) Tax	0.00	0.00	0.00	0.00	4114.12
(4) Ending Basis (1) + (2) − (3)	10800.00	11664.00	12597.12	13604.89	10579.16

C. Switch to Consumption Tax in 1996, without Transition Relief

	1995	1996	1997	1998	1999
(1) Beginning Basis	7200.00	7614.72	8223.90	8881.81	9592.35
(2) Income	576.00	609.18	657.91	710.54	767.39
(3) Tax	161.28	0.00	0.00	0.00	2900.73
(4) Ending Basis (1) + (2) − (3)	7614.72	8223.90	8881.81	9592.35	7459.01

Note: The assumed tax rate is 28 percent and the assumed pretax rate of return is 8 percent.

- **Overtaxation.** The problem of overtaxation of existing assets is prevalent under all consumption taxes. Under a retail sales tax or a VAT, relief in the form of basis adjustment is not practical (under these options, all tax collections are from businesses, and individuals do not even file returns). Thus, under other types of consumption taxes, the additional burden on taxpayers who have already saved is ignored or relief is directed toward the elderly (for example, by exempting prescription drugs).

Under the Nunn-Domenici plan, there are methods for recovering preeffective-date basis. One is available only to investors with no more than $50,000 of preeffective date basis. These taxpayers will be eligible to ratably include basis during the first three years the consumption tax is in effect. This is referred to as the "transition basis deduction." But this option is not realistic for all taxpayers because of the severe revenue losses that would result (existing aggregate basis in the economy is probably greater than an entire year's taxable income). Thus, under the Nunn-Domenici proposal, savers would only be allowed to deduct basis when there are net withdrawals from savings. The practical effect of this rule is that many who must use their savings will get some tax relief.

THE NUNN-DOMENICI BUSINESS TAX

The Nunn-Domenici Business Tax is a "subtraction method" VAT levied at 11 percent. Under this type of VAT, the tax base starts with business receipts and then subtracts purchases from other businesses. All businesses, not just corporations, must pay the tax. Wages and interest are not deductible, but capital equipment costs are expensed rather than depreciated.

A Credit for Payroll Taxes

Under the USA tax, businesses can subtract the employer portion of payroll taxes as a credit against the business tax. This credit deserves careful attention for two reasons. First, it's important to understand how this works to gauge the tax's overall impact on wage costs. As noted, wages are not deductible under the general 11 percent tax. However, this is substantially offset by having a tax credit for the employer-portion of the payroll tax (7.65 percent up to a per employee annual ceiling—$62,700 in 1995 and an additional 1.45 percent tax on all wages without limit).

Second, the credit has an impact on the international competitiveness of domestically produced goods. The ability to credit the entire portion of the payroll tax against the business tax is equivalent to repealing the employer-portion of the payroll tax and using the business tax to restore lost revenues. Under the rules of the General Agreements on Tariffs and Trade (GATT), border adjustments are allowed for "indirect" sales and value-added taxes, but are not allowed for "direct" taxes on wages and profits. By replacing payroll tax revenue with VAT revenues, the Nunn-Domenici proposal effectively replaces a nonborder-adjustable tax with a border adjustable tax. This will be true to the extent the burden of payroll taxes is passed forward to consumers in higher prices (and not backward to employees in lower after-tax wages). In general, economists believe that the burden of wage taxes is born by labor in the form of lower after-tax wages.

Making the Transition for Business Property

The Nunn-Domenici Business Tax provides a large incentive for capital formation by allowing all purchases of new capital equipment to be expensed. However, if no depreciation deductions are allowed for the remaining basis of existing capital, this capital will be subject to a tax penalty. To prevent imposing an undue burden on existing capital, the Nunn-Domenici proposal allows a "transition basis deduction" for amortizing the remaining basis on the effective date for any assets placed in service before the effective date. The deduction amount is found based on the following schedule:

Type of Property	Remaining Amortization on Effective Date under Current Law	Amortization Period under Nunn-Domenici
Category I basis	Less than 15 years	10 years
Category II basis	More than 15 years	30 years
Category III basis	Not depreciable	40 years

In addition, unrecovered inventory costs would be deducted ratably over three years.

Carryforwards of net operating losses, alternative minimum tax credit, and other business credits—including R&E tax credit—generated under the existing income tax could not be used to reduce liability under the new business tax. *Note:* This could impose a particularly large burden on start-up firms. Some have warned that, by removing corporate deductions, the tax liability of certain small high-tech companies would be significantly increased.

CONCLUSION

The Nunn-Domenici proposal is not as simple as the Flat Tax. Also, it's not as sweeping in its elimination of tax preferences. The argument can be made, however, that the plan contains the most important elements of consumption taxation, while at the same time, making realistic accommodations that may be necessary to ensure sufficient political support for enactment.

6

A NATIONAL SALES TAX

A national retail sales tax might be an attractive revenue source for the government. It's relatively simple and familiar to most Americans. After all, most of us encounter retail sales taxes every day in our normal shopping patterns; 45 states and many local jurisdictions levy a sales tax. Retail sales taxes are highly visible, since they're itemized on sales tickets. A national sales tax large enough to replace the income tax might well exceed 20 percent, making it highly conspicuous to consumers. At least customers don't have to deal with any computing, filing, or recordkeeping chores; that falls to the retailers, many of whom already file sales tax returns and make sales tax payments to state and local authorities. One of the major difficulties posed by a national sales tax is how to deal with retailer and state government resistance, especially with a tax of this magnitude.

Fairness issues also arise with a sales tax. On the one hand, states exempt many final goods and services, resulting in undertaxation of some sectors. On the other hand, states tax many intermediate goods, resulting in overtaxation of some sectors. So, in practice, states' retail sales taxes fall short of the ideal of taxing all consumption once.

EXEMPTING NECESSITIES AND OTHER THINGS

In practice, state governments exempt many types of goods and services from sales tax for a variety of reasons. Some products—such as food, clothing, and housing—are exempted because they're considered necessities. Since the poor generally spend a higher proportion of their income on necessities than the wealthy, lower-income households get proportionally more relief.

Another broad exemption often applies to services. Some services, including many types of financial services, are exempt because it's so difficult to identify their value. Other services, including government services at all levels, are exempt for the same reason—not to mention it's good politics. Finally, "merit" goods, such as those provided by charities, are exempt because they are considered deserving of public support.

But exemptions, however worthy they may be, often create additional administrative burdens for tax authorities and compliance burdens for taxpayers. Exemptions also impede economic efficiency. The administrative costs of a retail sale tax would be greatly reduced if no exemptions or special rates were allowed. Much time and debate are consumed in identifying exactly which items should be exempt. Once these items have been exempted, retail businesses must distinguish taxable from nontaxable sales. For service providers, invoices to customers must allocate total charges between taxable products and nontaxable services.

This complexity is not inherent in a retail sales tax; it's the result of political considerations. It seems unrealistic to assume that a consumption tax would not include tax relief for certain sectors. And it seems reasonable to expect that political considerations will in fact more than likely complicate the administration of any retail sales tax. The fact is that all states with sales taxes—as well as almost every country with a national retail sales tax or VAT—provide numerous instances of preferential treatment. There is nothing in the history of the federal tax legislative process to suggest that a federal consumption tax would be devoid of special interest provisions.

Cascading Taxes on Intermediate Sales

Even without favored treatment for certain products and services, the problem of separating taxable sales to consumers from nontaxable sales to businesses would remain. State governments generally use two methods—both imperfect—to help separate retail sales from nonretail sales. The first is to grant "exemption certificates" to business taxpayers. The second is to impose sales tax on some types of products whether sales are retail or not. Because of the bluntness of each of these tools, retail sales taxes overtax final sales of some products while undertaxing sales of other products.

When intermediate goods are taxed, the final product's purchase price embodies not only the tax on the final sale, but also the tax on inputs to the final product. Take this example: Say a 5 percent state sales tax is imposed on delivery services (for example, trucking and other methods of delivering goods) and that same sales tax also applies to the buying of gasoline and computers that account for 20 percent of the delivery services' cost (that is, an additional 1 percent on the tax). This means that the total state-imposed sales tax on delivery services is 6 percent. This is called tax "cascading," which can result in higher tax burdens on products that happen to use more intermediate goods subject to tax. It can also result in unfair competition within industries if some firms provide their own intermediate inputs (nontaxable) and their competitors must buy intermediate inputs in taxable transactions.

Cascading is not an issue under a VAT (either the credit-invoice or subtraction methods, explored in greater detail later). For example, under the credit-invoice method, any taxes paid on intermediate sales between businesses would be rebated to the business making sales to consumers. Look again at the preceding example; the taxes on gasoline (collected by the gas station) and on consumers (collected by the computer dealer) would be rebated to the company providing the delivery services to the consumers with individuals paying 5 rather than 6 percent.

Cheating on Business Purchases

Under a retail sales tax, it might be possible for businesses—especially those closely-held—to claim exemption on items that are completely used for personal consumption. States usually grant businesses "exemption certificates" that allow them to make purchases without paying sales tax. But there is little to stop exemption certificate holders from buying items and then using these for personal consumption. Beyond checking an exemption certificate's validity, it is not reasonable to expect sellers to add much in enforcement. To determine whether items should be taxable or tax-exempt, sellers would have to know the use to which the item would be put. Sellers of goods and services can't read buyers' minds to know the purchased items' intended use. First and foremost, sellers want to close the deal. Challenging buyers could result in not only the loss of a sale, but also in customer goodwill leading to future sales.

Unless special care is taken, a retail sales tax places little burden of proof on those in business making purchases. The only way these business purchases can be audited is if the seller retains records of the purchases, including the purchasers' ID numbers. Even with exhaustive recordkeeping, the threat of audit, in most cases, would be insignificant, given the small amount of tax any single taxpayer could evade with purchases from a single retailer. These issues now exist and mechanisms are in place to control avoidance, but attempts at evasion may increase at higher tax rate levels.

There may be a greater threat of audit for big-ticket items—such as autos and personal computers—that have extensive business and personal use. Here, it doesn't seem inappropriate to require the seller to keep a record of taxpayer IDs. One possible alternative is to use rebates instead of exemptions for large ticket items (like paybacks on receipt of valid invoices), although the downside is that such rebates would entail substantial administrative costs.

The problem of distinguishing business items from personal-use items is hardly restricted to retail sales taxation or to consumption taxes in general. Under the income tax, small business owners have similar incentives to claim business deductions for personal use items. The fact is the higher the marginal income tax rate, the greater the incentive for evasion. Under the income tax, however, the business must stand ready to defend all deductions claimed, and even a valid business deduction improperly documented can be disallowed. Under a credit-invoice VAT, businesses may attempt to claim credits on items bought for personal use. Similarly, under a personal consumption tax or a subtraction-method VAT, closely held businesses may attempt to deduct the cost of items bought for personal consumption as business expenses. Thus, evasion through overstating business expenses is a significant concern under almost any tax.

There is, however, a critical difference in detecting evasion under a retail sales tax versus other consumption taxes: evasion by retail sales tax buyers would require cross-checking and the auditing of multiple taxpayers. Under other types of taxation, evasion can be detected by auditing the buyer. Given the difficulty, even in the best of circumstances, of distinguishing business- from personal-use items, the problem of evasion by buyers of business-use items under a retail sales tax cannot be easily dismissed.

GETTING RETAILERS TO COLLECT

Perhaps the most cited difficulty with enacting a federal retail sales tax is the potential lack of compliance by retailers. The rate of a federal sales tax that would be necessary to replace income tax revenue would almost certainly exceed 20 percent. Most tax administrators believe that 10 percent or 12 percent of gross receipts is the maximum burden that may be reasonably placed on a sector comprised of numerous small businesses. Because tax is imposed only at the point of final sale, weaknesses in collections at that point would be particularly harmful to compliance compared to an income tax or VAT in which the compliance burden is spread more evenly across businesses and, in the case of the individual income tax, on tens of millions of individual taxpayers. Compliance by small business is already an issue under both the federal income tax and state sales taxes. In fact, under a VAT, many commentators argue that significant exemptions—or subsidies—should be granted to small businesses because of the high compliance costs. This would not be possible under a retail sales tax without a substantial loss of revenue.

Real-world experience seems to support tax administrators' comments that there's an upper limit on the rate of the retail sales tax. While most countries with VATs have standard rates of 15 percent to 20 percent, retail sales tax rates are usually less than 5 percent. Given this evidence, and given the existence of current state sales taxes, there seems to be little room for an additional federal sales tax that would not result in significant compliance problems for both state and federal tax collectors. Nevertheless, the retail sales tax cannot be ignored as an option as an add-on tax.

The Why of Retail Enforcement Problems

There are several reasons that enforcement is a problem at the retail level under any kind of tax:

- It is not usually possible to cross-check a retailer's sales with the buyers' records because taxable sales by retailers are made to consumers.
- The retail sector has a relatively large proportion of small businesses. Evasion by small businesses is more likely than by large businesses because audits are much less likely and the relative costs of compliance higher.
- The life expectancy of small business is short. Collections from a discontinued business can be difficult and costly.

The retail sales tax imposes its entire compliance burden on the sector from which collections are most troublesome. The retail sector must remit far greater amounts of revenue under a sales tax than under a VAT or an income tax. In addition, a retail sales tax imposes the unique compliance burden of requiring a separation of receipts between taxable sales to consumers and nontaxable sales to other businesses.

A national retail sales tax could impose a large new financial burden on state and local governemnts (see Appendix B).

7

VAT? WHAT'S THAT?

While Americans are focusing intently on a variety of innovative but untested consumption taxes, they're paying remarkably little attention to the consumption tax most widely used in other countries. That is the value-added tax, or VAT tax. While the VAT, and in particular the "credit invoice" method VAT, is the most popular consumption tax with foreign governments, it is not receiving any significant consideration on Capitol Hill.

But the credit-invoice VAT, while it has its own administrative problems, manages to bypass many of the problems inherent in other consumption taxes. Until recently, in fact, the credit-invoice method VAT was perhaps the most viable consumption tax option under consideration in the United States. The prospect for a credit-invoice method VAT could rise again, especially if compliance concerns increase or if Congress decides it must provide exemptions to governments, nonprofit organizations, and certain businesses. For the United States, it is an option that can't simply be written off.

EYE TROUBLE

What is "value added"? For each business, valued added is simply the contribution of its labor and its capital to national output. In general terms, that might be calculated either as the total earnings of the amounts contributed by the firm's investors and workers or as sales minus allowable costs. Either method should produce the same result. But the methods differ administratively, and different kinds of VATs are distinguished by exactly how they measure value added.

One reason the VAT gets short shrift in the national tax debate is that the whole notion of value added immediately makes American eyes glaze over. It tends to sound foreign and confusing, especially compared to familiar concepts like a tax on retail sales or a tax on income. In some ways, the VAT can be seen as a cross between a sales tax on consumers and an income tax on business. Like a sales tax, it's fundamentally assessed on the price of goods and services. If you buy a $1 item at the store, there would be a VAT tax on that $1.

But unlike the sales tax, the VAT is not initially imposed on the consumer (although it may be passed on through higher prices); instead, the VAT is charged to business. The VAT tax on that $1 item would be paid by all the businesses that made it and brought it to you—the store, the wholesaler, the trucking company, the manufacturer, and all the suppliers to the manufacturer. Each would pay a share of the tax in proportion to its share of the item's final $1 value. For each business, that's a lot like paying a tax on its income from that product. In practice, of course, the business wouldn't calculate the tax on every individual sale but on total sales over a full year.

The Farmer, the Miller, and the Baker

To illustrate the value-added chain, suppose that the $1 item is a loaf of bread. Here is the paradigm of a farmer, a miller, and a baker:

1. The farmer uses his own land and seed, buying no inputs from other businesses. He sells his wheat for 20 cents per bushel. This is the farmer's value added.

2. The miller buys the wheat from the farmer for 20 cents. This is ground into flour and sold to the baker for 50 cents. The miller's value added is 30 cents—the difference between the 50-cent sale and the 20 cents of cost.

3. Now, the baker buys the flour from the miller for 50 cents. The flour is then used to bake bread, which is sold to consumers for $1. The baker's value added is 50 cents— the difference between the $1 sales price and the 50 cents of cost.

Thus, the total value added at each stage of the production process equals the final sales price.

There are two fundamental ways to measure value added. One is to start with sales and subtract purchases from other businesses. This is known as the "subtraction method." Suppose a company has sales of

$100,000, and it pays $40,000 to other companies for raw materials, equipment, transportation, utilities, and other costs. Using the subtraction method, the company's value added would be $100,000 minus $40,000 or $60,000.

Another measure, called the "addition method," calculates a firm's value added as the sum of its payments to workers and return to its owners (and lenders). In this example, the company paid its workers $50,000. That leaves a profit, after paying $40,000 to other companies and $50,000 to its own workers, of $10,000. Using the addition method, the company's value added would be the $10,000 in profit plus the $50,000 in wages, or $60,000—the same as the result from the subtraction method. The addition method is used by the state of Michigan, but is rarely applied in other countries. The subtraction method, which is used in Japan, is currently getting the most consideration in the United States.

A third system, known as the credit-invoice method, is also widely accepted in much of the world but is getting less attention here. It's like the subtraction method but with an administrative twist. Rather than subtracting purchases from suppliers, a firm would get tax credits from those suppliers for the amount of tax the supplier paid. That makes the credit-invoice method more complex to administer, but it also makes it easier to enforce and adds flexibility by allowing the possibility of exemptions for some businesses.

Comparing Methods

Both the subtraction method and the credit-invoice method are taxes on consumption and have the same potential to boost capital formation and improve competitiveness. And either method could produce the same result in terms of distributing the tax burden. The main differences are in compliance costs, flexibility, and public perception. The subtraction method is simpler because buyers and sellers don't have to exchange and preserve tax information on every purchase. The subtraction method also may be more palatable to the general public because it looks more like a corporate income tax and less like a sales tax.

The credit invoice method, however, is harder to evade, just because of all that required documentation. The credit invoice method also offers the advantage—or disadvantage, depending on your point of view—of giving preferential treatment to farmers, health care providers, government entities, charities, or other favored groups. For more on the features of these two methods, see Appendix F.

8

THE POLICY ISSUES: SAVINGS, INFLATION, AND THE BUSINESS CYCLE

Saving is indisputably critical to economic growth. Saving provides the capital that buys the tools that let American workers be productive and competitive. It's also indisputable that the United States is saving less than it used to and saving less than other countries. One reason is that the current tax, despite some provisions designed to encourage saving, is fundamentally biased against saving. Switching to a consumption tax, especially one that exempts interest and other capital income, would increase after-tax returns. That in turn might get people to save more. Or it might not.

TAXES AND SAVING

Although a consumption tax may seem to favor saving, that's true only by comparison to an income tax that includes saving in its tax base. Two fundamental observations can be made about the effect of taxes on saving:

- An income tax penalizes saving—the more you save, the greater your lifetime tax burden.
- A consumption tax neither rewards nor penalizes saving.

With a consumption tax, saving doesn't alter the present value of your lifetime tax burden. The consumption—by itself—doesn't provide any incentive to increase savings. The benefit to a consumption tax is removing the tax from saving income until such time as that income is consumed.

Less Reason to Save

There is no guarantee that improving after-tax returns will improve the savings rate, although it is natural to expect that an increase in the returns to saving will increase saving. With greater rewards for saving, individuals will do more of it. The opposite, however, may also be true. This may be illustrated by considering the case of a "target saver." A target saver is an individual who saves to achieve a certain dollar amount of future consumption (such as tuition for a child's college education). An increase in the after-tax rate of return on saving would reduce the amount of savings necessary to achieve the desired amount of saving. For example, suppose the parents of a newborn wish to provide $100,000 of college tuition to their child on the child's eighteenth birthday. If the rate of interest is 8 percent and the parents' tax bracket is 30 percent, they would have to save $3,182 annually to accumulate $100,000 in eighteen years. If their savings is exempt from tax, they only need to save $2,472 annually in order to achieve their objective. Another example of target saving that *declines* with increases in rate of return is the funding of defined benefit pension plans: when interest rates increase, employers can more easily meet their pension obligations and therefore reduce their funding of pension plans.

INFLATION? RECESSION?

Keynesian economists may not wield the influence they did in the 1960s, but their views still deserve consideration. In a nutshell, Keynesian, or "demand-side" economics says increased government deficits and increased public spending can also help spur more private spending, at least in periods of significant unemployment and less than full-capacity utilization. Under this line of reasoning, a tax on consumption might seem to place a significant drag on the economy that could lead to recession. There are many arguments to dispute that idea. The main argument is that most consumption taxes under consideration would be offset by reductions in or elimination of income taxes. Assuming the new consumption tax is revenue-neutral, the deficit would not change, and the impact on overall demand would be small.

Because it is widely believed that the burden of consumption taxes will result in higher prices, there are concerns that a consumption tax will be accompanied by an increase in the rate of inflation. The choices faced by business will be: raise prices, absorb costs, or reduce wages (because there is no income tax). If consumption taxes imposed on businesses are passed forward in higher prices, the effect on the price level will depend on the rate of tax and the comprehensiveness of the tax base. If the rate of tax is 15 percent, and the tax applies to 80 percent of the goods and services in the economy, the increase in the price level that accompanies the imposition of the tax could be 12 percentage points.

Because changes in the price level are ultimately controlled by monetary policy, any increase in the price level from a consumption tax would have to be accommodated by the Federal Reserve (that is, a 12 percent increase in the price level would have to be accompanied by an increase in the money supply of approximately 12 percent). Because the Fed's actions are not under the direct control of Congress or the President, it is difficult to know how the Fed policy would react to the imposition of a large consumption tax. It is also important to stress that any changes in the price level due to the imposition of a new consumption tax (or an increase in the rate of an existing tax) are likely to be one-time changes in the price *level* and not permanent increases in the *rate* of inflation.

CONCLUSION

In terms of its impact on saving, there is substantial uncertainty surrounding the enactment of a replacement consumption tax. *Definitive* statements about a consumption tax's impact on saving and economic growth should be accepted warily. One thing that does seem clear is that even under the most optimistic assumptions, it is unlikely that a replacement consumption tax can increase U.S. saving to a level comparable to that of its major trading partners.

Potentially, the impact on long-term economic growth can be significant. If saving is not responsive to tax changes, however, the impacts on growth will be small. In summary, with regard to economic growth, a replacement consumption tax is unlikely to do any harm, and does have significant upside potential. Most conclude its impact on inflation will be a short-term initial increase only.

9

THE IMPACT ON INDIVIDUALS AND NONCORPORATE BUSINESSES

The leading consumption tax plans would be good news for taxpayers on the higher rungs of the income ladder but might not be such good news for those in the middle (nor possibly for unincorporated businesses and labor intensive industries). Under both the Nunn-Domenici and the Flat Tax proposals, upper-income households, which now pay the highest taxes per dollar of income, would see their burden eased.

Nunn-Domenici appears to provide relief to both the lowest and highest classes, making up lost revenue with a modest increase to middle-income taxpayers. The Flat Tax, by exempting capital income, would give substantial relief to higher-income households. The heaviest burdens would shift from upper-income households to the middle class, which would pay the highest taxes per dollar of income. Still, the Flat Tax would ease taxes for nearly all individual taxpayers. The big loser would be the Federal Treasury, since a 17 percent flat tax would raise far less revenue than the current individual income tax.

NEW TAX ON BUSINESS

For unincorporated businesses, both Nunn-Domenici and the Flat Tax add new taxes on the business itself, in addition to the tax on business income flowing to the individual tax returns of the owners. Those new taxes may or may not mean higher overall tax bills for the owners, however. The largest business tax burden comes under Nunn-Domenici. The combined business and individual tax generally would increase. High-income business owners would appear to face much higher tax bills than they do now. Low-income business owners might pay less, though, especially those whose business brings in only a small part of the total family income. The Flat Tax, on the other hand, generally would reduce combined tax burdens for unincorporated business owners.

INCOME TAX DEMOGRAPHICS

Let's review some basic facts about who pays the most and least under the current individual income tax (based on the latest available official information, from 1993). This is to help you gauge the impact of the proposals:

- The top 4 percent of taxpayers—those with adjusted gross incomes above $100,000—pay more than one-third of the total individual income tax revenue collected.

- People with adjusted gross incomes below $30,000 account for more than half of the returns filed. Those returns, however, account for only about 10 percent of the total individual income tax revenue collected.

- Personal exemptions and the standard deduction allow most low-income households to entirely escape tax.

- Many low-income households with children receive refunds—in effect, a "negative" income tax—as a result of the earned income credit.

- Only 29 percent of all individual tax filings include itemized deductions.

- As income increases, so do itemized deductions. Most taxpayers with adjusted gross income of more than $50,000 take itemized deductions. State and local taxes, mortgage interest, and charitable contribution deductions are the three largest.

- On the whole, tax as a percentage of AGI rises as income rises. In other words, the current tax system is effectively progressive.

- Although itemized deductions typically rise along with income, those deductions are not enough, on average, to off-set the impact of the progressive rate structure enacted into law in 1993. Nor are they enough to offset the phase-out of itemized deductions and personal exemptions on upper-income taxpayers enacted into law in 1990.

Nunn-Domenici Demographics

Let's examine the effects of the Nunn-Domenici Individual Tax proposal:

- The refundable payroll tax credit (like current earned income credit) gives substantial tax relief to low-income working households.

- Personal exemption amounts are slightly lower than current law (but they don't phase-out for high-bracket taxpayers as under current law).

- The "family allowance" provides a slight increase over the standard deduction we have now.

- The family allowance is available to all taxpayers, effectively giving everybody some of the benefit now reserved for itemizers.

- Tax rates rise quickly, with a 40 percent rate imposed even on middle-income households. Now, nobody pays the top 39.6 percent rate until their income reaches above $263,000 (although there's a lower threshold for married people filing separately).

- As a general rule, most saving is done by the wealthiest individuals. Low-income households generally do little or no saving.

- The great benefit to high-income households is the deduction for new saving.

- In general, Nunn-Domenici seems to place tax burdens on middle-income taxpayers that are comparable to current law and provides some relief to low- and high-income taxpayers.

Flat Tax Demographics

And here's a look at how the Flat Tax affects various segments of society:

- Perhaps the most prominent feature of the individual Flat Tax is the liberal personal allowances for all taxpayers. They're larger than the combined standard deduction and personal exemptions under current law and larger than the comparable allowances under Nunn-Domenici.

- The large personal allowance permits lower-income taxpayers to escape tax in far greater numbers than current law.

- Taxpayers with more deductions than income can claim a refund. At 17 percent, the tax on $1,000 of taxable income above the personal allowance would be $170. A taxpayer with income $1,000 under the personal allowance would claim a $170 refund. To some extent, this replaces the earned income credit, which would be eliminated.

- The single low rate gives high-income taxpayers a great advantage relative to either Nunn-Domenici or current law.

- Since high-income taxpayers get a far greater percentage of their income from capital than low-income taxpayers, high-income taxpayers enjoy significant tax relief under Flat Tax despite complete elimination of itemized deductions.

COMPARING ALTERNATIVES

With regard to the distribution of the tax burden, both the current individual income tax and the individual Nunn-Domenici tax appear to maintain progressivity through all income levels. Compared to current law, the Nunn-Domenici proposal provides more relief for the poor—primarily through the refundable payroll credit—and more relief for the wealthy—primarily through the deduction for savings. The individual component of the Flat Tax provides substantial relief to the poor—despite the repeal of the EITC—by allowing refunds when taxable compensation is negative. The highest income categories actually may have lower effective tax rates than upper-middle income taxpayers because income from capital is exempt from tax.

Three Cases

Let's examine the following scenarios involving three noncorporate businesses and their owners. Assume this is in year 2000.

Example 1: Two-earner couple, four children. One earner owns a small business clearing $15,000. One is an employee with an annual salary of $33,000. The business pays about $11,000 in wages to its sole employee. Table 9.1 shows the way the family's tax burden appears under current law, Nunn-Domenici, and the Flat Tax.

This family does better under either Nunn-Domenici or the Flat Tax than under current law. In the case of Nunn-Domenici, this is due to their getting the family allowance and personal deductions along with itemized deductions and a deduction for new saving. In the case of the Flat Tax, this is due to the generous family and dependency deductions.

Although the family faces additional taxes on the business, that tax is relatively modest. Since business income and business taxes make up a secondary part of the family finances, the family pays less overall than under current law.

> **Example 2:** Sole practitioner physician, spouse, two children. Income of $145,000 from two sources: $120,000 is generated by one spouse with a medical practice, and the remainder is income from investments. Part of the medical practice expenses are $22,000 of salary to its sole employee. The family deducts $14,500 of itemized expenses under current law. Table 9.2 shows the breakdown.

Under Nunn-Domenici, tax rates are generally higher, but the family benefits from having a family allowance and a deduction for additional saving. The net result is that this family pays virtually the same individual tax under current law and Nunn-Domenici. The Nunn-Domenici business tax, however, adds a large new tax burden for the medical practice. That, combined with the individual tax, leaves the family with a larger tax burden than under current law.

Under the Flat Tax, despite the denial of itemized deductions, the family is far better off then under current law because of family and dependency deductions and because of the lower tax rate imposed. The business component of the Flat Tax adds a new burden, but it's less than half the size of the Nunn-Domenici business tax. Even with the additional business tax, the family pays considerably less overall under the Flat Tax than under current law.

> **Example 3:** Partner at law firm, spouse, two children. Income of $230,000, mostly from one partner's share of law partnership profits. The family itemizes deductions. This partner's share of the firm's salary expense is $150,000, assuming salaries are allocated in proportion to partners' income. Table 9.3 has the details.

Table 9.1 Tax Burden for Two-Earner Couple, One Owning a Small Business

INDIVIDUAL TAX

	CURRENT LAW	NUNN-DOMENICI	FLAT TAX
Income from Noncorporate Business	$15,000	$15,000	$15,000
Other Wage Income	$33,000	$33,000	$33,000
Other Capital Income	$ 2,000	$ 2,000	$ 0
Total Gross Income	$50,000	$50,000	$48,000
Standard Deduction/Family Allowance	$ 7,600	$ 8,400	$24,250
Personal/Dependency Deduction—Number	4	4	2
Personal/Dependency Deduction—Amount	$11,800	$10,200	$11,300
Charitable Deduction	$ 0	$ 700	$ 0
Mortgage Deduction	$ 0	$ 2,700	$ 0
Deduction for Net Saving	$ 0	$ 3,000	$ 0
Tax Base	$30,600	$25,000	$12,450
Tax	$ 4,590	$ 4,079	$ 2,117
Payroll Credit	$ 0	$ 3,672	$ 0
Net Tax	**$ 4,590**	**$ 407**	**$ 2,117**

Table 9.1   Tax Burden for Two-Earner Couple, One Owning a Small Business *(continued)*

BUSINESS TAX

	CURRENT LAW	NUNN-DOMENICI	FLAT TAX
Wages to Employees		$10,950	$ 0
Fringe Benefits		$ 5,190	$ 5,190
Interest		$ 548	$ 548
Income to Owner		$15,000	$ 0
Tax Base		$31,688	$ 5,738
Tax Rate		11%	17%
Gross Tax		$ 3,486	$ 975
Payroll Credit		$ 1,530	$ 0
Net Tax	– none –	**$ 1,956**	**$ 975**
TOTAL INDIVIDUAL AND BUSINESS TAX	**$ 4,590**	**$ 2,363**	**$ 3,092**

Table 9.2 Tax Burden for Sole Practitioner

INDIVIDUAL TAX

	CURRENT LAW*	NUNN-DOMENICI	FLAT TAX
Income from Noncorporate Business	$120,000	$120,000	$120,000
Other Wage Income	$ 0	$ 0	$ 0
Other Capital Income	$ 30,000	$ 30,000	$ 0
Total Gross Income	$150,000	$150,000	$120,000
Standard Deduction/Family Allowance	$ 0	$ 8,400	$ 24,250
Personal/Dependency Deduction—Number	4	4	2
Personal/Dependency Deduction—Amount	$ 11,800	$ 10,200	$ 11,300
Charitable Deduction	$ 3,500	$ 3,500	$ 0
Mortgage Deduction	$ 11,000	$ 11,000	$ 0
Deduction for Net Saving	$ 0	$ 20,000	$ 0
Tax Base	$112,961	$ 96,900	$ 84,450
Tax	$ 25,803	$ 32,377	$ 14,357
Payroll Credit	$ 0	$ 6,703	$ 0
Net Tax	**$ 25,803**	**$ 25,674**	**$ 14,357**

Table 9.2 Tax Burden for Sole Practitioner *(continued)*

BUSINESS TAX

	CURRENT LAW	NUNN-DOMENICI	FLAT TAX
Wages to Employees		$ 21,600	$ 0
Fringe Benefits		$ 28,320	$ 28,320
Interest		$ 432	$ 432
Income to Owner		$120,000	$ 0
Tax Base		$170,352	$ 28,752
Tax Rate		11%	17%
Gross Tax		$ 18,739	$ 4,888
Payroll Credit		$ 8,215	$ 0
Net Tax	– none –	**$ 10,524**	**$ 4,888**
TOTAL INDIVIDUAL AND BUSINESS TAX	**$ 25,803**	**$ 36,198**	**$ 19,244**

*Not shown are an $11,000 deduction for state and local income taxes and property taxes, and a $261 deduction disallowance for high-income taxpayers.

Table 9.3 Tax Burden for Law Partner

INDIVIDUAL TAX

	CURRENT LAW*	NUNN-DOMENICI	FLAT TAX
Income from Noncorporate Business	$180,000	$180,000	$180,000
Other Wage Income	$ 0	$ 0	$ 0
Other Capital Income	$ 50,000	$ 50,000	$ 0
Total Gross Income	$230,000	$230,000	$180,000
Standard Deduction/Family Allowance	$ 0	$ 8,400	$ 24,250
Personal/Dependency Deduction—Number	4	4	2
Personal/Dependency Deduction—Amount	$ 11,800	$ 10,200	$ 11,300
Charitable Deduction	$ 5,000	$ 5,000	$ 0
Mortgage Deduction	$ 14,000	$ 14,000	$ 0
Deduction for Net Saving	$ 0	$ 30,000	$ 0
Tax Base	$188,618	$162,400	$144,450
Tax	$ 42,756	$ 58,577	$ 24,557
Payroll Credit	$ 0	$ 7,573	$ 0
Net Tax	**$ 42,756**	**$ 51,004**	**$ 24,557**

Table 9.3 Tax Burden for Law Partner (continued)

BUSINESS TAX

	CURRENT LAW	NUNN-DOMENICI	FLAT TAX
Wages to Employees		$153,000	$ 0
Fringe Benefits		$ 66,600	$ 66,600
Interest		$ 1,530	$ 1,530
Income to Owner		$180,000	$ 0
Tax Base		$401,130	$ 68,130
Tax Rate		11%	17%
Gross Tax		$ 44,124	$ 11,582
Payroll Credit		$ 18,283	$ 0
Net Tax	– none –	$ 25,841	$ 11,582
TOTAL INDIVIDUAL AND BUSINESS TAX	**$ 42,756**	**$ 76,845**	**$ 36,139**

*Not shown are a $16,000 deduction for state and local income taxes and property taxes, a $2,757 reduction in personal exemptions for high-income taxpayers, and a $2,661 reduction in itemized deductions for high-income taxpayers.

Under Nunn-Domenici, the family gets a family allowance and savings deduction in addition to itemized deductions, but these benefits do not offset the burdens of higher rates. The family pays significantly more individual tax than under current law. In addition, the partner faces a hefty tax on a business tax base comprised mostly of wages paid to employees and fringe benefits for both employees and partners. Overall, the family pays nearly 80 percent more under Nunn-Domenici.

Under the Flat Tax, on the other hand, the family benefits from lower rates and pays considerably less individual tax. Even with the business tax, largely imposed on fringe benefits, the family enjoys a tidy savings.

CONCLUSION

You can see how the major consumption tax alternatives substantially redistribute the tax burden. Low-income and high-income households fare especially well under both plans. Under Nunn-Domenici, a payroll tax credit reduces taxes for low-income households. High-income households pay less mainly because of the deduction for new saving. Under the Flat Tax, all individual taxpayers appear to pay less. This is particularly true for low-income households that could receive refunds for negative tax liability. The generous family deduction and dependency deductions would make such tax rebates commonplace. High-income households pay less because they pay tax only on wage income and no longer face a progressive rate structure.

Both plans add substantial new entity-level taxes on noncorporate businesses. Those business currently don't pay separate business taxes, instead paying individual income tax on profits flowing to the owners. The Nunn-Domenici tax is particularly harsh for "typical" noncorporate business because they are labor-intensive, and wages are not deductible under the tax. The Flat Tax would allow deductions for wages but not for fringe benefits.

10

CONSUMPTION TAXES AND BUSINESS

A replacement consumption tax would mean major changes in how businesses compute and pay taxes, and lead to a variety of changes rippling through the economy. Assessing the impact on business calls for considering a wide range of issues, including:

- Tax liability under a consumption tax (over several years)
- Potential changes in the economy
- Potential elimination of current tax preferences
- Transition provisions
- Changing impacts over business cycle
- Impact on financial statements

Some economists think the first is a simple issue: businesses should not be greatly concerned about their tax liability under a consumption tax. Once the economy has fully adjusted, business will face no burden at all. Instead, prices will rise in response to a consumption tax, and customers will pay the tax in the form of higher prices. There is no adverse effect on after-tax profits. Businesses, however, can't take for granted that consumption taxes can be automatically passed forward in the form of higher prices without adverse impact on their sales or market share. Therefore, businesses want to know:

- Whether they pay more or less under a consumption tax than an income tax.
- What is the relative burden of each consumption tax.

DIRECT BUSINESS TAXES

Retail Sales Taxes

Under a national sales tax, only retail businesses collect taxes. Therefore, if all income taxes were repealed, businesses without retail sales
would entirely escape tax liability (along with about 130 million individual tax filers). Retailers would bear the bulk of the burden in terms of
compliance costs as well as actual liability.

Value-Added Tax

The impact of a VAT tax is difficult to determine. Unlike gross receipts
(the base of the sales tax) or profits (the base of business taxes), value
added is not a concept routinely encountered by U.S. tax professionals.
The concept is not included on financial statements. The income tax
base and a VAT base are vastly different.

Individual Consumption Tax

Here, only individuals pay tax. If all income taxes are repealed, businesses would be entirely exempt from tax. In addition, there would be
no direct impact on prices since businesses wouldn't have any tax
burden to pass on to consumers in the form of higher prices. The major
differences between a VAT and an income tax are detailed in the next
subsections.

Interest and Wages Not Deductible

Unlike the income tax, a VAT does not allow deductions for wages or
interest expenses. For many leveraged firms, the loss of interest deduction could be a major setback. In dollars and cents, this could have an
enormous impact. In 1992, for example, corporations had taxable
income of about $570 billion and interest deductions of approximately
$597 billion. For the corporate sector as a whole, losing the interest
deduction could double the tax base. In general, however, losing the
deduction for wages and fringe benefits would have an even larger
impact. Shifting the burden from capital intensive to labor intensive
businesses is a significant change in domestic tax policy.

Temporary Benefits of Expensing

Businesses would immediately expense capital purchases in lieu of current capital recovery deductions. That's a significant benefit on newly

purchased capital. The tax benefit, under reasonable conditions, should be approximately equivalent to a tax exemption for all income generated by the capital being expensed.

In the context of the income tax, expensing provides enormous benefits. Newly bought capital is effectively exempt from tax. In addition, if that capital is financed with debt, the combined expensing and interest deductions can easily generate more deductions than income. Effective income tax rates in that case would be driven below zero. In other words, the purchase of new capital is not only exempt from tax, it generates deductions that may be used to shelter other income.

In the context of the VAT, however, the benefits of expensing—while significant—are not dominant. As under the income tax, expensing effectively exempts income from new capital. For highly leveraged firms, however, interest deductibility provided near total exemption from the income tax. For these firms, the loss of interest deductibility, by itself, may entirely offset any benefit from expensing. Still, the loss of deductions for wages is far more important. Since income from capital is a relatively small component of total value added for most firms, the favorable impact of expensing on a firm's tax liability in almost all cases will be more than completely offset by including labor costs in the tax base.

Permanent Effects of Expensing

While usually small compared to wage costs, the impact of expensing is still important. Over the long term, the benefit of expensing means replacing a depreciation deduction with a deduction for new capital purchases. On average, it can be expected that an expensing deduction will be somewhat larger than a depreciation deduction.

Temporary Impacts

A larger impact of a switch from depreciation to expensing occurs in the short term while taxpayers are able to deduct depreciation of existing capital in addition to expensing new capital purchases. Over time, of course, these effects become increasingly less important.

IMPACT OF A REPLACEMENT VAT ON NONCORPORATE BUSINESS

Here, all businesses—including S corporations, partnerships, sole proprietorships, as well as other pass-through entities—would be subject to tax. If VAT revenues were used solely to replace the corporate income tax, the new tax would undoubtedly represent a major new burden for noncorporate businesses, particularly service businesses with few inputs other than nondeductable labor.

Most consumption tax proposals, however, usually also include individual and payroll tax relief. In these cases, it's not always clear if a replacement consumption tax would hurt noncorporate business. Under many reasonable scenarios, it is possible for noncorporate business owners to be better off under a replacement consumption tax. For example, in a system that repealed the current individual and corporate income tax system, replacing it with a 25 percent VAT (and assuming no changes in payroll taxes), a sole proprietorship with $1 million of wage and profits paid to its owner would incur $250,000 of tax liability (and no individual tax). Under current law, the owner would pay well over $300,000 of individual income tax.

TAX RATES

It's easy to get lost in technicalities and forget about the important, but simple details. Obviously, the rate of consumption tax is critical. What rate is it reasonable to expect?

Nunn-Domenici

Initial reports indicated the rate of tax for the Nunn-Domenici plan's business subtraction method VAT could be as low as 9 percent. Its rate on introduction was 11 percent. (The Nunn-Domenici plan also includes an individual consumption tax with rates as high as 40 percent.)

Armey Flat Tax

The Armey Flat Tax has a 17 percent rate, after a transition period with an initial 20 percent rate. The Armey legislation, however, also includes substantial controls on government spending, so the tax provisions, by themselves, are not revenue neutral. The Treasury Department has estimated that a revenue-neutral rate for the Armey plan would be over 20 percent.

Broad-Based VAT

As noted earlier, a broad-based VAT would need a 25 percent rate to make up revenues lost by repealing both the individual and corporate income tax. If payroll taxes were also repealed, the rate would have to be about 33 percent. If preferential treatment were granted, rates could be even higher.

In summary, legislation introduced to date has used rates far below the current 35 percent corporate rate. Replacing revenues lost due to the individual income tax's repeal would require imposing a VAT with a 19.5 percent rate. Replacing the corporate income tax would add 4.2 percent to the VAT rate, and replacing the payroll taxes would add 15.6 percent to the VAT rate. To totally replace the current tax system would require a consumption tax rate in excess of 40 percent. This doesn't include higher rates that might be required to account for any permanent or transitional relief.

UNCERTAIN ECONOMIC GROWTH

The most cited economic reason for enacting a replacement consumption tax is its overall positive impact on economic growth. The underlying reasoning is basically this: replacing an income tax with a consumption tax increases the after-tax return to saving and removes the penalty income taxes impose on saving. To the extent this increase in after-tax returns increases saving, it's likely that interest rates will drop and domestic capital formation will increase. Increases in domestic capital formation mean that workers will have more capital to work with and thus will be more productive. In the long run, this means a higher standard of living and a larger economy. The following are the potential economic changes that might result from a replacement consumption tax:

- Increased saving
- Reduced consumer spending
- Increased capital formation
- Increased overall long-term growth
- High prices (short term)

Still, these outcomes are not necessarily absolutes. For example, the numerous tax incentives for saving and investment already in the current tax code leave some question as to whether the switch from the current system (which many economists characterize as a "hybrid income-consumption tax") to a pure consumption tax will really have that serious an impact on the overall cost of new capital. Second, increased domestic saving may just be used to fund overseas investment that would have little impact on domestic capital formation and growth. Third, interest rates may be more influenced by the flow of international capital than domestic savings, therefore interest rates may not be significantly affected by changes in domestic saving.

After decades of analysis and debate, it seems fair to say that no consensus has emerged as to the impact of a replacement consumption tax on saving. If there is a large impact on saving, then it's likely that interest rates will drop, domestic capital formation will increase, and productivity, wages, and the size of the overall economy will all increase. If there is no significant impact on saving, there will be little impact on interest rates, productivity, wages, and economic growth.

The problem for business planning is that either of the scenarios described is possible. Predictions are precarious because they depend on empirical analyses that are subject to dispute. Models used by economists are simply not reliable. In addition, there is often a remarkable consistency between an economist's political views and the results of his or her economic analysis. Despite the conviction of many economists as to a consumption tax's impact, economic modeling has not sufficiently advanced to predict results with any degree of certainty, and the analysis using existing models is inconclusive.

TAX EXPENDITURES: SOME GO, SOME REMAIN

While the 1986 Tax Reform Act reduced or eliminated numerous special interest provisions, many remain. Their annual dollar value totals in the hundreds of billions. Their elimination would have a major impact on certain businesses, either directly on tax liability or indirectly through the impact on customers and suppliers.

Most consumption tax proposals currently under consideration eliminate numerous special tax benefits (known as "tax expenditures") available under existing law. To many businesses, preferential treatment under current law can provide significant benefits, and each business' overall appraisal of a new consumption tax may be dependent on whether preferential treatment is maintained under the new system. To help you sort out some of these issues, it's useful to divide current tax expenditures into two categories:

- Obsolete tax expenditures
- Consumption tax expenditures

OBSOLETE TAX EXPENDITURES

There are those tax rules that provide treatment considered preferential under an income tax. These would become standard under a consumption tax system. For example, there is interest on most municipal bonds. Under current law, the interest is exempt—viewed as a major tax benefit. What happens within a consumption tax? All interest income would be exempt (or provide tax treatment that's largely equal to exemption). Thus, under a consumption tax, municipal bond interest would continue to be tax-free. However, this would no longer be considered a tax benefit, since all other interest income would also be exempt. This type of tax expenditure can be called an "obsolete tax expenditure." A list of tax expenditures whose status would no longer be special is provided in Table 10.1. Most of these tax benefits are made obsolete by eliminating tax on income from capital under a consumption tax.

Those who benefited before from tax expenditures that would become obsolete under a consumption tax might be hurt by the

Table 10.1   Obsolete Tax Expenditures under a Consumption Tax

1. Exclusion of Employer Pension Contribution and Earnings
2. Step-Up Basis on Capital Gains at Death
3. Accelerated Depreciation
4. Deferral of Capital Gains on Home Sales
5. Exclusion of Interest on State and Local Debt
6. Exclusion of Interest on Life Insurance Saving
7. Preferential Treatment of Capital Gains
8. Exception from the Passive Loss Rules for $25,000 of Rental Loss
9. Net Exclusion of Individual Retirement Account Contributions
10. Exclusion of Capital Gains on Home Sales for Persons Over the Age of 55
11. Possessions Tax Credit
12. Expensing of Research and Development
13. ESOP Benefits
14. Deferral of Unrepatriated Foreign Source Income
15. Expensing for Certain Small Investments
16. Exclusion of Income of Foreign Sales Corporations
17. Favorable Source Rules for Exported Goods
18. Deferral of Interest on Savings Bonds
19. Deferral of Income on Installment Sales
20. Exclusion of Income Earned Abroad by U.S. Citizens
21. Expensing of Multiperiod Timber Growing Costs
22. Deferral of Gains from Sales of Broadcasting Facilities to Minority-Owned Business
23. Special Rules for Allocation of Research Expenditures
24. Expensing of Exploration and Development Costs

change. This would be true even though they received the same tax benefits under the new tax law, because relative advantages have been eliminated by a consumption tax. For example, under current law, many insurance company products provide unique tax advantages not available from products provided by banks and other financial firms. Eliminating these special rules can affect businesses by sweeping away competitive advantages.

It's still possible to restore these items to situations of relative tax advantage by providing them even greater benefits than they receive under current law. It seems likely that there will be political pressures to keep preferential treatment for certain types of investments under a consumption tax. Under the Nunn-Domenici plan, municipal bond interest would remain exempt even though the bonds' purchase price is deductible. Retaining this preferential treatment may solve some political difficulties. Nevertheless, it would leave the new consumption tax with the same economic distortions and administrative costs as current law.

CONSUMPTION TAX EXPENDITURES

There are items that could still be considered tax benefits after a switch to a consumption tax. Take, for example, tax credits for research expenditures. These are equally viable under a consumption tax and an income tax. The ones listed in Table 10.2 are the types of tax expenditures called "consumption tax expenditures."

Table 10.2   Consumption Tax Expenditures That Could Survive

1. Exclusion of Employer Contributions for Medical Insurance Premiums and Medical Care
2. Deductibility of Mortgage Interest on Owner-Occupied Homes
3. Deductibility of State and Local Taxes
4. Deductibility of Charitable Contributions
5. Exclusion of Social Security Benefits for Retired Workers
6. Earned Income Credit
7. Credit for Child and Dependent Care Expenses
8. Low-Income Housing Credit
9. Exclusion of Benefits for Armed Forces Personnel
10. Exclusion of Employer-Provided Parking
11. Exclusion of Veterans Disability Compensation

12. Exclusion of Social Security Disability Benefits
13. Additional Deduction for the Elderly
14. Percentage Depletion
15. R&E Credit
16. Alternative Fuel Production Credit
17. Exclusion of Scholarship and Fellowship Income
18. Exclusion of Employer-Provided Child Care
19. Exclusion of Public Assistance Benefits
20. Exclusion of Employee Meals and Lodging
21. Parental Personal Exemption for Students Age 19 and Over
22. Exclusion of Railroad Retirement System Benefits
23. Targeted Jobs Credit
24. Exemption of Credit Union Income
25. Empowerment Zones
26. Exclusion of Parsonages Allowances
27. Special Rules for Allocation of Research Expenditures
28. Deductibility of Casualty Losses
29. Credit for Disabled-Access Expenditures
30. Exclusion from Income of Conservation Subsidies Provided by Public Utilities
31. Exclusion of Employer Premiums on Accident and Disability Insurance
32. Small Life Insurance Company Deduction
33. Exclusion of Military Disability Pensions
34. Special Blue Cross/Blue Shield Deduction
35. Tax Incentives for Preservation of Historic Structures
36. Cancellation of Indebtedness
37. Tax Exemption for Certain Insurance Companies
38. Exclusion of Special Benefits for Disabled Coal Miners
39. Exclusion of Employer-Provided Educational Assistance
40. Investment Credit for Rehabilitation of Structures
41. Exclusion of Veterans Pensions
42. Expending of Certain Agricultural Outlays
43. Exclusion of GI Bill Benefits
44. New Technology Credit
45. Tax Credit for Elderly and Disabled
46. Special Rules for Mining Reclamation Reserves
47. Tax Credit and Deduction for Clean-Burning Fuels

While obsolete tax expenditures are, in effect, automatically repealed by a replacement consumption tax, there is no mechanical linkage between a replacement consumption tax and repeal of consumption tax expenditures. As to the credit for research expenditures mentioned, all of the policy reasons for enacting the credit remain intact under a consumption tax. Current rules for this credit could remain largely unchanged. The only difference is that it would be used to reduce consumption rather than income taxes.

TRANSITION TREATMENT

The tax rules governing the transition from an income tax to a new consumption tax can be of critical importance to some businesses. In the past, so-called "transition relief" has often been a euphemism for exceptions that postpone or otherwise lessen adverse tax changes. These rules have served to lubricate the political process rather than address inconsistencies in the tax law. In contrast, special rules during a transition from an income tax to a consumption tax often are necessary to prevent retroactive tax increases on existing business operations. In many cases, without special transition rules, businesses could be subject to tax penalties.

There is no doubt that transition relief makes a replacement consumption tax much more complex and costly to the government. During the transition, taxpayers might have to keep records to comply with rules relating to both old and new tax regimes. Thus, even if the new tax system will ultimately be more simple than current law, during the transition period it might be more complicated. Most consumption tax proposals have at least some transition relief. The major stumbling block to more complete transition relief is the steep revenue cost. To pay for transition provisions, most tax plans that include them must have higher tax rates during the transition period. Let's examine the areas where transition relief would apply:

- Depreciation
- Amortization of existing inventories
- Carryover of net operating losses and credits
- Accrual-to-cash method accounting

Depreciation

If businesses can't deduct unrecovered depreciation outstanding on a replacement consumption tax's enactment date, they may be hit by a large tax penalty. This burden seems particularly harsh when contrasted with how newly bought capital would be treated—that, due to expensing, it would effectively be exempt from tax. Without transition relief, a business making an investment in an asset shortly before the effective date will face a sharp tax increase as compared to those making that same investment afterward.

Because of the inherent difficulties of switching to an entirely new system, it is likely that many months or even years might transpire between the time of enactment (or the time when the likelihood of enactment seems certain) and the effective date of a new replacement consumption tax. In this case, the stiff penalty on preenactment investment that would result from the absence of transition relief could cause a severe slowdown in business investment. This slowdown would likely be followed by a rapid burst in business investment once the favorable tax rules of the new regime became effective.

Amortization of Existing Inventories

Most consumption tax proposals would allow items put into inventory and similar capitalized items to be deducted when purchased instead of when used. Thus, unlike an income tax, a consumption tax allows deductions for additions to inventory. However, also unlike an income tax, reductions to inventory are not deductible unless special transition rules are put into effect. In order not to penalize businesses, the balance of inventories and other capital items existing on the date of enactment should be deductible when balances drop below the date-of-enactment level. Otherwise, businesses will be denied deductions for legitimate costs.

Carryover of Net Operating Losses and Tax Credits

The availability of net operating losses can be an important source of value for a firm that expects to be profitable in the future. If net operating losses could not be used under a new business tax, there could be a substantial reduction in a firm's value. Similarly, the inability to utilize unused business tax credits against a new business consumption tax could represent a substantial reduction in value for a business. On financial statements, unused operating losses and tax credits are shown as prepaid tax assets. Their elimination would require a write-off of that asset. The most prominent business credits under existing law are the alternative minimum tax credit, the foreign tax credit, the credit for research expenditures, the alternative fuels credit, and the targeted jobs tax credit.

Accrual-to-Cash Method Accounting

Many consumption tax proposals purport to place all businesses on the cash method of accounting. Special transition rules will have to be implemented to prevent double taxation. For example, income accrued on a transaction prior to the effective date of a cash method consumption tax but subsequently determined uncollectable might not be allowed a bad debt deduction because such deductions are inconsistent with the cash method.

LESS CUSHION FOR THE BUSINESS CYCLE

Because profits are highly procyclical, taxes on profits have served as an "automatic stabilizer" for the economy—disproportionately increasing taxes when the economy is strong and disproportionately reducing taxes during recessions. Under an income tax, when business is bad, many firms can escape income tax entirely. Some are even able to collect refunds of prior-year taxes paid.

Although collections from a consumption tax are likely to follow the business cycle, their variability (in percentage terms) will likely be far less than that of a profits tax. The good news for business is that when profits are high, the burden of the consumption tax will not increase dramatically. However, because the largest component of value-added is wages, businesses experiencing severe financial difficulties might still be liable for substantial business taxes.

No Tax Holiday for Startups

Lack of profitability is also characteristic of startup firms. Typically, a new business doesn't generate income tax liability for several years. If the new business is not taxed as a corporation, losses are generally deductible against owners' other income reported on their individual tax returns. For new businesses that are taxed as corporations, losses may not be used on owners' returns, but net operating losses and tax credits generated during the start-up years can keep the firm free of income tax years after profitability has been achieved. This is a stark difference to what firms may expect under a VAT. New businesses—whether incorporated or not—will have no start-up tax holiday under a

VAT. Unless losses are very large, start-up firms are likely to generate tax liabilities from the beginning of their existence.

Major Tax Changes for Reorganizing Businesses

Under current law, tax specialists go to great pains to minimize both corporate and individual income tax liability that may be triggered during business reorganizations. Reorganizations involving changes of ownership of a business (for example, merger or sale of the business) or change in entity (for example, partnership to corporation) will not be taxable events under a new consumption tax. As noted earlier, this is a major simplification relative to current law. If, however, assets—rather than ownership shares—are sold or exchanged, the entire proceeds from the sale of tangible assets (for example, inventories, plant, and equipment) would generally be taxable to the seller and deductible for business buyers.

Four Key Factors

The four most important factors for determining overall liability are:

- **Wages.** Amount of each firm's wages and how they are treated under the alternative proposal.
  Point: For almost all businesses, wage payments are the tax base's largest component. However, wage treatment can be vastly different (that is, included in base, deductible, or creditable) under each proposal.

- **Transition relief.** This can have an enormous impact on tax liabilities.
  Point: This revenue loss may or may not be offset by temporarily higher tax rates. Transition relief may come in a variety of forms, and it's possible for it to be entirely omitted from the plans.

- **Rates.** The range of possible tax rates for different reasonable proposals is enormous.
  Point: Sometimes the simple impact of differences in tax rates is neglected because so much effort must be devoted to understanding the differences in the tax base.

- **Exports and imports.** It was noted that, in the aggregate, the impact of border tax adjustments on the tax base is relatively small—about 2 percent of the total consumption tax burden.

Point: Underlying these aggregate figures, though, there lies a wide degree of variation. For example, it's not uncommon for a firm's exports to exceed 10 percent of its sales. For many firms, even with this low exports-to-sale ratio, the deductibility of exports can be a dominant factor in determining tax liability.

In many cases, tax liability can be eliminated.

Calculating Consumption Liabilities

The Flat Tax

Here are the key points to remember in figuring the Flat Tax (see Table 10.3):

- Businesses include all receipts from domestic business—including exports—in gross income.
- Wages are deductible, but not fringe benefits.
- Capital expenditures are expensed.
- Interest income is not includeable and interest expense is not deductible.
- Property or state income taxes are not deductible.
- There are no tax credits.
- The tax rate is 17 percent.
- Payroll taxes are unaffected by the tax.

Nunn-Domenici

Here are the key points to remember in figuring the tax using Nunn-Domenici USA plan (see Table 10.4):

- Exports are excluded from the tax base and imports are subject to tax at the border.
- The rate of tax and rate of import duty are both 11 percent.
- Capital expenditures are expensed.
- Interest expense, fringe benefits, and property and state income taxes are not deductible.
- Wages are not deductible.
- Employer portion of the payroll tax is a tax credit.

Table 10.3   Armey Flat Tax Plan: Business Tax Worksheet

Gross Active Income:

Gross Receipts from Sales of Goods and Services	_____	
Proceeds from Sales of Business Assets	_____	
TOTAL INCOME		_____
Deductions:	_____	
Compensation	_____	
Contributions to Qualified Retirement Plans	_____	
Capital Equipment	_____	
Inventory Items	_____	
Real Estate	_____	
Other Business Property	_____	
Supplies	_____	
Services	_____	
Travel and Entertainment	_____	
Excise Taxes	_____	
Transition Deductions	_____	
TOTAL DEDUCTIONS		(_____)
NET RECEIPTS		_____
Business Tax Rate (17%)		x .17
TOTAL TAX LIABILITY		=========

CONCLUSION

Businesses want to know:

- If they pay more or less under a consumption tax than under an income tax; and
- The relative burden of each consumption tax.

Unfortunately, the wide range of variables and their uncertain and conflicting analyses leave businesses unclear about how the consumption tax would affect their liability.

Table 10.4   Nunn-Domenici USA Plan: Business Tax Worksheet

Receipts:

Gross Receipts from Domestic Sales of Goods and Services	_____	
Proceeds from Sales of Business Assets	_____	
TOTAL RECEIPTS		_____

Business Purchases:

Capital Equipment	_____
Inventory Items	_____
Real Estate	_____
Other Business Property	_____
Rent	_____
Supplies	_____
Services	_____
Bad Debts	_____
Travel and Entertainment	_____
Excise Taxes	_____
Transition Deductions	_____
TOTAL PURCHASES	(_____)

	_____
GROSS PROFIT (not less than zero)	_____
Business Tax Rate (11%)	x .11
Tax Liability	_____
Payroll Tax Credit	(_____)
TOTAL BUSINESS TAX DUE (a)	_____

Imports:

Total Cost of Imported Products and Services Purchased	_____
Import Tax (11%)	x .11
TOTAL IMPORT TAX DUE (b)	_____
TOTAL TAX LIABILITY	(a)+(b)

11

THE IMPACT ON VARIOUS BUSINESS SECTORS

Changing to any form of consumption tax would completely rearrange all the accidental and deliberate incentives and disincentives in the current income tax code. The effects would be wide-ranging and not entirely predictable. But some broad conclusions can be drawn at this point:

- About two-thirds of the total value added in the economy is employee compensation. This means an ordinary VAT primarily is a tax on wages.

- The business portions of the Flat Tax and the Nunn-Domenici proposals are similar to a "plain vanilla" VAT, with these exceptions: the Flat Tax allows a deduction for wages, and Nunn-Domenici provides a tax credit for wages. While this relief is substantial, these proposals generally still favor capital-intensive relative to labor-intensive industries.

- Excluding exports from the calculation of a firm's gross receipts gives exporters a large tax benefit. Under Nunn-Domenici, unlike the Flat Tax, with the border tax adjustment available, a typical manufacturing exporter could cut its tax bill in half.

Some cautions ought to be addressed here, because generalizations can be misleading. The effects of new consumption tax proposals would often depend on each business's unique circumstances. Take these situations:

Example 1: Acme Corp., with high profits, might opt for a consumption tax over its current corporate tax.

Example 2: Baker Corp., Acme's competitor, has substantial outstanding debt. It might prefer current law since loss of the interest deduction could put it in an unfavorable tax position.

Example 3: Champion Corp., a rival of Acme and Baker, pays relatively little corporate income tax. However, it does some export business. It might choose a border-adjustable consumption tax if it were able to completely eliminate its tax liability (or even generate refunds).

WAGES: THE KEY INGREDIENT

Commerce Department statistics (1993) provide a good starting point for evaluating and comparing the proposals. For the U.S. economy as a whole, value added can be figured as the sum of total employee compensation (including wages and fringe benefits), corporate profits, net interest paid, net nonincome taxes paid by business, and net income received by owners of noncorporate business. This calculation uses the addition method of figuring value added, although many VAT proposals use the subtraction method. It also should be noted that it's not possible to differentiate between "wages" and "profits" that owners of closely held businesses pay to themselves. Thus, no distinction is made between the two in Table 11.1.

Table 11.1   Total Private Sector Value Added (billions of dollars)

Wages	$2,517	51.2%
Fringe Benefits	$ 498	10.1%
Corporate Profits	$ 391	7.9%
Net Interest	$ 460	9.4%
Payments to Owners of Noncorporate Business	$ 520	10.6%
Net Indirect Business Taxes	$ 529	10.8%
Total	$4,915	100%

The preceding table makes an important point. Employee compensation (wages plus fringe benefits) is at least 60 percent of all private-sector value added. Considering that some significant portion of payments to noncorporate business owners is also wages, you can reasonably assume that about two-thirds of all private-sector value added are payments for labor services. Thus, in a "plain vanilla" VAT, employee compensation is the dominant factor in determining business tax liability.

Let's now look at the ratio of employee compensation to total value added for some major industry groups. The main point of the next listing is that not only is employee compensation an important component of value added for the economy as a whole, it's also important for most major industry groups. Note that only for three of the groups (agriculture, utilities, and real estate) is the employee compensation to value added ratio less than 50 percent (except for utilities; these are low since much of the return to labor is in the form of payments to owners of noncorporate business). Even for industries that are commonly considered "capital-intensive" (such as manufacturing, mining, and construction), wages and fringe benefits are still the largest component of value added.

Employee Compensation as Percentage of Total Value Added

Agriculture	35%
Communication	53%
Construction	72%
Finance	62%
Manufacturing—durables	86%
Manufacturing—nondurables	66%
Mining	62%
Real estate	7%
Retail trade	63%
Services	75%
Transportation	76%
Utilities	38%
Wholesale trade	64%

Given these statistics, it's not too surprising, from a political perspective, that the leading consumption tax proposals provide substantial relief for the wage component of the consumption tax.

FIGURING THE TAX BASE

The preceding facts measure value added, but several adjustments must be made to get a reasonable approximation of the total tax base under alternative proposals. Depending on the proposal, adjustments must be made for the following items:

- Expensing
- Deductible business taxes
- Exports and imports

Also, although in theory not related to value added, transition depreciation and the payroll tax credit are very important to determining the impact of some consumption tax proposals.

Another major issue in consumption taxation is whether or not tax should be levied on domestic production or on domestic sales. If imposed on domestic production, exports would be taxed and imports would be exempt from tax. If imposed on domestic sales, the reverse is true. The difference may have important implications for international trade.

Table 11.2 shows the results of all these adjustments, and uses them to calculate the tax liability for the economy as a whole for:

- A 5 percent broad-based VAT
- Nunn-Domenici Business Tax
- Flat Tax

The last two are chosen since they are the proposals currently getting the most attention. While not now in favor, an ordinary VAT serves as a useful benchmark for comparison.

THE 5 PERCENT VAT

To calculate the total amount collected under a "plain vanilla" VAT, three adjustments must be made to the earlier measure of value added (see Table 11.1).

- When expensing is allowed instead of depreciation, value added is reduced by the excess of current capital expenditures over current depreciation.
- Since VATs usually operate under the destination principle (see Appendix D, "Consumption Taxes and International Trade"), you reduce the tax base by the amount of exports and increase it by the amount of imports. Since the United States routinely runs trade deficits, the net effect of implementing the destination principle is to enlarge the tax base.
- Value added includes sales and excise taxes. However, these taxes are often deductible in value-added taxes.

Table 11.2   Adjusting from Value Added to the Business Tax Base (billions of dollars)

	5% VAT	11% N-D USA Tax	17% Flat Tax
Value Added	4,915	4,915	4,915
Adjustments			
Wages			−2,517
Benefit of Expensing	−205	−205	−205
Benefit of Export Exemption	−457	−457	
Inclusion of Imports	538	538	
Benefit of Excise Tax Deduction	−258	−258	−258
Total Adjustments	382	382	2,980
Tax Base	**4,533**	**4,533**	**1,935**
Tax Rate	5%	11%	17%
Gross Tax	227	499	329
Payroll Credit		−177	
Net Tax (w/o Transition Depreciation)	**227**	**322**	**329**
Note: Maximum Transition Depreciation	580	580	580
Note: Tax Benefit of Transition Depreciation	29	64	99
Net Tax (with Transition Depreciation)	**198**	**258**	**230**

THE NUNN-DOMENICI BUSINESS TAX

As already noted, this is similar to an ordinary broad-based VAT. Thus, the same adjustments are made here as in the 5 percent VAT. The big difference is the payroll tax credit (generally, 7.65 percent of most wages). By what percentage this reduces the overall take of a VAT depends on the tax rate. For Nunn-Domenici with an 11 percent rate, the amount of revenue raised is reduced from $499 billion to $322 billion—a 35 percent reduction.

Business Flat Tax

This tax has two important differences from Nunn-Domenici:

- The Flat Tax doesn't have border tax adjustments. While this will make an enormous difference to individual firms, it results only in a net increase of about 2 percent on the overall tax base.

- Wages are entirely deductible. This is probably the Flat Tax's defining characteristic. The business portion of the Flat Tax has a narrower base than Nunn-Domenici, but the Flat Tax has a higher tax rate (that is, 17 percent when fully in place) and no payroll tax credit.

Transition Relief

As noted earlier, transition relief is a significant issue. You can see how this importance is underscored from Table 11.2.

- For the regular VAT, transition relief reduces total taxes by about one-eighth at the start of the transition.

- For Nunn-Domenici, transition relief reduces total taxes by about one-seventh.

- For the Flat Tax, transition relief reduces total tax by about one-third.

It should be noted that to offset this revenue reduction, Nunn-Domenici has higher individual tax rates during its first four years of existence. Initially, the Flat Tax would impose a 20 percent rate for both individuals and businesses.

The transition relief shown in Table 11.2 would be larger if additional items were included, such as:

- Inventories could be written off (as proposed under Nunn-Domenici).

- Certain credits could be carried forward (such as the research or AMT credits) and credited against the new tax.

- Operating losses could be carried forward and deducted against the new tax base.

But transition relief could be less if statutory rules simply reduce the amount of existing capital that may be deducted. In any case, keep in mind, to the extent there is any relief, its importance diminishes over time.

NEW PLANS VS. CORPORATE INCOME TAX

In addition to comparing various tax proposals with each other, it's important to look at differences between those proposals and current tax law. In Table 11.3, the corporate and noncorporate portions of value added are not always separately stated. While corporate profits and corporate depreciation are separate, there's no distinction made, for example, between interest and wages paid by corporations and interest and wages paid by noncorporate businesses. Remember, these are Commerce Department estimates. (It should be noted that, in fact, in 1993, the corporate income tax actually raised $117.5 billion. The lower actual figure is not surprising given the more accelerated depreciation allowed for tax purposes and the availability of tax credits.)

Table 11.3   Estimated Corporate Tax Liability (billions of dollars)

	Current Law	5% VAT	Nunn-Domenici	Armey Flat Tax
Wages		2,011	2,011	0
Fringe Benefits		409	409	409
Interest		131	131	131
Profit	391	391	391	391
Nondeductible Taxes		188	188	188
Benefit of Expensing		−139	−139	−139
Imports Less Exports		69	69	69
Tax Base	391	3,060	3,060	1,049
Tax Rate	35%	5%	11%	17%
Gross Tax	137	153	337	178
Payroll Credit			141	
Net Tax	**137**	**153**	**196**	**178**
Maximum Transition Depreciation		394	394	394
Tax Benefit of Transition Depreciation	0	20	43	67
Tax with Transition	137	133	153	111

The figures invite some comments:

- They show that if these tax proposals were fully effective in 1993, they each would have raised revenues in the same order of magnitude—between $153 billion and $178 billion.
- As noted, a 5 percent VAT raises a little more than would have been needed to replace the revenue lost from the corporate tax's repeal.
- For the corporate sector, the benefit of the payroll tax credit (Nunn-Domenici) does not compensate for higher rates (11 percent for Nunn Domenici versus 5 percent for VAT).
- The Flat Tax full deduction for wages is a greater benefit than the Nunn-Domenici payroll credit.
- To compensate for this lost revenue, the Flat Tax proposal would need to have a higher rate than Nunn-Domenici.
- Transition rules could provide substantial temporary relief under all alternatives. The proportionate benefit of transition relief is related to the tax rate. Thus, transition rules under the Flat Tax provide the greatest percentage reduction in tax.

12

HOUSING AND OTHER CONSUMER DURABLES

The good news is your home isn't normally subject to income tax. In fact, if you have a mortgage, the interest can actually reduce your income tax. Housing could, however, be subject to a consumption tax, just like anything else you buy (or rent) and use. Housing, as well as other consumer durables, poses substantial administrative and political problems under a consumption tax. Appliances, furniture, tools, computer equipment, and automobiles—when used for personal consumption—are all examples of consumer durables. This chapter focuses on housing, the most important consumer durable of all, but most of the discussion also applies to consumer durables in general. There are basically two ways your housing can be taxed under a consumption tax:

- Your annual rental value
- Your purchase price (the more common of the two)

The threshold issue is whether housing ought to be taxed at all. Specifically, tax relief for housing is often under consideration since this relief can help ease some of a consumption tax's inherent regressiveness. In addition, deducting mortgage interest is the most cherished of middle-class tax preferences. There's no particular reason to expect that the switch from an income to a consumption tax will remove the political need to maintain housing prices and the happiness of homeowners.

It's likely that housing will get some sort of preferential treatment under any consumption tax that has a realistic chance of being enacted.

The relief can take a variety of forms, yet any that's granted will possibly be uneven. The fact is that the tax benefits can depend on whether the housing is debt- or equity-financed and whether it's owner-occupied or for rent. Also, as with changes under an income tax, there's likely to be different treatment for housing built before and after the consumption tax's effective date.

TAXING RENTAL VALUE

By definition, a consumer durable provides services to consumers for more than one year. Some economists maintain that, in theory, housing and other consumer durables should be treated this way: tax the consumption provided by these durables, measured by their annual rental values. (Don't confuse consumption services with depreciation, which is sometimes referred to as "capital consumption.")

For rental housing, owners can be taxed directly on the market rents charged to residents. For owner-occupied housing, however, rental value must be imputed and then taxed. Think of the major valuation problems this could pose. When you realize the high rates of tax (for example, 25 percent) being considered for a national consumption tax, disputes in this area could be serious. The notion that a home generates "services" that should be taxed is foreign to most people.

TAXING THE PURCHASE PRICE

The alternative treatment of housing under a consumption tax includes its purchase price in the tax base. In fact, under certain circumstances, the taxation of rent and the taxation of purchase price are economically equal. It's a basic tenet of economics and appraisal that a home's purchase price equals the present value of expected future rents. Thus, if tax rates are equal over time, taxation of a home's purchase price is equivalent to taxing all the future rents. For this reason, tax imposed on a home's purchase price is sometimes referred to as a "prepayment" of tax.

The prepayment approach opens up a Pandora's box of new issues. For example, imposing tax all in one year can create serious cash flow problems for home buyers. Another major difficulty arises as to the taxing of existing housing. Equitable treatment of existing and new homes would require that owners of existing houses be taxed on their home's value at the time of the law's enactment. This approach means burdensome administrative, not to mention political, problems.

THE PROBLEM WITH EXISTING HOUSING

Neither the rental value nor purchase price approaches provide good ways of taxing existing housing. One method that's been suggested is to tax the market value of existing homes on the consumption tax's enactment date. The other method is to tax existing housing on the first sale following enactment, which would result in a lock-in effect; that is, you could avoid tax on your home as long as you did not sell. It's easy to see why this is not an approach that's used by most industrialized countries with consumption taxes. These countries only impose tax on new homes—and improvements to existing ones. Under this approach, all rental payments are exempt from tax.

It is contended that exempting existing homes would provide a windfall to existing owners: prices of existing houses would rise along with the new housing subject to tax.

TAXING NEW HOUSING

When a builder sells a new home to a final consumer, the sale proceeds should be included in the builder's taxable receipts. Under a retail sales tax or a VAT, excluding these proceeds would exempt this housing from tax. Under any real-world consumption tax, the homeowner is "outside of the system." Thus, buyers effectively don't deduct their investment in housing, nor do they include their rental returns in gross receipts. Or, buyers could be allowed to deduct their investment and include their rents—a much more complex regime. Thus, it's the treatment of sellers, not buyers, that generally determines whether owner-occupied housing receives preferential treatment. Most countries with a consumption tax require full inclusion of sales by builders.

Taxing new rental housing is a bit more complex. One possibility would be to treat owners of rental housing like any other business: purchases of building (like other capital purchases) would be fully deductible, and rents collected from the lessee would be included in taxable receipts. The problem with this method is that taxing small landlords would impose large compliance and administrative costs. This has prompted most industrialized countries to entirely exempt owners of residential rental real estate from tax.

For a retail sales tax, builders selling homes are considered retailers (instead of building owners collecting rent). For a VAT, the last link in the chain subject to tax is sales to owners of housing, not providing housing to renters. This creates the problem of excluding from tax any value added by owners (for example, services—such as maintenance—provided by owners' employees).

Mortgage Interest

Under a VAT or a retail sales tax, deducting mortgage interest is not at issue for individual taxpayers because only sales of goods or services are taxed. Under general rules of interest payments under a VAT, businesses that own residential real estate are not allowed deductions for interest costs (or credits for a credit-invoice VAT).

Under an individual consumption tax system, the situation is more complex. To explain the implications of mortgage interest deductibility, it's necessary to review the general treatment of indebtedness under the tax. Under an individual consumption tax, net additions to savings are deductible. Under a theoretical individual consumption tax:

1a. Increases in debt are included in the tax base (since they present opportunities for increased consumption); and

1b. payment of interest and principal are deductible (because this is income that is not consumed).

Equivalent treatment of debt can be achieved by:

2a. Not including increases in debt in the tax base; and

2b. not allowing deductions of interest and principal.

Table 12.1   Treatment of Consumer Debt under a Personal Consumption Tax

	New Indebtedness	Payments of Interest and Principal
Standard Approach	1a. Include	1b. Deduct
Equivalent Approach	2a. Exclude	2b. Do Not Deduct

As shown in Table 12.1 (that assumes a 10 percent rate of interest), the loan's value on its beginning date equals the present discounted value of future interest and principal payments. Thus, the inclusion in taxable income of either the loan amount at the start of the loan or interest and principal over the life of the loan is economically equivalent.

Therefore, whether mortgage-financed housing is favorably treated under a personal consumption tax does not hinge entirely on whether mortgage interest is deductible, but depends as well on the treatment of debt and retirement of existing debt. Under Nunn-Domenici, mortgage financed housing is favored because new debt is not included in income, and mortgage interest (but not principal) is deductible.

EXISTING HOUSING AND USED GOODS

Under a consumption tax, if your entire purchase price is taxed, your present value of all future rentals is taxed. This holds true even if you sold the consumer durable. Therefore, if you've paid tax on a new consumer durable's purchase price, sales of used goods that had been subject to tax when new should not be subject to tax on resale. Thus, housing built after the consumption tax's effective date and then resold should not be subject to tax. This shouldn't create major administrative problems.

For other consumer durables, the recordkeeping and other compliance costs might be significant in comparison to the amount of tax collected. Dealers in used goods would have to keep records of which goods are subject to tax. It should be noted that a used good bought before the effective date then sold afterwards shouldn't be taxed if it's resold again. Thus, if a consumption tax came into effect, say in 1999, it wouldn't be enough to merely know an automobile's vintage (for example 1996) to determine if that vehicle should be taxed on resale; you should also know the date you purchased it.

CONCLUSION

If housing is not entirely exempt from a retail sales tax or a VAT, only new housing would be subject to tax. For housing to receive preferential treatment under the individual consumption tax, it's not enough for mortgage interest to be exempt from tax. Mortgage debt must be exempted from the general rule that new debt be included in income.

13

CONSUMPTION TAX TRADE-OFFS

Each type of consumption tax (like any tax) has its own strengths and weaknesses. Here are some comparative observations about consumption taxes:

- There is a tough trade-off between simplicity and regressivity. A consumption tax that can accommodate progressive rates has an important advantage: it can readily solve the regressivity problem. But it also has a major drawback: it would be more complex than a single-rate tax, especially in computing a deduction for saving.

- A retail sales tax has several important strikes against it. The public would see it as regressive; at the high rates necessary to replace the income tax, it may be unenforceable; state and local governments would probably oppose it. Still, the perceived simplicity of a retail sales tax is attractive to voters.

- Many of the enforcement problems prevalent under a retail sales tax disappear under a credit-invoice VAT. Like a retail sales tax, however, a credit-invoice VAT is highly visible and viewed as regressive by the public. In addition, it imposes substantial new compliance burdens on businesses. This kind of VAT also could accommodate exemptions for favored products and businesses. That may be an advantage, or, if you oppose special tax breaks, as a disadvantage.

- Politically, a subtraction-method VAT may be the most viable consumption tax. Administrative and compliance costs seem relatively low. Its effect on growth and income distribution would be comparable to other consumption taxes (except that it wouldn't be as flexible as an individual consumption tax in beating back regressiveness). But since it's promoted as a tax on business, the public may have some trouble recognizing its regressivity—no matter how much economists may insist this is the case.

- The subtraction-method VAT would radically shift the direct burden of paying taxes from individuals to businesses, although individuals might pay indirectly in the form of higher prices. In addition, within the business sector, it radically shifts the burden from capital- to labor-intensive industries.

- The Flat Tax alters the subtraction-method VAT to more closely resemble the current income tax. Instead of taxing only businesses, the Flat Tax distributes the tax burden between individuals and business—and across businesses—in a way that roughly mimics the present system, although some major differences would remain. The Flat Tax accomplishes this by removing the wage component of value added from the business tax base and, instead, imposing a wage tax on individuals.

Given that a consumption tax with less radical alteration in tax collections is likely to have more political viability, the Flat Tax may be viewed as a political refinement of the subtraction-method VAT. Table 13.1 compares attributes of the major types of consumption tax.

Table 13.1 Summary Comparison of Major Types of Consumption Taxes

Replacement Tax	(A) Complexity	(B) Perception	(C) Probable Effect on Growth	(D) Probable Effect on Inflation	(E) Probable Effect on Trade	(F) Impact on Income Distribution
(1) Retail Sales Tax	Enforcement Problems at High Rates	Like State Sales Taxes	Promotes Growth (to Extent Saving Increases)	One-time Increase in Price Level (if Fed Goes Along)	May Improve Trade Balance (if Saving Increases)	Regressive
(2) Credit-Invoice VAT	High Compliance Costs (Particularly with Multiple Rates)	Like State Sales Taxes	Promotes Growth (to Extent Saving Increases)	One-time Increase in Price Level (if Fed Goes Along)	May Improve Trade Balance (if Saving Increases)	Regressive
(3) Subtraction VAT	Most Information from Existing Books	Like Corporate Income Tax	Promotes Growth (to Extent Saving Increases)	One-time Increase in Price Level (if Fed Goes Along)	May Improve Trade Balance (if Saving Increases)	Regressive
(4) Individual Consumption Tax	Problems with Deduction for Saving	Like Individual Income Tax	Promotes Growth (to Extent Saving Increases)	Tax on Individuals Less Likely to Increase Prices	May Improve Trade Balance (if Saving Increases)	Depends on Rate Structure

96

Appendix A

Since it's difficult to identify and value services provided by financial institutions, no country with a consumption tax has been able to tax financial services in a manner consistent with consumption tax principles. But exempting financial institutions from consumption tax generally results in overtaxing financial services provided to businesses and undertaxing of services provided to consumers.

Problems with Placing Financial Institutions outside VAT System

The main problem caused by removing financial institutions from a VAT system is that this special treatment may result in economic distortions. Some bank customers will be favored and others penalized; also, certain types of financial institutions may be given a competitive advantage. In addition, the nature of the distortion will depend on the type of VAT—credit-invoice or subtraction (see Appendix F)—the method of relief (zero-rating or exemption), and the type of bank customer (business or consumer).

For the credit-invoice VAT, the problems of exemption and zero-rating for financial institutions are largely the same as those covered earlier (see the discussion on the credit-invoice method). Under the credit-invoice method, exemption does provide some relief for financial services provided to consumers, but at the same time can result in overtaxation of (or cascading of tax on) services provided to business customers. Zero-rating solves the overtaxation problem of business customers under the credit-invoice VAT, but it exacerbates the distortions on consumer financial services by entirely eliminating tax.

Under the subtraction method, business customers are unable to deduct implicit fees for financial services because these fees cannot be identified. This offsets any benefit to the bank from exemption, and the net result is that business services with implicit charges are fully taxed. Financial services for explicit charges still enjoy the benefit of exemption. For financial services provided to consumers, exemption eliminates the tax associated with bank value added.

METHODS OF INCLUDING FINANCIAL INSTITUTIONS IN A VAT SYSTEM

Most countries have abandoned attempts to include financial institutions in their VAT systems. There are, however, many aspects of the new consumption taxes currently under consideration in the United States that differ from the experience of other countries. It's possible, in theory, to figure bank value added under either the subtraction or addition method. Both methods require estimates and attributions to approximate the correct amount of liability. Under the addition method, a bank's tax base would equal wages plus profit plus net interest paid. Under the subtraction method, bank liability would equal explicit and implicit fee income less purchases from other business.

The reason for the enormous errors in calculating bank value added under standard approaches is that implicit fees for financial services are often embedded in interest charges and netted against interest payments. For example, banks provide a range of services (for example, free checking) to depositors without explicit charges. Banks receive payment for these services by paying depositors lower rates of interest than would be charged on financial exchanges for more convenient sources of funds, such as commercial paper. Banks also provide services to borrowers (for example, processing, assumption of risk) often without explicit fees. In these cases, banks receive payment for these services by charging borrowers higher rates of interest than would be paid for less cumbersome investments, such as corporate bonds.

These implicit fees for financial services provided to customers should be included in gross receipts when figuring VAT liability. The central problem concerning the treatment of banks under a consumption tax is that these charges usually are not separately identified.

TAXING INSURANCE COMPANIES UNDER A CONSUMPTION TAX

Any attempts to bring insurance companies into the system are thwarted by measurement problems. Premiums paid to insurance companies often have three elements:

- Funding for current and future claims
- Savings for the policyholder
- Compensation for the insurance companies' owners (profits), their lenders (net interest), and their employees (wages)

Only the last element is value added.

Because of the difficulty in identifying pure interest, it's problematic to measure net interest under the addition method; and because of the difficulty in identifying the value of implicit fees, it is troublesome to measure gross receipts under the subtraction method. Thus, taxation of insurance under a VAT is largely similar to the problems of taxing other financial services.

CONCLUSION

Presently, most other nations with VATs simply exempt financial institutions (or most of their value added) from tax. It may be possible, however, to implement some rules that reasonably approximate the correct amount of VAT liability for financial services. Unfortunately, such rules would almost certainly be complex and cumbersome.

Appendix B

WHAT HAPPENS TO STATE
AND LOCAL GOVERNMENTS
UNDER A CONSUMPTION TAX?

State and local governments could be subject to large, new financial burdens as a result of a new federal consumption tax. They have several concerns. For one, they'd suffer financial hardship if their taxes were not deductible against federal taxable income and if their services were subject to tax under a comprehensive consumption tax. There is a particular concern that a federal VAT or sales tax would encroach on state and local governments' ability to levy their own sales taxes.

The five most significant potential effects of a replacement tax are:

- Infringement on state and local governments' sales tax base
- Loss of federal income tax deduction to state and local citizens and resident for state and local property and income taxes
- Taxation of government activities
- Loss of tax-favored status to investors in state and local government debt
- Loss of ability of state income tax systems to "piggyback" on federal system once federal income tax system is repealed

Clearly, any one of these changes could pose a major new burden for state and local governments. The impact of the loss of all five of these benefits could be devastating. Thus, it's likely that a consumption tax that did not provide relief from these problems could face stiff opposition from state and local governments. Suppose state and local governments keep existing income tax systems. Then taxpayers will still have the cost of complying with multiple systems.

INFRINGING ON SALES TAX BASE

As noted earlier, a retail sales tax and credit-invoice VAT would pose problems for state and local governments in a variety of ways.

- As a political matter, it may be more difficult for these government units to raise additional revenue through sales tax increases if the combined federal and sales tax rate is high. Imagine how little tolerance there would be for a state sales increase say from 5 to 6 percent if the federal government had just imposed a 15 percent—let alone a 25 percent—federal sales tax.

- It's widely believed by tax administrators that enforcement problems begin to be unmanageable when retail sales tax rates get into double digits.

- State and local governments would be under much pressure to conform to federal sales tax rules to simplify taxpayer compliance. However, this would greatly lessen the ability of state and local governments to achieve policy objectives through adjustments in the sales tax base.

- Even with total conformity in the tax base, there must be some coordination of the tax rates between the federal and local tax bases. It must be decided whether, for example, the federal tax will include local tax in the federal tax base.

Almost all of these problems disappear under a subtraction method VAT or an individual consumption tax. Concerns remain only if public perception likens them to a sales tax. While the equivalence of consumption taxes is widely recognized by economists, this is not the case for the public at large—particularly if the tax is not separately stated at the cash register.

Conversely, losing federal income tax deductions for income and property taxes would be particularly hard for taxpayers in high-tax states, like New York and California.

TAXATION OF GOVERNMENT ACTIVITIES

In theory, there is no reason that goods and services provided by governments should not be subject to a retail sales tax or a VAT at the same rate as goods and services provided by the private sector. In practice, however, government goods and services are almost always excluded from tax. This gives government an unfair competitive advantage over private industry.

An individual consumption tax effectively taxes all government services. There is relief, though, to the extent that state and local services are financed by income and property taxes, and the individual consumption tax does not allow them to be deducted. It's also relevant to note that the Flat Tax is partially effective in taxing governments, because wages are subject to tax under the individual component of the Flat Tax and—because government is extremely labor-intensive—wages paid are a relatively accurate measure of value added in the government sector.

Loss of Tax-Favored Status for State and Local Debt

Under a retail sales tax, value-added tax, and the Flat Tax, all interest income would be exempt from tax. Thus, state and local governments, as well as investors in their securities, would not lose the benefit of tax exemption of interest on their indebtedness (and, in fact, they'd benefit from removal of regulations and restrictions dictated by federal tax rules).

But under these taxes, state and local governments would lose the special status that allows them to issue securities providing yields approximately 35 percent less than yields on taxable securities of comparable maturity and risk. The interest on all debt would be tax-exempt, so there would no longer be large interest-rate spreads between yields on private bonds and state and local bonds. How much this lack of distinction hurts state and local government depends on how much interest rates in general decline as a result of a new tax regime. Probably, interest rates will decline; however, it is unlikely that they will decline to such a level that would be available to state and local governments if they were the only type of tax-exempt security. In addition, it removes the competitive advantage governments currently enjoy over various private offerings.

The impact of an individual consumption tax on the municipal bond market may be more problematic. Under the general principles of individual consumption taxation, all interest income would be subject to tax, but purchases of new securities—if they represented new saving—would be deductible. (In contrast, all interest income is exempt under the Flat Tax, but purchases of securities are not deductible.) Without special transition rules retaining tax-exemption for the interest income they generate, previously issued bonds—now facing the prospects of taxation—would decline in value. Because newly issued purchased securities could be deducted, they would effectively be tax-exempt.

The individual consumption tax included in the Nunn-Domenici proposal retains tax exemption for all state and local government bond interest and, allows purchases of newly issued securities to be deductible. Thus, state and local bonds retain a special status under the Nunn-Domenici proposal despite the general relief from taxation on all capital income.

Relationship between Federal and State Income Taxes

Most states that collect income taxes rely heavily on the federal income tax. Taxable income for state income tax purposes often is based on taxable income for federal tax purposes. States also benefit indirectly from federal enforcement efforts. The elimination of federal income taxation will increase the complexity of state income taxation. The probable heightened dissatisfaction with state income taxes will no doubt increase pressure on states to reduce or reform their income taxes.

Appendix C

WHAT HAPPENS TO CHARITIES UNDER A CONSUMPTION TAX?

It has been contended that eliminating the charitable contribution deduction could be a serious blow to the charitable sector. In 1993, deductions against individual income tax for charitable contributions totaled about $100 billion. If the average marginal tax rate is 30 percent, this might mean a loss in value of approximately $30 billion annually to charities. Still, Flat Tax advocates maintain that the real motivators for giving are personal income and personal feelings. Opponents of the Flat Tax reform point out that the proposed changes come at a time when there is likely to be less government spending for social service programs. At the same time, there may be a corresponding increase in demand for privately funded charity.

As noted in the case of deductions for state and local taxes, you would lose the charitable deduction with a replacement sales tax or VAT. It could be made available under the individual component of the Flat Tax (but no version of the Flat Tax has yet been offered that does so). In Nunn-Domenici, the deduction is available and is, in fact, enhanced because of the generally higher marginal tax rates and the availability to those of you who currently are precluded from taking the charitable deduction because of the standard deduction.

POSSIBLE TAXING OF ACTIVITIES OF CHARITABLE ORGANIZATIONS

As you may know, under current law, the business activities of charities not related to their exempt purpose are subject to the unrelated business income tax (UBIT). These activities would almost certainly continue in the same way under any consumption tax imposed on businesses. The real question is whether activities related to charitable purposes (for example, educational services provided by universities, or medical services provided by hospitals) would be included in the new consumption tax base. Some experts assert that it would be more efficient to tax all provided services—whether done by a nonprofit or by a private firm—equally. But this proposition is also true under the current tax system with little impact on policy. Tax-exempt hospitals, for example, continue to enjoy a competitive advantage over taxable hospitals. It's unclear whether the political dynamics of a new consumption tax would result in including all charitable activities in the consumption tax base.

Even if all activities of all charitable organizations are not subject to tax, some curtailing of tax advantages to certain types of tax-exempt organizations may be on the horizon. For example, Nunn-Domenici repeals the tax exemption for certain types of educational organizations (more commonly called "think tanks") as well as certain organizations whose activities may be in the public interest but aren't considered to be purely charitable.

OTHER ISSUES FOR CHARITIES

Many charitable organizations, like hospitals and universities, have been able to issue tax-exempt securities. As noted earlier in the discussion relating to state and local government debt, a new consumption tax may result in some new burdens for entities currently issuing—and investors currently holding—tax-exempt debt. Nunn-Domenici allows you to deduct post-secondary tuition (limited to $2,000 annually per eligible student). This may give some relief to universities and other institutions of higher learning that wish to raise tuition.

CONCLUSION

As with state and local governments, tax-exempt organizations could be severely affected by the imposing of a federal consumption tax. This would be especially burdensome in light of possible reduced direct government support to these institutions and potential increased needs for their services given other government cutbacks. Still, as demonstrated by Nunn-Domenici, it's possible to design a tax that's generally favorable to tax-exempts.

Appendix D

CONSUMPTION TAXES AND INTERNATIONAL TRADE

A major issue in consumption taxation is whether tax should be levied on domestic *production*—in which case, exports would be taxed and imports would be exempt—or on domestic *sales*—in which case, exports would be exempt and imports would be taxed. The difference may have important implications for international trade.

Taxes on production are said to follow the "origin principle." Taxes on sales are said to follow the "destination principle." From an economic perspective, the destination principle is superior to the origin principle because it is less likely to distort consumers' choices between domestic and imported goods. In practice, most consumption taxes are imposed only on domestic sales. In addition, most consumption tax proposals—with the notable exception of the Flat Tax—are imposed on domestic sales. Income taxes, on the other hand, are typically imposed on domestic production.

Throughout this book it has been emphasized that it is important when evaluating a consumption tax to distinguish the case of an add-on consumption tax from a replacement consumption tax. This is particularly true in evaluating international issues. Most economists believe that consumption taxes levied on the destination principle are neutral with regard to international trade. Therefore, an *add-on* consumption tax operating under the destination principle does *not* have any major effect on the trade balance. In contrast, many economists believe that income taxes, levied on the origin principle, can be detrimental to international trade. Therefore, it is only when a consumption tax *replaces* an income tax that there may be a benefit to international trade.

Appendix E

DEALING WITH FINANCIAL STATEMENT IMPLICATIONS

The impact on financial reporting of new consumption taxes is likely to be an issue of major importance to the business community. There are many aspects of a replacement consumption tax that have the potential to adversely affect the firm's financial health as reported on financial statements. Investors, bankers, appraisers, and regulators rely heavily on these statements to check a business' financial health.

Without some kind of transition relief, the impact of a new consumption tax on the income and net worth reported on financial statements in many cases would be highly adverse. This could have a detrimental or even disruptive impact on financial markets. Without transition, significant special charges to income statements and reductions in shareholder equity might result.

ACCOUNTING

What are the benefits from eliminating deferred tax liability? Take this very simple illustration:

1. Acme Corp. has book profits of $100.

2. With, say a 35 percent corporate income tax rate, Acme's after-tax book profits are $65.

3. Suppose the availability of accelerated depreciation for tax purposes reduces tax income to $90 and the actual current tax liability to $31.50.

4. Acme's after-tax profits are still recorded at $65. The $3.50 of tax reduction is really only a tax deferral (to be paid over time). Accountants record this $3.50 tax effect of the temporary difference of $10 in taxable income resulting from the excess of tax over book depreciation as a deferred tax liability.

A reduction in the rate of income tax reduces deferred tax liabilities. Similarly, without transition provisions, total elimination of the income tax reduces deferred tax liabilities. Under the accounting rules for treating income taxes—Financial Accounting Standards Board (FASB) Statement 109: Accounting for Income Taxes—businesses would eliminate their deferred tax liabilities and increase their recorded book income (and resulting shareholders' equity) by the amount of deferred tax liability all in the accounting period in which the tax was repealed.

THE BURDEN OF ELIMINATING TAX ASSETS

Deferred tax liabilities arise when a tax deduction is taken in a year preceding that of the corresponding book expense. Similarly, when the book expense comes in an earlier year than the tax deduction, a deferred tax asset is created.

Without transition rules, eliminating the income tax would eliminate deferred tax assets. In the year in which the income tax was eliminated, businesses would have to eliminate their deferred tax assets and decrease their recorded book income by the amount of deferred tax assets. This tax asset elimination would then be a dollar-for-dollar reduction in book income and shareholders' equity possibly resulting in a detrimental impact on financial matters.

OTHER TAX ASSETS: CARRYFORWARDS OF LOSSES AND CREDITS

Besides deferred tax assets arising from temporary differences, businesses may carry other tax assets on their books. These arise from unused net operating losses (NOLs), alternative minimum tax credits, foreign tax credits, research tax credits, and other business credits. If it's more likely that these credits can be used against future tax liability, these unused tax benefits are book assets. Eliminating the income tax assets for unused losses and credits against any new tax would result in the write-off of those assets and an immediate reduction in book income and shareholders' equity by the amount of the write-off.

Note that even if NOLs could be deducted under a new consumption tax, their value would have to be reduced if the rate of tax were reduced. For example, a $100 NOL for a corporation could result in a $35 deferred tax asset under current law. Take Nunn-Domenici: NOLs generated under the current tax system can't be deducted against the new business tax. But even if they could, their value in this example would have to be reduced from $35 to $11, given the 11 percent tax rate under Nunn-Domenici.

CONCLUSION ABOUT ELIMINATING THE INCOME TAX

For firms that have accumulated a net deferred tax liability, the elimination of the income tax taken in isolation would result in a major improvement to balance sheets and a one-shot improvement to the income statement as these liabilities were eliminated. Over the long term, the impact on income statements of the elimination from the income tax could be favorable: a firm that previously would record $100 of before-tax and $65 of after-tax income might now record considerably more than $65 of after-tax income, depending on the new consumption tax rate and mix of factors comprising the tax base. Still, on an overall basis, business would benefit since tax liabilities significantly exceed tax assets. But for any specific firm, the change could be of crucial impact.

IMPOSING A NEW CONSUMPTION TAX

The accounting treatment of any new consumption tax depends critically on whether the new tax would be considered an income tax or a sales tax for accounting purposes. If the new business tax is considered an income (or profits) tax, FASB Statement No. 109 would apply. In this case, permanent differences between book and tax income—such as the lack of deductions for wages under a value-added tax—would be reflected in the income statement every year. Temporary differences—such as immediate tax deductions for items capitalized for financial statements—would be reflected on the balance sheet.

As a collection agent, the business would establish a liability account for any taxes collected until such time as they are sent in to the government. There would be no impact on revenue or expenses. As a sales tax, the new consumption tax would not give rise to deferred tax assets or deferred tax liabilities. If the new consumption tax enacted is a retail sales tax or a credit-invoice VAT, it seems probable that this tax will not be considered an income tax. Conversely, the FASB could provide that some of the FASB Statement No. 109 concepts be applied as described next.

Although, in many ways similar to a credit-invoice VAT, the case might be made that a subtraction method VAT is akin to a business income tax, and that the principles of FASB Statement No. 109 should apply. Certainly there is a legitimate question about whether a tax that disallows deductions for interest expenses, wages, salaries, and fringe benefits is an income tax. On the other hand, proponents of subtraction method VAT (and related proposals) stress that the tax is based on income concepts and accounting, and they often refer to the tax base as "gross profit." (It should also be noted that, because the Flat Tax allows deductions for wages and salaries, the Flat Tax is even more likely to be categorized as an income tax than would be a regular subtraction method VAT.)

If the new tax is accounted for under the principles of FASB Statement No. 109, there would be numerous important effects on financial statements. Some of the more notable effects are listed here. The first of these effects has potentially significant implications for financial statements.

Treating Transition Basis

Basis refers to the part of an asset's cost that isn't subject to tax. For depreciable assets, the remaining basis may be deducted over the asset's useful life. For assets that are sold, only sale proceeds in excess of basis are income and therefore subject to tax.

What happens under a consumption tax without transition relief? All of the book basis in existence on enactment date would eventually be subject to tax. Without transition relief, deductions for depreciation of existing assets would not be allowed under the new tax, and the entire proceeds from a theoretical sale of assets at the end of the reporting year for the initial application of the new tax law would be included in the tax base. These future tax payments would be set up as deferred tax liabilities equal in amount to the book value of these assets times the new tax rate with a corresponding charge against book income.

Treating Expensing and Other Temporary Differences

As just noted, without transition rules, old assets might be treated harshly under a new consumption tax. In contrast, new asset purchases receive favorable treatment. These costs can be deducted—expensed—entirely in the year of purchase. Under income tax accounting principles, expensing allows tax payment to be deferred on an equal sum of value-added or consumption tax base. This tax liability is like a loan from the government and, like a loan, is recorded as a liability on the balance sheet since the assets are capitalized for financial statement purposes.

Treatment of Permanent Differences

Under a subtraction-method VAT, like the Nunn-Domenici business tax, interest expense, wages, and employee benefits are not deductible (under the Flat Tax, wages are deductible, but not interest and employee benefits). For most firms, the inability to deduct these result in the tax base being far in excess of book income. In this case, the firm's effective tax rate (that is, the ratio of tax to book income) will far exceed the statutory rate of the new tax (for example, 17 percent under the proposed Armey Flat Tax). Whether the firm's effective tax rate will exceed the statutory corporate rate of 35 percent under current law will depend on how many expenses for financial purposes are not deductible and also—on the plus side—on how much of gross receipts (for example, exports and interest income) is excluded from the tax base.

CONCLUSION

To determine the impact of eliminating the income tax on financial statements, businesses need to determine:

- Net balance of their deferred tax assets and liabilities on their balance sheet
- New tax rate
- Amount of transition relief (if any)

To determine the impact of a new consumption tax, firms need to determine:

- Book basis of their existing assets
- New tax rate
- Amount of transition relief (if any)
- Net balance of their existing deferred taxes
- If the new tax would be considered an income tax for accounting purposes in which case FASB Statement No. 109

applies. However, if there is no transition relief and FASB 109 does indeed apply, there could be significant financial reporting effects in the year the new tax was enacted.

These issues are summarized in Table E.1.

Table E.1   Major Impacts on Financial Statements

I. Repeal of Current Income Tax	With No Transition Results in . . .	With Full Transition Results in . . .
A. Transition Depreciation and Other Temporary Differences	. . . Elimination of Deferred Tax Liability (Assets) That Increases (Reduced) Equity and Income in Year of Enactment	. . . Reduction in Deferred Tax Liability (Assets) Value Due to Reduction in Tax Rate
B.1 Carryforwards: Losses	. . . Elimination of Tax Asset That Reduces Equity and Income in Year of Enactment	. . . Reduction in Tax Asset Amount Due to Reduction in Tax Rate
B.2 Carryforwards: Tax Credits	. . . Elimination of Tax Asset That Reduces Equity and Income in Year of Enactment	. . . No Impact on Financial Statement
C.1 Unremitted Foreign Earnings: Remittance Assumed	. . . Elimination of Deferred Tax Liability That Increases Equity and Income in Year of Enactment	. . . Reduction in Tax Liability Amount Due To Reduction in Tax Rate
C.2 Unremitted Foreign Earnings: Indefinite Reinvestment Overseas	No Impact	No Impact

II. Imposition of Consumption Tax *(Assuming FASB 109 Applies)* Existing Assets	With No Transition Results in . . .	With Full Transition Results in . . .
A. Book Basis of *Existing* Assets	. . . Creation of Deferred Tax Liability That Reduces Equity and Income in Year of Enactment	. . . No Impact on Financial Statement

Appendix F

Two VAT Methods: Credit-Invoice and Subtraction

The Credit-Invoice Method VAT

The Basic Mechanics

Under the credit-invoice method, tax is imposed on each firm's gross receipts. Tax credits are available to the extent each business can show that its suppliers paid tax on their sales to the business. The amount of creditable taxes appears on the invoice provided by suppliers to the business.

Following the example in Chapter 7, suppose the miller had $50 of sales and $20 of purchases from the farmer. If the rate of tax is 10 percent, the miller pays $5 of tax on gross receipts and also receives $2 of credit. The $2 of credit corresponds to the tax paid by the farmer and this $2 is reported on the invoice provided by the farmer to the miller. The following summarizes a 10 percent credit-invoice method VAT's basic operation, compared to a 10 percent retail sales tax, as it would apply to our illustration:

Business	Sales	Gross VAT	Credits	Net VAT	Retail Tax
Chain					
Farmer	$ 20	$ 2	$ 0	$ 2	$ 0
Miller	$ 50	$ 5	$ 2	$ 3	$ 0
Baker	$100	$10	$ 5	$ 5	$10
Total		$17	$ 7	$10	$10

The illustration also shows that, because total value added equals the retail sales prices, a comprehensive value-added tax imposes the same total burden as a comprehensive retail sales tax (with the same tax rate).

Comparison to Retail Sales Tax

Because a retail sales tax and a credit-invoice VAT (with the same rate) generally impose the same amount of tax on the same tax base (that is, total final sales), economists believe that the taxes will have largely the same impact on saving, international trade, and income distributions. To economists, the differences between a retail sales tax and a credit-invoice VAT are primarily matters of administration and compliance.

To better understand the credit-invoice method, it is useful to divide calculating tax liability into two parts:

- Calculating gross VAT
- Calculating credit

Calculating Gross VAT

The calculation is largely similar to a retail sales tax. Both taxes apply the tax rate to gross taxable sales. Because both taxes are usually stated separately at the cash register, they are both highly visible to consumers. This separate statement is a feature of all retail sales taxes and many VATs. It would be possible, with some minor adjustments, to impose both taxes without this feature. To the extent that there are exemptions or special rates for certain types of products, you must differentiate between sales of exempt and nonexempt products under both taxes.

There are, however, some important differences between calculating gross VAT and retail sales tax. In one respect, a retail sales tax is simpler than calculating gross VAT—a retail sales tax only applies to retail business while a VAT applies to all business. On the other hand, a retail sales tax is more complicated than gross VAT because under a VAT, it's not necessary to make a distinction between sales to business or sales to consumers. Under a VAT, all sales are taxable. If the buyer is a business, the tax will be creditable. Thus, one of the most vexing administrative problems of a retail sales tax is absent under a VAT.

The credit-invoice method's most important distinguishing feature is the second part of the calculation, calculating credits. There are no tax credits under a retail sales tax. Under the credit-invoice method, gross liabilities of businesses are substantially reduced by credits. It's noteworthy that businesses earn credits only for taxes paid by other businesses. The credits are allowed only if the taxpayer has a verified record of taxes paid by the seller. This unique interdependence of tax liability is important for two reasons:

- **Administration and compliance.** All transactions between businesses are subject to tax and both buyer and seller must keep detailed records. What happens if a buyer doesn't keep records of tax liability associated with a transaction—purchase date, product type, seller ID, and tax paid by seller? VAT credit can be denied for that transaction. Note that all credit claims by buyers can be cross-checked with the sellers' records. This places an enormous new compliance burden on businesses not present under a retail sales tax or an income tax.

- **Effect on tax exemption.** Under an income tax or almost any other type of consumption tax, exemption affects only the exempted taxpayer, and exemptions generally reduce overall tax receipts. However, under the credit-invoice method of figuring VAT, the impacts of exemption can extend far beyond the exempted party. Tax exemption can even have the unintended side effect of increasing taxation. We'll examine this in the following discussion.

In learning about value-added taxation, it's important to understand how tax relief may be implemented. In practice, VATs usually have many special rates and exemptions. There are two basic methods of providing tax relief under a VAT: exemption and zero-rating (the sale is taxed, but at a zero rate). Recognizing the impact of these is critical to understanding the effect of a credit-invoice VAT on those sectors and products often provided VAT relief—food, housing, medical care, small business (including farmers), exports, used goods, state and local governments, financial intermediaries, and charitable organizations. In addition, the differences between exemption and zero-rating also serve to highlight some important differences between the credit-invoice and subtraction methods of calculating VAT.

Exemption from a Credit-Invoice VAT

Exemption of a business under a credit-invoice VAT removes tax liability and the availability of credit, leaving the business in a zero-tax position. This is not, however, the end of the story. It's still possible for an exempt business to face a significant burden from a VAT. The overall burden may increase because business customers of an exempt business will be unable to receive tax credits on purchases from the exempt business. In a competitive market, the exempt business that gives its customers invoices without credits will have to reduce its prices or lose sales.

While exemption can increase the burden, it can also reduce it or leave it unchanged from what it would be without exemption. Whether exemption from a credit-invoice VAT increases, reduces, or does not affect the burden depends on where in the production-distribution chain exemption is granted:

- If a business at the beginning of the production chain is exempt, no tax is paid by the exempt business, but an additional amount of tax is paid by the next business in the chain that exactly offsets this. In this case, total VAT liability is the same as in the case without exemptions.

- If an intermediate business is exempt from tax, the business making purchases from that exempt business is not able to credit any taxes paid by the business earlier in the chain. Thus, the buyer from an exempt business pays as much tax as if no tax were previously paid. In this case, total VAT liability is greater than the case without exemptions.

- If a retailer making final sales is exempt from tax, all taxes on value added prior to purchases by the retailer are properly paid and the value added by the retailer is exempt from tax. Here, total VAT liability is less than the case without exemptions.

While exemption is seemingly the most straightforward way of relieving administrative burden, its impact on the tax burdens associated with different products can be markedly uneven. As a rough rule of thumb, however, businesses providing goods and services to other businesses will generally be hurt by exemption. Businesses providing goods and services to consumers will generally benefit from exemption.

Zero-Rating as an Alternative to Exemptions

The large and uneven economic distortions that can result from exemptions have led to using zero-rating as an alternative to exemption. When the sales of a business are zero-rated, the business must still become part of the VAT system and file annual returns. However, the business's compliance burden is not so much an issue because zero-rated taxpayers receive refunds. In fact, under most VAT systems where exemptions are allowed, many businesses opt to remain zero-rated taxpayers. A zero-rated business pays no gross VAT, but is eligible for credits. Besides being good for the zero-rated firm, the economic impacts are much more even than under a system of exemptions. Any zero-rating before the retail stage does not impact a final product's total liability. Zero-rating at the retail stage results in a product's complete exemption.

What Makes a VAT a Consumption Tax?

One of the most prominent features of a consumption tax imposed on businesses is the immediate write-off of the full price of capital purchases. Under a credit-invoice VAT, the equivalent of expensing is achieved by allowing a tax credit for the full price of capital purchases. Expensing does more than just simplify the tax and enhance its political appeal. It is the feature of a VAT that makes it a consumption tax.

Despite widespread acceptance throughout the rest of the industrialized world, perceived high-compliance costs and the recognized similarity to sales taxation have kept the credit-invoice method from playing a prominent part in the current consumption tax debate in the United States. Instead, a somewhat similar alternative—the subtraction-method VAT—lies at the core of almost all current consumption tax proposals.

THE SUBTRACTION METHOD VAT

While its proponents may not like to admit it, the subtraction-method VAT has a great deal in common with the credit-invoice VAT. The tax base is calculated as the difference between business receipts and purchases from other businesses. So, like the credit-invoice method, the starting point in figuring tax liability is gross business receipts. Instead of credits, however, the subtraction method uses deductions to modify the tax on gross receipts to a VAT. Given the same tax rate, you pay the same amount of tax under either method.

There are some general thoughts to consider regarding the subtraction-method VAT:

- This is the general type of consumption tax now getting the most attention on Capitol Hill.

- No country except Japan (with a 3 percent rate) has any experience implementing this method.

- It's likely to be simpler to administer than a credit-invoice VAT.

- It may be more politically viable than a credit-invoice VAT. A subtraction-method VAT has an appearance similar to that of the corporate income tax, while a credit-invoice VAT more closely resembles a sales tax.

What are the similarities between the two methods?

- Like the retail sales tax, both methods are taxes on consumption (assuming immediate deductions for capital expenditures).
- Both methods equally have the ability to increase capital formation and improve competitiveness.
- Both potentially have the same impacts on distributing the tax burden.

What are the significant differences in the economic impacts between a subtraction-method and credit-invoice method VAT? There are three important ones between the two methods:

- Different compliance and administrative costs
- Different degrees of flexibility
- Differences in the recognized similarity to retail sales taxes

Administration and Compliance

The basic difference between the credit-invoice method and the subtraction-method VAT is this: tax liability under the subtraction-method tax paid by the buyer may be figured without reference to taxes paid by sellers. Generally, proponents argue that this greatly reduces the compliance burden in two ways:

- Businesses selling products don't have to provide tax information on invoices to business customers or keep records of these invoices.
- Businesses buying products don't have to retain special tax records of each purchase to claim credits.

Under the subtraction method, businesses can use annual accounting flows similar to those used under current financial and tax accounting rules to calculate tax liability. Businesses would not have to keep detailed records of each transaction. It is important to note, however, that current accounting records would have to be supplemented to determine the subtraction-method liability. For example, you would have to divide cost categories such as cost of goods sold and advertising between (nondeductible) internal costs and (deductible) purchases from other businesses.

Despite these adjustments, it seems likely that a subtraction-method VAT entails lower compliance costs for business taxpayers than a credit-invoice VAT. This simplification comes at the cost of increased potential for evasion and less flexibility.

Under a subtraction-method VAT, compliance might be lower than under a credit-invoice VAT because it is more difficult for tax collectors to cross-check business tax returns under the subtraction method. Duplicate records of invoices held by sellers and business buyers make it much easier to identify unreported sales under a credit-invoice VAT. Tax evasion by retailers not reporting sales to consumers, however, is still a problem under the subtraction method as it is under the credit-invoice method and the income tax. It should be noted that if VAT rates are lower than current income tax rates, the incentives to under-report sales would be fewer.

Flexibility

Many commentators have pointed out that a credit-invoice VAT is much better able to accommodate tax relief for particular products and particular business sectors than the subtraction method. Yet, the subtraction-method VAT's lack of flexibility is considered by some to be an advantage. Here, an absence of preferential treatment would reduce complexity and improve economic efficiency. On the other hand, flexibility is seen as a disadvantage by those who believe some types of special relief are desirable or inevitable. Without being able to accommodate certain sectors of the economy (for example, farmers, health care providers, state and local governments, charitable and cultural organizations), a VAT should not or could not be enacted. This point deserves serious attention because it is important in determining how the tax will be administered and in determining the political dynamics surrounding its passage (as well as post-enactment modifications).

Like a retail sales tax and credit-invoice VAT, preferential treatment of products (for example, food, exports) under a subtraction-method VAT is effectuated by identifying those products at the retail level and excluding them from the tax base. As noted, preferential treatment adds significant administrative and compliance costs, but no more so for the subtraction-method VAT than for a retail sales tax or a credit-invoice VAT. Therefore, a subtraction-method VAT can be effectively administered at multiple rates as long as preferential rates are imposed at the retail level. If preferential rates were provided at the retail level, a subtraction-method VAT would face the problem of distinguishing retail from nonretail sales similar to that encountered under a retail sales tax. However, the items likely to get preferential treatment under a VAT—clothing, public transportation, medical care, and off-premise consumption of food—are much easier to identify as retail sales than those at issue under a retail sales tax—such as tools, personal computers, and autos.

The critical difference between the subtraction and credit-invoice methods is preferential treatment before the retail level. A credit-invoice VAT is particularly well suited to provide preferential treatment for nonretail sales (for example, small farmers). Unlike zero-rating under a credit-invoice VAT, preferential treatment of nonretail sales under a subtraction-method VAT results in uneven taxation of final products. If nonretail sales are exempt (or subject to preferential rates), there is no tax on the seller's value added. But, unlike a subtraction-method VAT, the lost revenue is not made up further along the production chain. Thus, exemption at the intermediate level does provide relief for the final product.

However, if there is preferential treatment of nonretail sales under a subtraction-method VAT and final sales are excluded (for example, exports and food), the preferentially treated final sales do better than being exempt or zero-rated. Their tax is not only eliminated, but they get a subsidy. They are, in effect, being granted a rebate for taxes not paid at prior levels.

There are three responses to the problem of exemption of intermediate product sales under the subtraction-method VAT:

- No preferential rates or product exemptions allowed before the retail level. This seems to be favored by most proponents of subtraction-method VATs. It's important to note that such a restriction doesn't hinder implementing policies intending to promote trade (for example, exempting exports) and policies meant to provide relief for low-income households (that is, exempting food and medical care). Such a restriction, however, would be an impediment to giving relief for small businesses and small farmers who often face a disproportionate compliance burden and are, at the same time, politically influential.

- Disallowing deductions for business purchases on which no tax was paid. This would require that sellers report to buyers that tax was paid, and that buyer and seller keep records of all transactions. The administration of such a system would be much different from that of a credit-invoice VAT.

- Allowing deductions even though there have been exemptions before the retail level. Here, the problem—particularly if not of a large magnitude—can simply be ignored.

Perceived Similarity to Retail Sales Taxes

Economists are often indifferent in their choice of consumption taxes since different types of consumption taxes are widely believed to have similar economic impacts. Politicians, on the other hand, are acutely sensitive to the differences between consumption taxes. This is because the public has a very different understanding of the various types of consumption taxes. Thus, politicians realize that it's the public perception of consumption taxes that will drive the political debate.

There are two notions of a subtraction-method VAT that make it more attractive to the general public than a credit-invoice VAT. The first is its dissimilarity in appearance to a sales tax. The second is its similarity in appearance to a corporate income tax. Retail sales taxes are widely viewed as regressive taxes; that is, taxes that become proportionately lower as the tax base increases. Thus, it has a greater impact on low-income taxpayers. From the final consumer's point of view, a retail sales tax and a credit-invoice VAT are indistinguisable. Both types of tax are collected at the cash register and are generally separately stated from the retail prices.

If a subtraction-method VAT is not separately stated (as under all recent proposals), it doesn't have the appearance of a sales tax. In addition, the subtraction-method VAT imposes significant tax liabilities on large businesses, as does the corporate income tax. This similarity in appearance to the corporate income tax should not be discounted. Many current proposals would use the revenues from a subtraction-method VAT to replace the corporate income tax. Much of the current public affinity for the corporate income tax and the corporate alternative minimum tax is due to the perceived unfairness of large corporations not paying tax. Given the history of the corporate income tax and the corporate alternative minimum tax (AMT), it is likely there would be a significant public outcry if large corporations paid no tax. It should be noted that even though almost all economists believe the burden of a consumption tax falls on consumption, and thus the consumer, and many economists believe the burden of corporate income tax is borne by capital, replacing the corporate income tax with a subtraction-method VAT might be politically acceptable. It probably is more palatable than replacing the corporate income tax with a retail sales tax—even though economists consider both proposals economically equivalent.

It is not only the public's perceptions that matters in the choice between the credit-invoice and subtraction methods. State governments may be more willing to accept a "hidden" subtraction-method VAT that doesn't visibly compete with its retail sales tax base than a credit-invoice VAT that does.

Glossary of Key Terms

Addition method: One of the two methods for purposes of measuring the "value added" (see value added). Under the addition method, value added is calculated as the sum of a firm's payments to its workers and return to the firm's owners (and lenders) for using their invested capital.

Add-on consumption tax: A consumption tax system that is implemented in conjunction with the current tax system as opposed to a consumption tax that replaces the existing tax system (see Replacement consumption tax).

Armey-Shelby Flat Tax: The proposal by Congressman Richard Armey and Senator Richard Shelby to repeal the current tax system, replacing it with a flat tax (see Flat Tax).

Basic standard deduction: The flat allowance that is part of the Flat Tax. This is similar to the standard deduction in the current law in that it is in lieu of itemized deductions.

Consumption tax: A tax on spending, not on income. This kind of a tax exempts investment or savings from taxation.

Consumption tax expenditure: Items that might be also known as "tax benefits" or "preferences" such as the mortgage interest deduction. Most consumption tax proposals call for doing away with most preferences.

Credit-invoice method: A method under which tax is imposed on each firm's gross receipts. Credits are available to the extent each business can show that its suppliers paid tax on their sales to that business.

Exemption certificate: A form granted by the state that exempts the holders from having to pay sales taxes on the purchases they make.

Expensing: Deducting the cost of an item in the year it is purchased or placed in service.

Family living allowance: A flat allowance that is comparable to the standard deduction in the current tax system. As with the current law's standard deduction, its amount is based on the taxpayer's filing status.

Flat tax: A type of value-added tax. Under this tax, a flat rate is applied to wage income on the individual side and to net sales (sales less business expenses) on the business side.

Indexing: The adjustment of basic amounts as a result of inflation.

Individual consumption tax: Also referred to as the "personal consumption tax." The difference between the current income tax and the individual consumption tax is that the latter would allow an unlimited deduction for net annual additions to saving.

New saving: Additions to net wealth after enactment of the new tax law.

Nunn-Domenici proposal: The proposal put forth by Senators Nunn and Domenici. It has a progressive rate structure for the individual tax and a flat rate for the business tax.

Obsolete tax expenditures: Items that under a consumption tax would no longer be considered a tax benefit (for example, municipal bond interest).

Old saving: Saving collected before enactment of the new tax law.

Payroll tax credit: This is the credit against tax liability for the employee portion payroll taxes (for 1996, 7.65 percent of the first $62,700 plus 1.45 percent of the excess).

Progressive taxes: A system where the tax, as a percentage of income, is greater for high-income households than for low-income households.

Proportional taxes: A system where the tax, as a percentage of income, is the same for all taxpayers.

Regressive taxes: A system where taxes become proportionately lower as the tax base increases.

Replacement consumption tax: This is a tax system that is implemented in place of the existing system.

Retail sales tax: A tax levied at a certain percentage when certain goods or services are purchased.

Savings-Exempt Income Tax (SEIT): A label given to the individual portion of the Nunn-Domenici proposal.

Subtraction-method value added: Under this method, value added is measured as the difference between a business firm's sales and its purchases from other businesses.

Tax base: The total sum to which the tax rate is applied.

Tax expenditures: Special tax benefits in the current law system (for example, accelerated depreciation).

Transition relief: Relief provided to ease or otherwise lessen the adverse effects of changes implemented by a new tax system.

Unlimited Savings Allowance (USA) Tax: The proposal put forth by Senators Nunn and Domenici.

Value added: For business, the contribution of its labor and its capital to national output.

Value-added tax (VAT): A tax applied to goods and services at each production stage at the retail level.

Zero-rating: When the tax is removed. It is an alternative to an exemption from tax.

104TH CONGRESS

NAMES, ADDRESSES, AND TELEPHONE NUMBERS

Rep. Neil Abercrombie (D), Representative from Hawaii, District 1

DC Office: 1233 Longworth House Office Building, Washington, DC 20515, 202-225-2726.

District Offices: 300 Ala Moana Blvd., Honolulu 96850, 808-541-2570.

Sen. Spencer Abraham (R), Senator from Michigan

DC Office: 245 Dirksen Senate Office Building, Washington, DC 20510, 202-224-4822; Fax: 202-224-8834.

State Offices: 30800 Van Dyke Ave., Warren 48093, 810-573-9017; and 720 Fed. Bldg., 110 Michigan Ave., NW, Grand Rapids 49503, 616-456-2592.

Rep. Gary L. Ackerman (D), Representative from New York, District 5

DC Office: 2243 Rayburn House Office Building, Washington, DC 20515, 202-225-2601; Fax: 202-225-1589.

District Offices: 218-14 Northern Blvd., Bayside 11361, 718-423-2154; and 229 Main St., Huntington 11743, 516-423-2154.

Sen. Daniel K. Akaka (D), Senator from Hawaii

DC Office: 720 Hart Senate Office Building, Washington, DC 20510, 202-224-6361; Fax: 202-224-2126.

State Offices: 3104 Prince Kuhio Fed. Bldg., 300 Ala Moana Blvd., Honolulu 96850, 808-541-2534.

Rep. Wayne Allard (R), Representative from Colorado, District 4

DC Office: 422 Cannon House Office Building, Washington, DC 20515, 202-225-4676; Fax: 202-225-8630.

District Offices: Greeley Natl. Plz., 822 7th St., Greeley 80631, 303-351-7582; 315 W. Oak, Ft. Collins 80521, 303-493-9132; 212 E. Kiowa, Ft. Morgan 80701, 303-867-8909; and 19 W. 4th Ave., La Junta 81050, 719-384-7370.

Rep. Robert E. Andrews (D), Representative from New Jersey, District 1

DC Office: 2439 Rayburn House Office Building, Washington, DC 20515, 202-225-6501; Fax: 202-225-6583; e-mail: randrews@hr.house.gov.

District Offices: 16 Somerdale Sq., Somerdale 08063, 609-627-9000; and 63 N. Broad St., Woodbury 08096, 609-848-3900.

Rep. Bill Archer (R), Representative from Texas, District 7

DC Office: 1236 Longworth House Office Building, Washington, DC 20515, 202-225-2571; Fax: 202-225-4381.

District Offices: 1003 Wirt Rd., Houston 77055, 713-467-7493.

Rep. Richard K. (Dick) Armey (R), Representative from Texas, District 26

DC Office: 301 Cannon House Office Building, Washington, DC 20515, 202-225-7772; Fax: 202-225-7614.

District Offices: 9901 Valley Ranch Pkwy. E., Irving 75063, 214-556-2500.

Sen. John Ashcroft (R), Senator from Missouri

DC Office: 170 Russell Senate Office Building, Washington, DC 20510, 202-224-6154; Fax: 202-228-0998; e-mail: john_ashcroft@ashcroft.senate.gov.

State Offices: 1736 Sunshine, Springfield 65804, 417-881-7068; 339 Broadway, Cape Girardeau 63701, 314-334-7044; 600 Broadway, Kansas City 64105, 816-471-7141; 312 Monroe St., Jefferson City 65101, 314-634-2488; and 8000 Maryland Ave., St. Louis 63105, 314-727-7773.

Rep. Spencer Bachus (R), Representative from Alabama, District 6

DC Office: 127 Cannon House Office Building, Washington, DC 20515, 202-225-4921; Fax: 202-225-2082; e-mail: sbachus@hr.house.gov.

District Offices: 1900 Intl. Park Dr., Birmingham 35243, 205-969-2296; and 3500 McFarland Blvd., P.O. Drawer 569, Northport 35476, 205-333-9894.

Rep. Scotty Baesler (D), Representative from Kentucky, District 6

DC Office: 113 Cannon House Office Building, Washington, DC 20515, 202-225-4706; Fax: 202-225-2122.

District Offices: 401 W. Main St., Lexington 40507, 606-253-1124.

Rep. Bill Baker (R), Representative from California, District 10

DC Office: 1724 Longworth House Office Building, Washington, DC 20515, 202-225-1880; Fax: 202-225-1868.

District Offices: 1801 N. California Blvd., Walnut Creek 94596, 510-932-8899; and Dublin City Hall, 100 Civic Plz., Dublin 94568, 510-829-0813.

Rep. Richard H. Baker (R), Representative from Louisiana, District 6

DC Office: 434 Cannon House Office Building, Washington, DC 20515, 202-225-3901; Fax: 202-225-7313.

District Offices: 5555 Hilton Ave., Baton Rouge 70808, 504-929-7711; 3406 Rosalino St., Alexandria 71301, 318-445-5504.

Rep. John Elias Baldacci (D), Representative from Maine, District 2

DC Office: 1740 Longworth House Office Building, Washington, DC 20515, 202-225-6306.

District Offices: 202 Harlow St., P.O. Box 858, Bangor 04402, 207-942-6935; 157 Main St., Lewiston 04240, 207-782-3704; and 445 Main St., Presque Isle 04769, 207-764-1036.

Rep. Cass Ballenger (R), Representative from North Carolina, District 10

DC Office: 2238 Rayburn House Office Building, Washington, DC 20515, 202-225-2576; Fax: 202-225-0316; e-mail: cassmail@hr.house.gov.

District Offices: P.O. Box 1830, Hickory 28603, 704-327-6100; and P.O. Box 1881, Clemmons 27012, 919-766-9455.

Rep. James A. Barcia (D), Representative from Michigan, District 5

DC Office: 1410 Longworth House Office Building, Washington, DC 20515, 202-225-8171; Fax: 202-225-2168.

District Offices: 503 N. Euclid, Bay City 48706, 517-667-0003; 5409 Pierson Rd., Flushing 48433, 313-732-7501; and 301 E. Genessee St., Saginaw 48607, 517-754-6075.

Rep. Bob Barr (R), Representative from Georgia, District 7

DC Office: 1607 Longworth House Office Building, Washington, DC 20515, 202-225-2931; Fax: 202-225-2944.

District Offices: 1001 Whitlock Ave., Marietta 30061, 404-429-1776; 200 Ridley Ave., LaGrange 30240, 706-812-1776; 600 E. 1st St., Rome 30161, 706-290-1776; and 423 College St., Carrollton 30117, 404-836-1776.

Rep. William (Bill) Barrett (R), Representative from Nebraska, District 3

DC Office: 1213 Longworth House Office Building, Washington, DC 20515, 202-225-6435; Fax: 202-225-0207.

District Offices: 312 W. 3d St., Grand Island 68801, 308-381-5555; and 1502 2d Ave., Scottsbluff 69361, 307-632-3333.

Rep. Thomas M. Barrett (D), Representative from Wisconsin, District 5

DC Office: 1224 Longworth House Office Building, Washington, DC 20515, 202-225-3571; Fax: 202-225-2185.

District Offices: 135 W. Wells St., Milwaukee 53203, 414-297-1331.

Rep. Roscoe G. Bartlett (R), Representative from Maryland, District 6

DC Office: 322 Cannon House Office Building, Washington, DC 20515, 202-225-2721; Fax: 202-225-2193.

District Offices: 5831 Buckeystown Pk., Frederick 21701, 301-694-3030;15 E. Main St., Westminster 21157, 410-857-1115; 100 W. Franklin St., Hagerstown 21740, 301-797-6043; and 50 Broadway, Frostburg 21532, 301-689-0034.

Rep. Joe L. Barton (R), Representative from Texas, District 6

DC Office: 2264 Rayburn House Office Building, Washington, DC 20515, 202-225-2002; Fax: 202-225-3052; e-mail: barton06@hr.house.gov.

District Offices: 2019 E. Lamar Blvd., Arlington 76006, 817-543-1000.

Rep. Charles F. Bass (R), Representative from New Hampshire, District 2

DC Office: 1728 Longworth House Office Building, Washington, DC 20515, 202-225-5206; Fax: 202-225-2946.

District Offices: 142 N. Main St., Concord 03301, 603-226-0249.

Rep. Herbert H. Bateman (R), Representative from Virginia, District 1

DC Office: 2350 Rayburn House Office Building, Washington, DC 20515, 202-225-4261; Fax: 202-225-4382.

District Offices: 739 Thimble Shoals Blvd., Newport News 23606, 804-873-1132; 4712 Southpoint Pkwy., Fredericksburg 22407, 703-898-2975; and P.O. Box 447, Accomac 23301, 804-787-7836.

Sen. Max Baucus (D), Senator from Montana

DC Office: 511 Hart Senate Office Building, Washington, DC 20510, 202-224-2651; e-mail: max@baucus.senate.gov.

State Offices. Granite Bldg., 23 S. Last Chance Gulch, Helena 59601,406-449-5480; 202 Fratt Bldg., 2817 2d Ave. N., Billings 59101, 406-657-6970; Fed. Bldg., 32 E. Babcock, P.O. Box 1689, Bozeman 59715, 406-586-6104; Silver Bow Ctr., 125 W. Granite, Butte 59701, 406-782-8700; 107 5th St. N., Great Falls 59401, 406-761-1574; 715 Main St., Kalispell 59901; and 211 N. Higgins, Missoula 59802, 406-329-3123.

Rep. Xavier Becerra (D), Representative from California, District 30

DC Office: 1119 Longworth House Office Building, Washington, DC 20515, 202-225-6235; Fax: 202-225-2202.

District Offices: 2435 Colorado Blvd., Los Angeles 90041, 213-550-8962.

Rep. Anthony C. Beilenson (D), Representative from California, District 24

DC Office: 2465 Rayburn House Office Building, Washington, DC 20515, 202-225-5911; Fax: 202-225-0092.

District Offices: 21031 Ventura Blvd., Woodland Hills 91364, 818-999-1990; and 200 N. Westlake Blvd., Thousand Oaks 91362, 805-496-4333.

Sen. Robert F. Bennett (R), Senator from Utah

DC Office: 431 Dirksen Senate Office Building, Washington, DC 20510, 202-224-5444.

State Offices: 4225 Wallace F. Bennett Fed. Bldg., Salt Lake City 84138, 801-524-5933; 51 S. University Ave., Provo 84601, 801-379-2525; 324 24th St., Ogden 84401, 801-625-5676; and Fed. Bldg., 196-E Tabernacle St., St. George 84770, 801-628-5514.

Rep. Ken Bentsen (D), Representative from Texas, District 25

DC Office: 128 Cannon House Office Building, Washington, DC 20515, 202-225-7508; Fax: 202-225-2947.

District Offices: 515 Rusk St., Houston 77002, 713-229-2244; and 100 E. Southmore St., Pasadena 77502, 713-473-4334.

Rep. Doug Bereuter (R), Representative from Nebraska, District 1

DC Office: 2348 Rayburn House Office Building, Washington, DC 20515, 202-225-4806; Fax: 202-226-1148.

District Offices: 1045 K St., Lincoln 68508, 402-438-1598; and 502 N. Broad St., Fremont 68025, 402-727-0888.

Rep. Howard L. Berman (D), Representative from California, District 26

DC Office: 2231 Rayburn House Office Building, Washington, DC 20515, 202-225-4695.

District Offices: 10200 Sepulveda Blvd., Mission Hills 91345, 818-891-0543.

Rep. Tom Bevill (D), Representative from Alabama, District 4

DC Office: 2302 Rayburn House Office Building, Washington, DC 20515, 202-225-4876; Fax: 202-225-1604.

District Offices: 107 Fed. Bldg., Gadsden 35901, 205-546-0201; 1710 Alabama Ave. Fed. Bldg., Jasper 35501, 205-221-2310; and 102 Fed. Bldg., Cullman 35055, 205-734-6043.

Sen. Joseph R. Biden, Jr. (D), Senator from Delaware

DC Office: 221 Russell Senate Office Building, Washington, DC 20510, 202-224-5042; Fax: 202-224-0139; e-mail: senator@biden.senate.gov.

State Offices: Fed. Bldg., 844 King St., Wilmington 19801, 302-573-6345; 1101 Fed. Bldg, 300 S. New St., Dover 17901, 302-678-9483; and Box 109, The Circle, Georgetown 19947, 302-856-9275.

Rep. Brian P. Bilbray (R), Representative from California, District 49

DC Office: 1004 Longworth House Office Building, Washington, DC 20515, 202-225-2040; Fax: 202-225-2948.

District Offices: 1011 Camino de Rio South, San Diego 92108, 619-291-1430.

Rep. Michael Bilirakis (R), Representative from Florida, District 9

DC Office: 2240 Rayburn House Office Building, Washington, DC 20515, 202-225-5755; Fax: 202-225-4085.

District Offices: 1100 Cleveland St., Clearwater 34615, 813-441-3721; and 4111 Land O'Lakes Blvd., Land O'Lakes 34639, 813-996-7441.

Sen. Jeff Bingaman (D), Senator from New Mexico

DC Office: 703 Hart Senate Office Building, Washington, DC 20510, 202-224-5521; Fax: 202-224-2852; e-mail: senator_bingaman@bingaman.senate.gov.

State Offices: 119 E. Marcy St., Santa Fe 87501, 505-988-6647; 625 Wilver Ave., SW, Albuquerque 87102, 505-766-3636; 505 S. Main St., Las Cruces 88001, 505-523-6561; and 114 E. 4th St., Roswell 88201, 505-622-7113.

Rep. Sanford D. Bishop, Jr. (D), Representative from Georgia, District 2

DC Office: 1632 Longworth House Office Building, Washington, DC 20515, 202-225-3631; Fax: 202-225-2203.

District Offices: 225 Pine St., Albany 31701, 912-439-8067; 17 10th St.,Columbus 31901, 706-323-6894; City Hall, Dawson 31742, 912-995-3991;682 Cherry St., Macon 31201, 912-741-2221; and 401 N. Patterson St.,Valdosta 31601, 912-247-9705.

Rep. Thomas J. Bliley, Jr. (R), Representative from Virginia, District 7
DC Office: 2241 Rayburn House Office Building, Washington, DC 20515, 202-225-2815.
District Offices: 4914 Fitzhugh Ave., Richmond 23230, 804-771-2809.

Rep. Peter I. Blute (R), Representative from Massachusetts, District 3
DC Office: 1029 Longworth House Office Building, Washington, DC 20515, 202-225-6101; Fax: 202-225-2217.
District Offices: 100 Front St., Worcester 01608, 508-752-6789; 1039 S. Main St., Fall River 02724, 508-675-3400; and 7 N. Main St., Attleboro 02703, 508-223-3100.

Rep. Sherwood Boehlert (R), Representative from New York, District 23
DC Office: 2246 Rayburn House Office Building, Washington, DC 20515, 202-225-3665; Fax: 202-225-1891; e-mail: boehlert@hr.house.gov.
District Offices: 10 Broad St., Utica 13501, 315-793-8146; 41 S. Main St., Oneonta 13820, 607-432-5524; and 42 S. Broad St., Norwich 13815 607-336-7160.

Rep. John A. Boehner (R), Representative from Ohio, District 8
DC Office: 1011 Longworth House Office Building, Washington, DC 20515, 202-225-6205; Fax: 202-225-0704.
District Offices: 5617 Liberty-Fairfield Rd., Hamilton 45011, 513-894-6003; and 12 S. Plum St., Troy 45373, 513-339-1524.

Sen. Christopher S. (Kit) Bond (R), Senator from Missouri
DC Office: 293 Russell Senate Office Building, Washington, DC 20510, 202-224-5721; Fax: 202-224-8149.
State Offices: 1736 Sunshine, Springfield 65804, 417-881-7068; 339 Broadway, Cape Girardeau 63701, 314-334-7044; 600 Broadway, Kansas City 64105, 816-471-7141; 312 Monroe St., Jefferson City 65101, 314-634-2488; and 8000 Maryland Ave., St. Louis 63105, 314-727-7773.

Rep. Henry Bonilla (R), Representative from Texas, District 23
DC Office: 1427 Longworth House Office Building, Washington, DC 20515, 202-225-4511; Fax: 202-225-2237.
District Offices: 11120 Wurzbach, San Antonio 78230, 210-697-9055; 1300 Matamoros St., Laredo 78040, 210-726-4682; 100 E. Broadway, Del Rio 78840, 210-774-6547; 4400 N. Big Spring, Midland 79705, 915-686-8833.

Rep. David E. Bonior (D), Representative from Michigan, District 10
DC Office: 2207 Rayburn House Office Building, Washington, DC 20515, 202-225-2106; Fax: 202-226-1169.
District Offices: 59 N. Walnut, Mt. Clemens 48043, 313-469-3232; and 526 Water St., Port Huron 48060, 313-987-8889.

Rep. Sonny Bono (R), Representative from California, District 44
DC Office: 512 Cannon House Office Building, Washington, DC 20515, 202-225-5330; Fax: 202-225-2961.

District Offices: 1555 S. Palm Canyon Dr., Palm Springs 92264, 619-320-1076; and
23119-A Cottonwood Ave., Moreno Valley 92553, 909-653-4466.

Rep. Robert A. Borski (D), Representative from Pennsylvania, District 3
DC Office: 2182 Rayburn House Office Building, Washington, DC 20515,
202-225-8251; Fax: 202-225-4628.
District Offices: 7141 Frankford Ave., Philadelphia 19135, 215-335-3355; and
2630 Memphis St., Philadelphia 19125, 215-426-4616.

Rep. Rick Boucher (D), Representative from Virginia, District 9
DC Office: 2245 Rayburn House Office Building, Washington, DC 20515,
202-225-3861; Fax: 202-225-0442; e-mail: ninthnet@hr.house.gov.
District Offices: 188 E. Main St., Abingdon 24210, 703-628-1145; 311 Shawnee
Ave., Big Stone Gap 24219, 703-523-5450; and 112 N. Washington Ave., Pulaski
24301, 703-980-4310.

Sen. Barbara Boxer (D), Senator from California
DC Office: 112 Hart Senate Office Building, Washington, DC 20510, 202-224-3553;
Fax: 202-228-0026; e-mail: senator@boxer.senate.gov.
State Offices: 1700 Montgomery St., San Francisco 94111, 415-403-0100; and
2250 E. Imperial Hwy., El Segundo 90245, 310-414-5700.

Sen. Bill Bradley (D), Senator from New Jersey
DC Office: 731 Hart Senate Office Building, Washington, DC 20510, 202-224-3224;
Fax: 202-224-8567; e-mail: senator@bradley.senate.gov.
State Offices: 1 Newark Ctr., Newark 07102, 201-639-2860; and 1 Greentree Ctr.,
Rte. Marlton 08053, 609-983-4143.

Sen. John B. Breaux (D), Senator from Louisiana
DC Office: 516 Hart Senate Office Building, Washington, DC 20510, 202-224-4623;
Fax: 202-224-4268; e-mail: senator@breaux.senate.gov.
State Offices: 705 Jefferson, Lafayette 70501, 318-264-6871; Hale Boggs Fed. Bldg.,
501 Magazine St., New Orleans 70130, 504-589-2531; and 211 N. 3d St., Monroe
71201, 318-325-3320.

Rep. Bill Brewster (D), Representative from Oklahoma, District 3
DC Office: 1727 Longworth House Office Building, Washington, DC 20515,
202-225-4565; Fax: 202-225-9029.
District Offices: 201 Post Office Bldg., Ada 74820, 405-436-1980; 118 Fed. Bldg.,
McAlester 74501, 918-423-5951; 123 W. 7th Ave., Stillwater 74074, 405-743-1400;
and 101 W. Main St., Ardmore 73401, 405-266-6300.

Rep. Glen Browder (D), Representative from Alabama, District 3
DC Office: 2344 Rayburn House Office Building, Washington, DC 20515,
202-225-3261; Fax: 202-225-9020.
District Offices: 107 Fed. Bldg., Opelika 36801, 205-745-6221; P.O. Box 2042,
Anniston 36202, 205-236-5655; and 115 E. Northside, Tuskegee 36083,
205-727-6490.

Sen. Hank Brown (R), Senator from Colorado

DC Office: 716 Hart Senate Office Building, Washington, DC 20510, 202-224-5941; Fax: 202-224-6471; e-mail: senator_brown@brown.senate.gov.

State Offices: 1200 17th St., Denver 80202, 303-844-2600; 1100 10th St., Greeley 80631, 303-352-4112; 228 N. Cascade, Colorado Springs 80903, 719-634-6071; 411 Thatcher Bldg., Pueblo 81003, 719-545-9751; and 215 Fed. Bldg., 400 Rood Ave., Grand Junction 81501, 303-245-9553.

Rep. George E. Brown, Jr. (D), Representative from California, District 42

DC Office: 2300 Rayburn House Office Building, Washington, DC 20515, 202-225-6161; Fax: 202-225-8671.

District Offices: 657 La Cadena Dr., Colton 92324, 909-825-2472.

Rep. Corrine Brown (D), Representative from Florida, District 3

DC Office: 1610 Longworth House Office Building, Washington, DC 20515, 202-225-0123; Fax: 202-225-2256.

District Offices: 815 S. Main St., Jacksonville 32207, 904-398-8567; 250 N. Beach St., Daytona Beach 32114, 904-254-4622; 75 Ivanhoe Blvd., Orlando 32806, 407-872-0656; and 401 SE First Ave., Gainesville 32601, 904-375-6003.

Rep. Sherrod Brown (D), Representative from Ohio, District 13

DC Office: 1019 Longworth House Office Building, Washington, DC 20515, 202-225-3401; Fax: 202-225-2266.

District Offices: 5201 Abbe Rd., Elyria 44035, 216-934-5100.

Rep. Sam Brownback (R), Representative from Kansas, District 2

DC Office: 1313 Longworth House Office Building, Washington, DC 20515, 202-225-6601; Fax: 202-225-2983; e-mail: brownbak@hr.house.gov.

District Offices: 612 S. Kansas St., Topeka 66603, 913-233-2503; 1001 N. Broadway, Pittsburg 66762, 316-231-6040.

Sen. Richard H. Bryan (D), Senator from Nevada

DC Office: 364 Russell Senate Office Building, Washington, DC 20510, 202-224-6244; Fax: 202-224-1867.

State Offices: 300 Las Vegas Blvd. S., Las Vegas 89101, 702-388-6605; 300 Booth St., Reno 89509, 702-784-5007; and 600 E. William St., Carson City 89701, 702-885-9111.

Rep. Ed Bryant (R), Representative from Tennessee, District 7

DC Office: 1516 Longworth House Office Building, Washington, DC 20515, 202-225-2811; Fax: 202-225-2989.

District Offices: 5909 Shelby Oaks Dr., Memphis 38134, 901-382-5811; 330 N. 2nd St., Clarksville 37040, 615-503-0391; and 810 1/2 S. Garden St., Columbia 38401, 615-381-8100.

Rep. John Bryant (D), Representative from Texas, District 5

DC Office: 2330 Rayburn House Office Building, Washington, DC 20515, 202-225-2231; Fax: 202-225-0327.

District Offices: 8035 E. R.L.Thornton Freeway, Dallas 75228, 214-767-6554.

Sen. Dale Bumpers (D), Senator from Arkansas

DC Office: 229 Dirksen Senate Office Building, Washington, DC 20510, 202-224-4843; Fax: 202-224-6435; e-mail: senator_bumpers.senate.gov.

State Offices: 2527 Fed. Bldg., 700 W. Capitol, Little Rock 72201, 501-324-6286.

Rep. Jim Bunn (R), Representative from Oregon, District 5

DC Office: 1517 Longworth House Office Building, Washington, DC 20515, 202-225-5711; Fax: 202-225-2994.

District Office: 738 Hawthorne Ave. NE, Salem 97301, 503-588-9100.

Rep. Jim Bunning (R), Representative from Kentucky, District 4

DC Office: 2437 Rayburn House Office Building, Washington, DC 20515, 202-225-3465; Fax: 202-225-0003; e-mail; bunning4@hr.house.gov.

District Offices: 1717 Dixie Hwy., Ft. Wright 41011, 606-341-2602; 1408 Greenup Ave., Ashland 41101, 606-325-9898; and 704 W. Jefferson St., La Grange 40031, 502-222-2188.

Sen. Conrad Burns (R), Senator from Montana

DC Office: 187 Dirksen Senate Office Building, Washington, DC 20510, 202-224-2644; Fax: 202-224-8594; e-mail; conrad_burns@burns.senate.gov.

State Offices: 2708 First Ave. N., Billings 59101, 406-252-0550; 208 N. Montana Ave., Helena 59601, 406-449-5401; 415 N. Higgins, Missoula 59802, 406-329-3528; 321 1st Ave. N, Great Falls 59401, 406-252-9585; 324 W. Towne, Glendive 59330, 406-365-2391; 10 E. Babcock, Fed. Bldg. Bozeman 59715, 406-586-4450; 125 W. Granite, Butte 59701, 406-723-3277; and 575 Sunset Blvd., Kalispell 59901, 406-257-3360.

Rep. Richard M. Burr (R), Representative from North Carolina, District 5

DC Office: 1431 Longworth House Office Building, Washington, DC 20515, 202-225-2071; Fax: 202-225-2995; e-mail: mail2nc5@hr.house.gov.

District Offices: 2000 W. 1st St., Winston-Salem 27104, 910-631-5125.

Rep. Dan Burton (R), Representative from Indiana, District 6

DC Office: 2411 Rayburn House Office Building, Washington, DC 20515, 202-225-2276; Fax: 202-225-0016.

District Offices: 8900 Keystone-at-the-Crossing, Indianapolis 46240, 317-848-0201; and 435 E. Main St., Greenwood 46142, 317-882-3640.

Rep. Steve Buyer (R), Representative from Indiana, District 5

DC Office: 326 Cannon House Office Building, Washington, DC 20515, 202-225-5037.

District Offices: 120 E. Mulberry St., Kokomo 46901, 317-454-7551; 204-A N. Main St., Monticello 47960, 219-583-9819.

Sen. Robert C. Byrd (D), Senator from West Virginia
DC Office: 311 Hart Senate Office Building, Washington, DC 20510, 202-224-3954;
Fax: 202-228-0002.
State Offices: Fed. Bldg., 500 Quarrier St., Charleston 25301, 304-342-5855.

Rep. H. L. (Sonny) Callahan (R), Representative from Alabama, District 1
DC Office: 2418 Rayburn House Office Building, Washington, DC 20515,
202-225-4931; Fax: 202-225-0562.
District Offices: 2970 Cottage Hill Rd., Mobile 36606, 334-690-2811.

Rep. Ken Calvert (R), Representative from California, District 43
DC Office: 1034 Longworth House Office Building, Washington, DC 20515,
202-225-1986; Fax: 202-225-2004.
District Offices: 3400 Central Ave., Riverside 92506, 909-784-4300.

Rep. Dave Camp (R), Representative from Michigan, District 4
DC Office: 137 Cannon House Office Building, Washington, DC 20515,
202-225-3561; Fax: 202-225-9679; e-mail: davecamp@hr.house.gov.
District Offices: 135 Ashman St., Midland 48640, 517-631-2552; 308 W. Main St.,
Owosso 48867, 517-723-6759; and 3508 W. Houghton Lake Dr., Houghton Lake
48629, 517-366-4922.

Rep. Tom Campbell (R), Representative from California, District 15
DC Office: 2221 Rayburn House Office Building, Washington, DC 20515;
202-225-2631; Fax: 202-225-6788.
District Offices: 100 N. Winchester Blvd., Santa Clara CA 95050, 408-983-1291.

Sen. Ben Nighthorse Campbell (R), Senator from Colorado
DC Office: 380 Russell Senate Office Building, Washington, DC 20510,
202-224-5852; Fax: 202-224-1933.
State Offices: 1129 Pennsylvania St., Denver 80203, 303-866-1900; 720 N. Main St.,
Pueblo 81003, 719-542-6987; 105 E. Vermijo, Colorado Springs 80903,
719-636-9092; 743 Horizon Ct., Grand Junction 81506, 303-241-6631; 835 2nd Ave.,
Durango 81301, 303-247-1609; and 19 Old Town Sq, Ft. Collins 80524,
303-224-1909.

Rep. Charles T. Canady (R), Representative from Florida, District 12
DC Office: 1222 Longworth House Office Building, Washington, DC 20515,
202-225-1252.
District Offices: Fed. Bldg., 124 S. Tennessee Ave., Lakeland 33801, 813-688-2651.

Rep. Benjamin L. Cardin (D), Representative from Maryland, District 3
DC Office: 104 Cannon House Office Building, Washington, DC 20515,
202-225-4016; Fax: 202-225-9219; e-mail: cardin@hr.house.gov.
District Offices: 540 E. Belvedere Ave., Baltimore 21212, 410-433-8886.

Rep. Michael N. Castle (R), Representative from Delaware, District 1
DC Office: 1207 Longworth House Office Building, Washington, DC 20515,
202-225-4165; Fax: 202-225-2291; e-mail: delaware@hr.house.gov.

District Offices: 3 Christina Ctr., 201 N. Walnut St., Wilmington 19801, 302-428-1902; and Freer Fed. Bldg., 300 S. New St., Dover 19901, 302-736-1666.

Rep. Steve Chabot (R), Representative from Ohio, District 1

DC Office: 1641 Longworth House Office Building, Washington, DC 20515, 202-225-2216; Fax: 202-225-3012.

District Offices: 105 W. 4th St., Cincinnati 45202, 513-684-2723.

Sen. John H. Chafee (R), Senator from Rhode Island

DC Office: 505 Dirksen Senate Office Building, Washington, DC 20510, 202-224-2921; e-mail: senator_chafee@chafee.senate.gov.

State Offices: 10 Dorrance St., Providence 02903, 401-528-5294.

Rep. Saxby Chambliss (R), Representative from Georgia, District 8

DC Office: 1708 Longworth House Office Building, Washington, DC 20515, 202-225-6531; Fax: 202-225-3013; e-mail: saxby@hr.house.gov.

District Offices: 3312 Northside Dr., Macon 31210, 912-475-0665; 1707 1st. Ave. SE, Moultrie 31768, 912-891-3474.

Rep. Jim Chapman, Jr. (D), Representative from Texas, District 1

DC Office: 2417 Rayburn House Office Building, Washington, DC 20515, 202-225-3035; Fax: 202-225-7265; e-mail: jchapman@hr.house.gov.

District Offices: P.O. Box 538, Sulphur Springs 75482, 903-885-8682; Fed. Bldg., 100 E. Houston St., Marshall 75670, 903-938-8386; and P.O. Box 248, New Boston 75510, 903-628-5594.

Rep. Helen Chenoweth (R), Representative from Idaho, District 1

DC Office: 1722 Longworth House Office Building, Washington, DC 20515, 202-225-6611.

District Offices: 304 N. 8th St., Boise 83702, 208-336-9831; 118 N. 2nd St., Coeur d'Alene 83814, 208-667-0127; and 621 Main St., Lewiston 83501, 208-746-4613.

Rep. Jon Christensen (R), Representative from Nebraska, District 2

DC Office: 1020 Longworth House Office Building, Washington, DC 20515, 202-225-4155; Fax: 202-225-3032.

District Offices: 8712 Dodge St., Omaha 68114, 402-397-9944.

Rep. Dick Chrysler (R), Representative from Michigan, District 8

DC Office: 327 Cannon House Office Building, Washington, DC 20515, 202-225-4872; Fax: 202-225-3034; e-mail: chrysler@hr.house.gov.

District Offices: 721 N. Capitol, Lansing 48906, 514-484-1770; 10049 E. Grand River Ave. Brighton 48116, 810-220-1002.

Rep. William (Bill) Clay (D), Representative from Missouri, District 1

DC Office: 2306 Rayburn House Office Building, Washington, DC 20515, 202-225-2406; Fax: 202-225-1725.

District Offices: 5261 Delmar Blvd., St. Louis 63108, 314-367-1970; and 49 Central City Shopping Ctr. N., St. Louis 63136, 314-388-0321.

Rep. Eva M. Clayton (D), Representative from North Carolina, District 1
DC Office: 222 Cannon House Office Building, Washington, DC 20515,
202-225-3101; Fax: 202-225-3354.
District Offices: 400 W. 5th St., Greenville 27834, 800-274-8672; and P.O. Box 676,
Warrenton 27589, 919-257-4800.

Rep. Bob Clement (D), Representative from Tennessee, District 5
DC Office: 2229 Rayburn House Office Building, Washington, DC 20515,
202-225-4311; Fax: 202-226-1035.
District Offices: 552 U.S. Crthse., Nashville 37203, 615-736 5205; 2701 Jefferson St.,
N. Nashville 37208, 615-320-1363; and 101 5th Ave. W., Springfield 37172,
615-384-6600.

Rep. William F. (Bill) Clinger, Jr. (R), Representative from Pennsylvania, District 5
DC Office: 2160 Rayburn House Office Building, Washington, DC 20515,
202-225-5121; Fax: 202-225-4681.
District Offices: 315 S. Allen St., State College 16801, 814-238-1776; and
605 Integra Bank Bldg., Warren 16365, 814-726-3910.

Rep. James E. Clyburn (D), Representative from South Carolina, District 6
DC Office: 319 Cannon House Office Building, Washington, DC 20515,
202-225-3315; Fax: 202-225-2313.
District Offices: 1703 Gervais St., Columbia 29201, 803-799-1100; 181 E. Evans St.,
Florence 29502, 803-622-1212; and 4900 LaCrosse Rd., N. Charleston 29418,
803-747-9660.

Sen. Daniel R. Coats (R), Senator from Indiana
DC Office: 404 Russell Senate Office Building, Washington, DC 20510,
202-224-5623; Fax: 202-228-4137.
State Offices: 1180 Market Tower, 10 W. Market St., Indianapolis 46204,
317-226-5555; Fed. Bldg., 1300 S. Harrison St., Fort Wayne 46802, 219-422-1505;
103 Fed. Ctr., 1201 E. 10th St., Jeffersonville 47132, 812-288-3377; 122 Fed. Bldg.,
101 NW M.L.K. Blvd., Evansville 47708, 812-465-6313; and 5530 Sohl Ave.,
Hammond 46320, 219-937-5380.

Rep. Howard Coble (R), Representative from North Carolina, District 6
DC Office: 403 Cannon House Office Building, Washington, DC 20515,
202-225-3065; Fax: 202-225-8611.
District Offices: 324 W. Market St., Greensboro 27401, 919-333-5005; P.O. Box
1813, 1404 Piedmont Dr., Lexington 27293, 704-246-8230; P.O. Box 814, 124 W.
Elm St., Graham 27253, 919-228-0159; 241 Sunset Ave., Asheboro 27203,
919-626-3060; and 1912 Eastchester Dr., High Point 27265, 919-886-5106.

Rep. Tom Coburn (R), Representative from Oklahoma, District 2
DC Office: 511 Cannon House Office Building, Washington, DC 20515,
202-225-2701; Fax: 202-225-3038.
District Offices: 215 State St., Muskogee 74401, 918-687-2533.

Sen. Thad Cochran (R), Senator from Mississippi

DC Office: 326 Russell Senate Office Building, Washington, DC 20510, 202-224-5054; e-mail: senator@cochran.senate.gov.

State Offices: 188 E. Capitol St., Jackson 39201, 601-965-4459; and 911 Jackson St., Oxford 38655, 601-236-1018.

Sen. William S. Cohen (R), Senator from Maine

DC Office: 322 Hart Senate Office Building, Washington, DC 20510, 202-224-2523; Fax: 202-224-2693; e-mail: billcohen@cohen.senate.gov.

State Offices: 150 Capitol St., P.O. Box 347, Augusta 04332, 207-622-8414; Fed. Bldg., 202 Harlow St., Bangor 04402, 207-945-0417; 109 Alfred St., Biddeford 04005, 207-283-1101; 11 Lisbon St., Lewiston 04240, 207-784-6969; 10 Moulton St., P.O. Box 1938, Portland 04104, 207-780-3575; and 169 Academy St., Presque Isle 04769, 207-764-3266.

Rep. Ronald D. Coleman (D), Representative from Texas, District 16

DC Office: 2312 Rayburn House Office Building, Washington, DC 20515, 202-225-4831; Fax: 202-225-4825.

District Offices: Fed. Bldg., 700 E. San Antonio St., El Paso 79901, 915-534-6200; and P.O. Bldg., Pecos 79772, 915-445-6218.

Rep. Mac Collins (R), Representative from Georgia, District 3

DC Office: 1130 Longworth House Office Building, Washington, DC 20515, 202-225-5901; Fax: 202-225-2515.

District Offices: 173 N. Main St., Jonesboro 30236, 404-603-3395; and 5704 Beallwood Connector, Columbus 31904, 706-327-7728.

Rep. Cardiss Collins (D), Representative from Illinois, District 7

DC Office: 2308 Rayburn House Office Building, Washington, DC 20515, 202-225-5006; Fax: 202-225-8396.

District Offices: 230 S. Dearborn St., Chicago 60604, 312-353-5754; and 328 Lake St., Oak Park 60302, 708-383-1400.

Rep. Barbara Rose Collins (D), Representative from Michigan, District 15

DC Office: 401 Cannon House Office Building, Washington, DC 20515, 202-225-2261; Fax: 202-225-6645.

District Offices: 1155 Brewery Park Blvd., Detroit 48207, 313-567-2233.

Rep. Larry Combest (R), Representative from Texas, District 19

DC Office: 1511 Longworth House Office Building, Washington, DC 20515, 202-225-4005.

District Offices: 1205 Texas Ave., Lubbock 79401, 806-763-1611; 5809 S. Western, Amarillo 79110, 806-353-3945; and 3800 E. 42d St., Odessa 79762, 915-362-2631.

Rep. Gary A. Condit (D), Representative from California, District 18

DC Office: 2444 Rayburn House Office Building, Washington, DC 20515, 202-225-6131; Fax: 202-225-0819.

District Offices: 415 W. 18th St., Merced 95340, 209-383-4455;and 920 16th St., Modesto 95354, 209-527-1914.

Sen. Kent Conrad (D), Senator from North Dakota

DC Office: 724 Hart Senate Office Building, Washington, DC 20510, 202-224-2043; Fax: 202-224-7776.

State Offices: Fed. Bldg., 3d & Rosser Ave., Bismarck 58501, 701-258-4648;657 2d Ave. N., Fargo 58102, 701-232-8030; 100 1st St. SW, Minot 58701,701-852-0703; and Fed. Bldg., 102 N. 4th St., Grand Forks 58201, 701-775-9601.

Rep. John Conyers, Jr. (D), Representative from Michigan, District 14

DC Office: 2426 Rayburn House Office Building, Washington, DC 20515, 202-225-5126; Fax: 202-225-0072; e-mail: jconyers@hr.house.gov.

District Offices: 669 Fed. Bldg., 231 W. Lafayette St., Detroit 48226, 313-961-5670.

Rep. Wes Cooley (R), Representative from Oregon, District 2

DC Office: 1609 Longworth House Office Building, Washington, DC 20515, 202-225-6730; Fax: 202-225-3046.

District Offices: 259 Barnett Rd., Medford 97501, 503-776-4646.

Rep. Jerry F. Costello (D), Representative from Illinois, District 12

DC Office: 2454 Rayburn House Office Building, Washington, DC 20515, 202-225-5661; Fax: 202-225-0285; e-mail: jfcil12@hr.house.gov.

District Offices: 327 W. Main St., Belleville 62221, 618-233-8026.

Sen. Paul Coverdell (R), Senator from Georgia

DC Office: 200 Russell Senate Office Building, Washington, DC 20510, 202-224-3643; Fax: 202-228-3783; e-mail: senator_coverdell@coverdell.senate.gov.

State Offices: 100 Colony Sq., 1175 Peachtree St., NE, Atlanta 30361, 404-347-2202.

Rep. Christopher Cox (R), Representative from California, District 47

DC Office: 2402 Rayburn House Office Building, Washington, DC 20515, 202-225-5611; Fax: 202-225-9177.

District Offices: 4000 MacArthur Blvd., Newport Beach 92660, 714-756-2244.

Rep. William J. Coyne (D), Representative from Pennsylvania, District 14

DC Office: 2455 Rayburn House Office Building, Washington, DC 20515, 202-225-2301; Fax: 202-225-1844.

District Offices: 2009 Fed. Bldg., 1000 Liberty Ave., Pittsburgh 15222, 412-644-2870.

Sen. Larry Craig (R), Senator from Idaho

DC Office: 313 Hart Senate Office Building, Washington, DC 20510, 202-224-2752; Fax: 202-224-2573; e-mail: larry_craig@craig.senate.gov.

State Offices: 304 N. 8th St., Boise 83702, 208-342-7985; 103 N. 4th St., Coeur d'Alene 83814, 208-667-6130; 846 Main St., Lewiston 83501, 208-743-0792; 1292 Addison Ave. E., Twin Falls 83301, 202-734-6780; 250 S. 4th Ave., Pocatello 83201, 208-236-6817; and 2539 Channing Way, Idaho Falls 83404, 208-523-5541.

Rep. Robert E. (Bud) Cramer (D), Representative from Alabama, District 5
DC Office: 236 Cannon House Office Building, Washington, DC 20515,
202-225-4801; Fax: 202-225-4392; e-mail: budmail@hr.house.gov.
District Offices: 737 E. Avalon Ave., Muscle Shoals 35661, 205-381-3450; 403
Franklin St., Huntsville 35801, 205-551-0190; and Morgan Cnty. Crthse.,
P.O. Box 668, Decatur 35602, 205-355-9400.

Rep. Philip M. Crane (R), Representative from Illinois, District 8
DC Office: 233 Cannon House Office Building, Washington, DC 20515,
202-225-3711; Fax: 202-225-7830.
District Offices: 1450 S. New Wilke Rd., Arlington Heights 60005, 708-394-0790;
and 300 N. Milwaukee Ave., Lake Villa 60046, 708-265-9000.

Rep. Michael Crapo (R), Representative from Idaho, District 2
DC Office: 437 Cannon House Office Building, Washington, DC 20515,
202-225-5531; Fax: 202-225-8216.
District Offices: 304 N. 8th St., Boise 83702, 208-334-1953; 250 S. 4th St., Pocatello
83201, 208-236-6734; 628 Blue Lakes Blvd., N., Twin Falls 83301, 208-734-7219; and
2539 Channing Way, Idaho Falls 83404, 208-523-6701.

Rep. Frank A. Cremeans (R), Representative from Ohio, District 6
DC Office: 1630 Longworth House Office Building, Washington, DC 20515,
202-225-5705; Fax: 202-225-3054.
District Offices: 200 Putnam St., Marietta 45750, 614-373-2120; 301 N. High St.,
Hillsboro 45133, 513-393-8688; and 308 Bank One Plz., Portsmouth 45662,
614-353-4006.

Rep. Barbara Cubin (R), Representative from Wyoming, District 1
DC Office: 1114 Longworth House Office Building, Washington, DC 20515,
202-225-2311; Fax: 202-225-3057.
District Offices: 4003 Fed. Bldg., 100 E. B St., Casper 82601, 307-261-5595;
2015 Fed. Bldg., 2120 Capitol Ave., Cheyenne 82001, 307-772-2595; and
2515 Foothills Blvd., Rock Springs 82901, 307-362-4095.

Rep. Randy (Duke) Cunningham (R), Representative from California, District 51
DC Office: 227 Cannon House Office Building, Washington, DC 20515,
202-225-5452; Fax: 202-225-2558.
District Offices: 613 W. Valley Pkwy., Escondido 92025, 619-737-6960.

Sen. Alfonse M. D'Amato (R), Senator from New York
DC Office: 520 Hart Senate Office Building, Washington, DC 20510, 202-224-6542;
Fax: 202-224-5871.
State Offices: 420 Fed. Bldg., Albany 12207, 518-472-4343; Fed. Bldg.,
111 W. Huron, Buffalo 14202, 716-846-4111; 7 Penn Plz., 7th Ave., New York
10001, 212-947-7390; 1259 Fed. Bldg., 100 S. Clinton St., Syracuse 13260,
315-423-5471; and 100 State St., 304 Fed. Bldg., Rochester 14614, 716-263-5866.

Rep. Pat Danner (D), Representative from Missouri, District 6

DC Office: 1323 Longworth House Office Building, Washington, DC 20515, 202-225-7041; Fax: 202-225-8221.

District Offices: 5754 N. Broadway, Bldg. 3, Kansas City 64118, 816-455-2256; and 201 S. 8th St., St. Joseph 64501, 816-233-9818.

Sen. Thomas A. Daschle (D), Senator from South Dakota

DC Office: 509 Hart Senate Office Building, Washington, DC 20510, 202-224-2321; Fax: 202-224-2047; e-mail: tom_daschle@daschle.senate.gov.

State Offices: P.O. Box 1274, Sioux Falls 57101, 605-334-9596; P.O. Box 1536, Aberdeen 57401, 605-225-8823; and P.O. Box 8168, Rapid City 57709, 605-348-3551.

Rep. Tom Davis (R), Representative from Virginia, District 11

DC Office: 415 Cannon House Office Building, Washington, DC 20515, 202-225-1492; Fax: 202-225-3071; e-mail: tomdavis@hr.house.gov.

District Offices: 7018 Evergreen Ct., Annandale 22003, 703-916-9610.

Rep. E (Kika) de la Garza (D), Representative from Texas, District 15

DC Office: 1401 Longworth House Office Building, Washington, DC 20515, 202-225-2531; Fax: 202-225-2534.

District Offices: 1418 Beech St., McAllen 78501, 210-682-5545; and Alice Fed. Bldg., 401 E. 2d St., Alice 78332, 512-664-2215.

Rep. Nathan Deal (R), Representative from Georgia, District 9

DC Office: 1406 Longworth House Office Building, Washington, DC 20515, 202-225-5211; Fax: 202-225-8272.

District Offices: P.O. Box 1015, Gainesville 30503, 404-535-2592; 415 E. Walnut Ave., Dalton 30720, 706-226-5320; and 109 N. Main St., La Fayette 30728, 706-638-7042.

Rep. Peter A. DeFazio (D), Representative from Oregon, District 4

DC Office: 2134 Rayburn House Office Building, Washington, DC 20515, 202-225-6416; Fax: 202-225-0373; e-mail: pdefazio@hr.house.gov.

District Offices: P.O. Box 1557, Coos Bay 97420, 503-269-2609; 151 W. 7th Ave., Eugene 97401, 503-465-6732; and P.O. Box 2460, Roseburg 97470, 503-440-3523.

Rep. Rosa L. DeLauro (D), Representative from Connecticut, District 3

DC Office: 436 Cannon House Office Building, Washington, DC 20515, 202-225-3661; Fax: 202-225-4890.

District Offices: 265 Church St., New Haven 06510, 203-562-3718.

Rep. Tom DeLay (R), Representative from Texas, District 22

DC Office: 203 Cannon House Office Building, Washington, DC 20515, 202-225-5951; Fax: 202-225-5241.

District Offices: 12603 Southwest Frwy., Stafford 77477, 713-240-3700.

Rep. Ronald V. Dellums (D), Representative from California, District 9
DC Office: 2108 Rayburn House Office Building, Washington, DC 20515, 202-225-2661; Fax: 202-225-9817.
District Offices: 1301 Clay St., Oakland 94612, 510-763-0370.
———————

Rep. Peter Deutsch (D), Representative from Florida, District 20
DC Office: 204 Cannon House Office Building, Washington, DC 20515, 202-225-7931; Fax: 202-225-8456; e-mail: pdeutsch@hr.house.gov.
District Offices: 10100 Pines Blvd., Pembroke Pines 33025, 305-437-3936.
———————

Sen. Mike DeWine (R), Senator from Ohio
DC Office: 140 Russell Senate Office Building, Washington, DC 20510, 202-224-2315; Fax: 202-224-6519; e-mail: senator_dewine@dewine.senate.gov.
State Offices: 200 N. High St., Columbus 43215, 614-469-6774; 550 Main St., Cincinnati 45202, 513-684-3894; 234 N. Summit St., Toledo 43604, 419-259-7535; 1240 E. 9th St., Cleveland 44199, 216-522-7272; and 200 Putnam St., Marietta 45750, 614-373-2120.
———————

Rep. Lincoln Diaz-Balart (R), Representative from Florida, District 21
DC Office: 431 Cannon House Office Building, Washington, DC 20515, 202-225-4211; Fax: 202-225-8576.
District Offices: 8525 N.W. 53d Terr., Miami 33166, 305-470-8555.
———————

Rep. Jay Dickey (R), Representative from Arkansas, District 4
DC Office: 230 Cannon House Office Building, Washington, DC 20515, 202-225-3772; Fax: 202-225-1314; e-mail: jdickey@hr.house.gov.
District Offices: 100 E. 8th St., Pine Bluff 71601, 501-536-3376; 100 Reserve, Hot Springs 71913, 501-623-5800; and 100 S. Jackson, El Dorado 71730, 501-862-0236.
———————

Rep. Norm Dicks (D), Representative from Washington, District 6
DC Office: 2467 Rayburn House Office Building, Washington, DC 20515, 202-225-5916; Fax: 202-226-1176.
District Offices: 1717 Pacific Ave., Tacoma 98402, 206-593-6536; and 500 Pacific Ave., Bremerton 98310, 206-479-4011.
———————

Rep. John D. Dingell (D), Representative from Michigan, District 16
DC Office: 2328 Rayburn House Office Building, Washington, DC 20515, 202-225-4071.
District Offices: 5465 Schaefer Rd., Dearborn 48126, 313-846-1276; and 23 E. Front St., Monroe 48161, 313-243-1849.
———————

Rep. Julian C. Dixon (D), Representative from California, District 32
DC Office: 2252 Rayburn House Office Building, Washington, DC 20515, 202-225-7084; Fax: 202-225-4091.
District Offices: 5100 W. Goldleaf Cir., Los Angeles 90056, 213-678-5424.
———————

Sen. Christopher J. Dodd (D), Senator from Connecticut

DC Office: 444 Russell Senate Office Building, Washington, DC 20510, 202-224-2823; Fax: 202-224-1083; e-mail: sen_dodd@dodd.senate.gov.

State Offices: 100 Great Meadow Rd., Wethersfield 06109, 203-240-3470.

Rep. Lloyd Doggett (D), Representative from Texas, District 10

DC Office: 126 Cannon House Office Building, Washington, DC 20515, 202-225-4865; Fax: 202-225-3073; e-mail: doggett@hr.house.gov.

District Offices: 763 Fed. Bldg., 300 E. 8th St., Austin 78701, 512-482-5921.

Sen. Robert Dole (R), Senator from Kansas

DC Office: 141 Hart Senate Office Building, Washington, DC 20510, 202-224-6521; Fax: 202-228-1245.

State Offices: 500 State Ave., Kansas City 66101, 913-371-6108; 444 S.E. Quincy, Topeka 66683, 913-295-2745; 100 N. Broadway, Wichita 67202, 316-263-4956.

Sen. Pete V. Domenici (R), Senator from New Mexico

DC Office: 328 Hart Senate Office Building, Washington, DC 20510, 202-224-6621; e-mail: senator_domenici@domenici.senate.gov.

State Offices: 625 Silver SW, Albuquerque 87102, 505-766-3481; New Postal Bldg., 120 S. Federal Pl., Santa Fe 87501, 505-988-6511; Sun Belt Plz., 1065 S. Main St., Bldg. Las Cruces 88005, 505-526-5475; and Fed. Bldg. Roswell 88201, 505-623-6170.

Rep. Calvin Dooley (D), Representative from California, District 20

DC Office: 1227 Longworth House Office Building, Washington, DC 20515, 202-225-3341; Fax: 202-225-9308.

District Offices: 224 W. Lacey Blvd., Hanford 93230, 209-585-8171.

Rep. John T. Doolittle (R), Representative from California, District 4

DC Office: 1526 Longworth House Office Building, Washington, DC 20515, 202-225-2511; Fax: 202-225-5444.

District Offices: 2130 Professional Dr., Roseville 95661, 916-786-5560.

Sen. Byron L. Dorgan (D), Senator from North Dakota

DC Office: 713 Hart Senate Office Building, Washington, DC 20510, 202-224-2551; Fax: 202-224-1193; e-mail: senator@dorgan.senate.gov.

State Offices: 312 Fed. Bldg., 3rd & Rosser Ave., Bismarck 58502, 701-250-4618; 112 Robert St., Fargo 58107, 701-239-5389.

Rep. Robert K. (Bob) Dornan (R), Representative from California, District 46

DC Office: 1201 Longworth House Office Building, Washington, DC 20515, 202-225-2965; Fax: 202-225-2762.

District Offices: 300 Plaza Alicante, Garden Grove 92642, 714-971-9292.

Rep. Mike Doyle (D), Representative from Pennsylvania, District 18

DC Office: 1218 Longworth House Office Building, Washington, DC 20515, 202-225-2135; Fax: 202-225-3084.

District Offices: 11 Duff Rd., Pittsburgh 15235, 412-241-6055; 541 5th Ave., McKeesport 15132, 412-664-4049.

Rep. David Dreier (R), Representative from California, District 28
DC Office: 411 Cannon House Office Building, Washington, DC 20515, 202-225-2305; Fax: 202-225-7018.
District Offices: 112 N. 2d Ave., Covina 91723, 818-339-9078.

Rep. John J. Duncan, Jr. (R), Representative from Tennessee, District 2
DC Office: 2400 Rayburn House Office Building, Washington, DC 20515, 202-225-5435; Fax: 202-225-6440.
District Offices: 501 W. Main St., Knoxville 37902, 615-523-3772; 200 E. Broadway, Maryville 37801, 615-984-5464; and Crthse., Athens 37303, 615-745-4671.

Rep. Jennifer B. Dunn (R), Representative from Washington, District 8
DC Office: 432 Cannon House Office Building, Washington, DC 20515, 202-225-7761; Fax: 202-225-8673; e-mail: dunnwa08@hr.house.gov.
District Offices: 50-116th Ave., SE, Bellevue 98004, 206-460-0161.

Rep. Richard J. Durbin (D), Representative from Illinois, District 20
DC Office: 2463 Rayburn House Office Building, Washington, DC 20515, 202-225-5271; Fax: 202-225-0170; e-mail: durbin@hr.house.gov.
District Offices: 525 S. 8th St., Springfield 62703, 217-492-4062; 221 E. Broadway, Centralia 62801, 618-532-4265; and 400 St. Louis St., Edwardsville 62025, 618-492-1082.

Rep. Chet Edwards (D), Representative from Texas, District 11
DC Office: 328 Cannon House Office Building, Washington, DC 20515, 202-225-6105; Fax: 202-225-0350.
District Offices: 710 University Tower, 700 S. University Parks Dr., Waco 76706, 817-752-9600.

Rep. Vernon J. Ehlers (R), Representative from Michigan, District 3
DC Office: 1717 Longworth House Office Building, Washington, DC 20515, 202-225-3831; Fax: 202-225-5144; e-mail: congehlr@hr.house.gov.
District Offices: 166 Fed. Bldg., 110 Michigan St. NW, Grand Rapids 49503, 616-451-8383.

Rep. Robert L. Ehrlich, Jr. (R), Representative from Maryland, District 2
DC Office: 315 Cannon House Office Building, Washington, DC 20515, 202-225-3061; Fax: 202-225-3094.
District Offices: 1407 York Rd., Lutherville 21093, 410-337-7222; and 45 N. Main St., Bel Air 21014, 410-838-2517.

Rep. Bill Emerson (R), Representative from Missouri, District 8
DC Office: 2268 Rayburn House Office Building, Washington, DC 20515, 202-225-4404; e-mail: bemerson@hr.house.gov.

District Offices: 339 Broadway, Cape Girardeau 63701, 314-335-0101; and 612 Pine, Rolla 65401, 314-364-2455.

Rep. Eliot L. Engel (D), Representative from New York, District 17

DC Office: 1433 Longworth House Office Building, Washington, DC 20515, 202-225-2464; e-mail: engeline@hr.house.gov.

District Offices: 3655 Johnson Ave., Bronx 10463, 718-796-9700.

Rep. Philip S. English (R), Representative from Pennsylvania, District 21

DC Office: 1721 Longworth House Office Building, Washington, DC 20515, 202-225-5406.

District Offices: 310 French St., Erie 16507, 814-456-2038; 306 Chestnut St., Meadville 16335, 814-724-8414; City Annex Bldg., Hermitage 16148, 412-342-6132; 327 N. Main St., Butler 16001, 412-285-5616.

Rep. John Ensign (R), Representative from Nevada, District 1

DC Office: 414 Cannon House Office Building, Washington, DC 20515, 202-225-5965; Fax: 202-225-3119.

District Offices: 1000 E. Sahara Ave., Las Vegas 89104, 702-731-1801.

Rep. Anna G. Eshoo (D), Representative from California, District 14

DC Office: 308 Cannon House Office Building, Washington, DC 20515, 202-225-8104; Fax: 202-225-8890; e-mail: annagram@hr.house.gov.

District Offices: 698 Emerson St., Palo Alto 94301, 415-323-2984.

Rep. Lane Evans (D), Representative from Illinois, District 17

DC Office: 2335 Rayburn House Office Building, Washington, DC 20515, 202-225-5905; Fax: 202-225-5396.

District Offices: 1535 47th Ave., Moline 61265, 309-793-5760; and 1640 N. Henderson St., Galesburg 61401, 309-342-4411.

Rep. Terry Everett (R), Representative from Alabama, District 2

DC Office: 208 Cannon House Office Building, Washington, DC 20515, 202-225-2901; e-mail: everett@hr.house.gov.

District Offices: 3500 Eastern Blvd., Montgomery 36116, 334-277-9113;100 W. Troy St., Dothan 36303, 334-794-9680; and City Hall Bldg., Opp 36487, 334-493-9253.

Rep. Thomas W. Ewing (R), Representative from Illinois, District 15

DC Office: 1317 Longworth House Office Building, Washington, DC 20515, 202-225-2371; Fax: 202-225-8071.

District Offices: P.O. Box 20, Pontiac 61764, 815-844-7660; 2401 E. Washington St., Bloomington 61704, 309-662-9371; 102 E. Madison, Urbana 61801, 217-328-0165; and 120 N. Vermillion, Danville 61832, 217-431-8230.

Sen. J. James Exon (D), Senator from Nebraska

DC Office: 528 Hart Senate Office Building, Washington, DC 20510, 202-224-4224; Fax: 202-224-5213.

State Offices: 1623 Farnam St., Omaha 68102, 402-341-1776; 287 Fed. Bldg., 100 Centennial Mall N., Lincoln 68508, 402-437-5591; 2106 1st St., Scottsbluff 69361, 308-632-3595; and 275 Fed. Bldg., North Platte 69101, 308-534-2006.

Sen. Lauch Faircloth (R), Senator from North Carolina

DC Office: 317 Hart Senate Office Building, Washington, DC 20510, 202-224-3154; Fax: 202-224-7406.

State Offices: Fed. Bldg., 310 New Bern Ave., Raleigh 27601, 919-856-4791; Fed. Bldg., 401 W. Trade St., Charlotte 28202, 704-375-1993; Fed. Bldg.,151 Patton Ave., Asheville 28801, 704-244-3099; and Fed. Bldg., 251 Main St., Winston-Salem 27101, 919-631-5313.

Rep. Sam Farr (D), Representative from California, District 17

DC Office: 1117 Longworth House Office Building, Washington, DC 20515, 202-225-2861; e-mail:samfarr@hr.house.gov.

District Offices: 380 Alvarado St., Monterey 93940, 408-649-3555; 701 Ocean Ave., Santa Cruz 95060, 408-429-1976; and 100 W. Alisal St., Salinas 93901, 408-424-2229.

Rep. Chaka Fattah (D), Representative from Pennsylvania, District 2

DC Office: 1205 Longworth House Office Building, Washington, DC 20515, 202-225-4001.

District Offices: 4104 Walnut St., Philadelphia 19104, 215-387-6404.

Rep. Harris W. Fawell (R), Representative from Illinois, District 13

DC Office: 2159 Rayburn House Office Building, Washington, DC 20515, 202-225-3515; Fax: 202-225-9420; e-mail: hfawell@hr.house.gov.

District Offices: 115 W. 55th St., Clarendon Hills 60514, 708-655-2052.

Rep. Vic Fazio (D), Representative from California, District 3

DC Office: 2113 Rayburn House Office Building, Washington, DC 20515, 202-225-5716; Fax: 202-225-5141; e-mail: dcaucus@hr.house.gov.

District Offices: 722-B Main St., Woodland 95695, 916-666-5521; and 332 Pine St., Red Bluff 96080, 916-529-5629.

Sen. Russell D. Feingold (D), Senator from Wisconsin

DC Office: 502 Hart Senate Office Building, Washington, DC 20510, 202-224-5323; Fax: 202-224-2725; e-mail: senator_feingold@feingold.senate.gov.

State Offices: 517 E. Wisconsin Ave., Milwaukee 53202, 414-276-7282; 8383 Greenway Blvd., Middleton 53562, 608-828-1200; 317 1st St., Wausau 54403, 715-848-5660; and 425 State St., LaCrosse 54603, 608-782-5585.

Sen. Dianne Feinstein (D), Senator from California

DC Office: 331 Hart Senate Office Building, Washington, DC 20510, 202-224-3841; Fax: 202-228-3954; e-mail: senator@feinstein.senate.gov.

State Offices: 1700 Montgomery St., San Francisco 94111, 415-249-4777; 750 B St., San Diego 92101, 619-231-9712; 11111 Santa Monica Blvd., Los Angeles 90025, 310-914-7300; and 1130 O St., Fresno 93721, 209-485-7430.

Rep. Cleo Fields (D), Representative from Louisiana, District 4

DC Office: 218 Cannon House Office Building, Washington, DC 20515, 202-225-8490; Fax: 202-225-8959.

District Offices: 700 N. 10th St., Baton Rouge 70802, 504-343-9773; 301 N. Main St., Opelousas 70570, 318-942-9691; and 610 Texas St., Shreveport 71101, 318-221-9924; 515 Murrey St., Alexandria 71301, 318-445-0632.

Rep. Jack M. Fields, Jr. (R), Representative from Texas, District 8

DC Office: 2228 Rayburn House Office Building, Washington, DC 20515, 202-225-4901; Fax: 202-225-2772.

District Offices: 111 E. University Dr., College Station 77840, 409-846-6068; 300 W. Davis, Conroe 77301, 409-756-8044; and 9810 FM1960 Bypass W., Deerbrook Plz., Humble 77338, 409-540-8000.

Rep. Bob Filner (D), Representative from California, District 50

DC Office: 504 Cannon House Office Building, Washington, DC 20515, 202-225-8045; Fax: 202-225-9073; e-mail: dfogle@hr.house.gov.

District Offices: 333 F St., Chula Vista 91910, 619-422-5963.

Rep. Floyd H. Flake (D), Representative from New York, District 6

DC Office: 1035 Longworth House Office Building, Washington, DC 20515, 202-225-3461; Fax: 202-226-4169.

District Offices: 196-06 Linden Blvd., St. Albans 11412, 718-849-5600; and 20-80 Seagirt Blvd., Far Rockaway 11691, 718-327-9791.

Rep. Michael Patrick Flanagan (R), Representative from Illinois, District 5

DC Office: 1407 Longworth House Office Building, Washington, DC 20515, 202-225-4061; Fax: 202-225-3128.

District Offices: 3538 W. Irving Park Rd., Chicago 60618, 312-588-2288.

Rep. Thomas M. Foglietta (D), Representative from Pennsylvania, District 1

DC Office: 341 Cannon House Office Building, Washington, DC 20515, 202-225-4731; Fax: 202-225-0088.

District Offices: Green Fed. Bldg., 600 Arch St., Philadelphia 19106, 215-925-6840; 1806 S. Broad St., Philadelphia 19125, 215-463-8702; and 2630 Memphis St., Philadelphia 19125, 215-426-4616.

Rep. Mark Foley (R), Representative from Florida, District 16

DC Office: 506 Cannon House Office Building, Washington, DC 20515, 202-225-5792; Fax: 202-225-3132.

District Offices: 4440 PGA Blvd., Palm Beach Gardens 33410, 407-627-6192; and 250 NW Country Club Dr., Port St. Lucie 34986, 407-878-3181.

Rep. Michael P. Forbes (R), Representative from New York, District 1

DC Office: 502 Cannon House Office Building, Washington, DC 20515, 202-225-3826; Fax: 202-225-3143; e-mail: mpforbes@hr.house.gov.

District Office: 1500 William Floyd Pkwy., Shirley 11967, 516-345-9000.

Sen. Wendell H. Ford (D), Senator from Kentucky

DC Office: 173-A Russell Senate Office Building, Washington, DC 20510, 202-224-4343; Fax: 202-224-0046; e-mail: wendell_ford@ford.senate.gov.

State Offices: 1072 New Fed. Bldg., Louisville 40202, 502-582-6251; 305 Fed. Bldg., Owensboro 42301, 502-685-5158; 343 Waller Ave., Lexington 40504, 606-233-2484; and 19 U.S. P.O. and Crthse., Covington 41011, 606-491-7929.

Rep. Harold E. Ford (D), Representative from Tennessee, District 9

DC Office: 2111 Rayburn House Office Building, Washington, DC 20515, 202-225-3265; Fax: 202-225-9215.

District Offices: 369 Fed. Bldg., 167 N. Main St., Memphis 38103, 901-544-4131.

Rep. Tillie K. Fowler (R), Representative from Florida, District 4

DC Office: 413 Cannon House Office Building, Washington, DC 20515, 202-225-2501; Fax: 202-225-9318.

District Offices: 4452 Hendricks Ave., Jacksonville 32207, 904-739-6600; and 533 N. Nova Rd., Ormond Beach 32174, 904-672-0754.

Rep. Jon D. Fox (R), Representative from Pennsylvania, District 13

DC Office: 510 Cannon House Office Building, Washington, DC 20515, 202-225-6111; Fax: 202-225-3155; e-mail: jonfox@hr.house.gov.

District Offices: 1768 Markley St., Norristown 19401, 610-272-8400; and Easton & Edge Hill Rds., Abington 19001, 215-885-3500.

Rep. Barney Frank (D), Representative from Massachusetts, District 4

DC Office: 2210 Rayburn House Office Building, Washington, DC 20515, 202-225-5931; Fax: 202-225-0182.

District Offices: 29 Crafts St., Newton 02158, 617-332-3920; 558 Pleasant St., New Bedford 02740, 508-999-6462; 222 Milliken Pl., Fall River 02721, 508-674-3551; and 89 Main St., Bridgewater 02324, 508-697-9403.

Rep. Gary A. Franks (R), Representative from Connecticut, District 5

DC Office: 133 Cannon House Office Building, Washington, DC 20515, 202-225-3822; Fax: 202-225-5085.

District Offices: 135 Grand St., Waterbury 06701, 203-573-1418; 30 Main St., Danbury 06810, 203-790-1263; 1 First St., Seymour Town Hall, Seymour 06483, 800-556-5089; 142 E. Main St., Meriden City Hall, Meriden 06450, 203-630-4130.

Rep. Bob Franks (R), Representative from New Jersey, District 7

DC Office: 429 Cannon House Office Building, Washington, DC 20515, 202-225-5361; Fax: 202-225-9460; e-mail: franksnj@hr.house.gov.

District Offices: 2333 Morris Ave., Union 07083, 908-686-5576; and 73 Main St., Woodbridge 07095, 908-602-0075.

Rep. Rodney P. Frelinghuysen (R), Representative from New Jersey, District 11

DC Office: 514 Cannon House Office Building, Washington, DC 20515, 202-225-5034; Fax: 202-225-3186.

District Offices: 1 Morris St., Morristown 07960, 201-984-0711; 18 W. Blackwell St., Dover 07801, 201-328-7413; and 3 Fairfield Ave., W. Caldwell 07006, 201-228-9262.

Rep. Dan Frisa (R), Representative from New York, District 4

DC Office: 1529 Longworth House Office Building, Washington, DC 20515, 202-225-5516; Fax: 202-225-3187.

District Office: 250 Old Country Rd., Mineola 11501, 516-739-1800.

Sen. William H. Frist (R), Senator from Tennessee

DC Office: 565 Dirksen Senate Office Building, Washington, DC 20510, 202-224-3344; Fax: 202-228-1264; e-mail: senate_frist@frist.senate.gov.

State Offices: U.S. Cthse., 801 Broadway, Nashville 37203, 615-736-7353.

Rep. Martin Frost (D), Representative from Texas, District 24

DC Office: 2459 Rayburn House Office Building, Washington, DC 20515, 202-225-3605; Fax: 202-225-4951; e-mail: frost@hr.house.gov.

District Offices: 3020 S.E. Loop 820, Ft. Worth 76140, 817-293-9231; 400 S. Zang Blvd., Dallas 75208, 214-948-3401; and 100 N. Main St.,Corsicana 75110, 903-874-0760.

Rep. David Funderburk (R), Representative from North Carolina, District 2

DC Office: 427 Cannon House Office Building, Washington, DC 20515, 202-224-4531; Fax: 202-225-3191.

District Office: 1207 W. Cumberland St., Dunn 28334, 910-891-1114; e-mail: funnc02@hr.house.gov.

Rep. Elizabeth Furse (D), Representative from Oregon, District 1

DC Office: 316 Cannon House Office Building, Washington, DC 20515, 202-225-0855; Fax: 202-225-9497; e-mail: furseor1@hr.house.gov.

District Offices: 2701 NW Vaughn, Portland 97210, 503-326-2901.

Rep. Elton Gallegly (R), Representative from California, District 23

DC Office: 2441 Rayburn House Office Building, Washington, DC 20515, 202-225-5811; Fax: 202-225-1100.

District Offices: 300 Esplanade Dr., Oxnard 93030, 805-485-2300.

Rep. Greg Ganske (R), Representative from Iowa, District 4

DC Office: 1108 Longworth House Office Building, Washington, DC 20515, 202-225-4426; Fax: 202-225-3193.

District Offices: Fed. Bldg., 210 Walnut St., Des Moines 50309, 515-284-4634; and 40 Pearl St., Council Bluffs 51503, 712-323-5976.

Rep. Samuel Gejdenson (D), Representative from Connecticut, District 2

DC Office: 2416 Rayburn House Office Building, Washington, DC 20515, 202-225-2076; Fax: 202-225-4977; e-mail: bozrah@hr.house.gov

District Offices: 74 W. Main, Norwich 06360, 203-886-0139; and 94 Court St., Middletown 06457, 203-346-1123.

Rep. George W. Gekas (R), Representative from Pennsylvania, District 17

DC Office: 2410 Rayburn House Office Building, Washington, DC 20515, 202-225-4315; Fax: 202-225-8440.

District Offices: 3605 Vartan Way, Harrisburg 17110, 717-541-5507; 222 S. Market St., Elizabethtown 17022, 717-367-6731; and 108-B Municipal Bldg., 400 S. 8th St., Lebanon 17042, 717-273-1451.

Rep. Richard A. Gephardt (D), Representative from Missouri, District 3

DC Office: 1226 Longworth House Office Building, Washington, DC 20515, 202-225-2671; Fax: 202-225-7452; e-mail: gephardt@hr.house.gov.

District Offices: 11140 S. Towne Sq., St. Louis 63123, 314-894-3400.

Rep. Pete Geren (D), Representative from Texas, District 12

DC Office: 2448 Rayburn House Office Building, Washington, DC 20515, 202-225-5071; Fax: 202-225-2786.

District Offices: 1600 W. 7th St., Ft. Worth 76102, 817-338-0909.

Rep. Sam M. Gibbons (D), Representative from Florida, District 11

DC Office: 2204 Rayburn House Office Building, Washington, DC 20515, 202-225-3376; Fax: 202-225-8016.

District Offices: 2002 N. Lois Ave., Tampa 33607, 813-870-2101.

Rep. Wayne T. Gilchrest (R), Representative from Maryland, District 1

DC Office: 332 Cannon House Office Building, Washington, DC 20515, 202-225-5311; Fax: 202-225-0254.

District Offices: 1 Plaza E., Salisbury 21801, 410-749-3184; 521 Washington Ave., Chestertown 21620, 410-778-9407; and 101 Crain Hwy., NW, Glen Burnie 21061, 410-760-3372.

Rep. Paul E. Gillmor (R), Representative from Ohio, District 5

DC Office: 1203 Longworth House Office Building, Washington, DC 20515, 202-225-6405; Fax: 202-225-1985.

District Offices: 120 Jefferson St., Port Clinton 43452, 800-541-6446; and 148 E. South Boundary St., Perrysburg 43551, 419-872-2500.

Rep. Benjamin A. Gilman (R), Representative from New York, District 20

DC Office: 2449 Rayburn House Office Building, Washington, DC 20515, 202-225-3776; Fax: 202-225-2541.

District Offices: 407 E. Main St., P.O. Box 358, Middletown 10940, 914-343-6666; 377 Rte. 59, Monsey 10952, 914-357-9000; and 32 Main St., Hastings-on-Hudson 10706, 914-478-5550.

Rep. Newt Gingrich (R), Representative from Georgia, District 6

DC Office: 2428 Rayburn House Office Building, Washington, DC 20515, 202-225-4501; Fax: 202-225-4656; e-mail: georgia6@hr.house.gov.

District Offices: 3823 Roswell Rd., Marietta 30062, 404-565-6398.

Sen. John H. Glenn Jr. (D), Senator from Ohio

DC Office: 503 Hart Senate Office Building, Washington, DC 20510, 202-224-3353; Fax: 202-224-7983.

State Offices: 200 N. High St., Columbus 43215, 614-469-6697; 1240 E. 9th St., Cleveland 44199, 216-522-7095; 550 Main St., Cincinnati 45202, 513-684-3265; and 234 N. Summit St., Toledo 43604, 419-259-7592.

Rep. Henry B. Gonzalez (D), Representative from Texas, District 20

DC Office: 2413 Rayburn House Office Building, Washington, DC 20515, 202-225-3236.

District Offices: 727 E. Durango St., San Antonio 78206, 512-229-6195.

Rep. Bob Goodlatte (R), Representative from Virginia, District 6

DC Office: 123 Cannon House Office Building, Washington, DC 20515, 202-225-5431; Fax: 202-225-9681; e-mail: talk2bob@hr.house.gov.

District Offices: 540 Crestar Plz., 10 Franklin Rd., SE, Roanoke 24011, 703-857-2672; 114 N. Central Ave., Staunton 24401, 703-885-3861; 2 S. Main St., Harrisonburg 22801, 703-432-2391; and 916 Main St., 804-845-8306.

Rep. Bill Goodling (R), Representative from Pennsylvania, District 19

DC Office: 2263 Rayburn House Office Building, Washington, DC 20515, 202-225-5836.

District Offices: Fed. Bldg., 200 S. George St., York 17405, 717-843-8887; 212 N. Hanover St., Carlisle 17013, 717-243-5432; 140 Baltimore St., Gettysburg 17325, 717-334-3430; 2020 Yale Ave., Camp Hill 17011, 717-763-1988; and 44 Frederick St., Hanover 17331, 717-632-7855, 800-631-1811.

Rep. Bart Gordon (D), Representative from Tennessee, District 6

DC Office: 2201 Rayburn House Office Building, Washington, DC 20515, 202-225-4231; Fax: 202-225-6887.

District Offices: P.O. Box 1986, 106 S. Maple St., Murfreesboro 37133, 615-896-1986; and 17 S. Jefferson, Cookeville 38501, 615-528-5907.

Sen. Slade Gorton (R), Senator from Washington

DC Office: 730 Hart Senate Office Building, Washington, DC 20510, 202-224-3441; Fax: 202-224-9393; e-mail: senator_gorton@gorton.senate.gov.

State Offices: 1350 Grandridge Blvd., Kennewick 99336, 509-783-0640;15600 Redmond Wy., Redmond 98052, 206-883-6072; and 402 E. Yakima Ave., Box 4083, Yakima 98901, 509-248-8084.

Rep. Porter Johnston Goss (R), Representative from Florida, District 14

DC Office: 108 Cannon House Office Building, Washington, DC 20515, 202-225-2536; Fax: 202-225-6820.

District Offices: 2000 Main St., Fort Myers 33901, 813-332-4677; and 3301 Tamiami Trail E., Bldg. F, Naples 33962, 813-774-8060.

Rep. Lindsey Graham (R), Representative from South Carolina, District 3

DC Office: 1429 Longworth House Office Building, Washington, DC 20515, 202-225-5301.

District Offices: P.O. Box 4126, Anderson 29622, 803-224-7401; 5 Fed. Bldg.,
211 York St., NE, Aiken 29801, 803-649-5571; and 129 Fed. Bldg., 120 Main St.,
Greenwood 29646, 803-223-8251.

Sen. Bob Graham (D), Senator from Florida

DC Office: 524 Hart Senate Office Building, Washington, DC 20510, 202-224-3041;
Fax: 202-224-2237; e-mail: bob_graham@graham.senate.gov.

State Offices: 44 W. Flagler St., Miami 33130, 305-536-7293; and 325 John Knox
Rd., Bldg. 600, Tallahassee 32303, 904-422-6100; and 101 E. Kennedy Blvd.,
Tampa 33602, 813-228-2476.

Sen. Phil Gramm (R), Senator from Texas

DC Office: 370 Russell Senate Office Building, Washington, DC 20510,
202-224-2934; Fax: 202-228-2856.

State Offices: 2323 Bryan, Dallas 75201, 214-767-3000; 222 E. Van Buren.,
Harlingen 78550, 512-423-6118; 712 Main, Houston 77002, 713-229-2766;
113 Fed. Bldg., 1205 Texas Ave., Lubbock 79401, 806-743-7533; 123 Pioneer Plz.,
El Paso 79901, 915-534-6896; 9311 San Pedro, San Antonio 78216, and
InterFirst Plz., 102 N. College St., Tyler 75702, 903-593-0902.

Sen. Rod Grams (IR), Senator from Minnesota

DC Office: 261 Dirksen Senate Office Building, Washington, DC 20510,
202-224-3244; Fax: 202-228-0956; e-mail: mail_grams@grams.senate.gov.

State Offices: 2013 2nd Ave., N., Anoka 55303, 612-427-5921.

Sen. Charles E. Grassley (R), Senator from Iowa

DC Office: 135 Hart Senate Office Building, Washington, DC 20510, 202-224-3744;
Fax: 202-224-6020.

State Offices: 721 Fed. Bldg., 210 Walnut St., Des Moines 50309, 515-284-4890;
210 Waterloo Bldg., 531 Commercial St., Waterloo 50701, 319-232-6657;
116 Fed. Bldg., 131 E. 4th St., Davenport 52801, 319-322-4331; 103 Fed. Bldg.,
320 6th St., Sioux City 51101, 712-233-3331; 307 Fed. Bldg., 8 S. 6th St.,
Council Bluffs 51501, 712-322-7103; and 206 Fed. Bldg., 101 1st St., SE,
Cedar Rapids 52401, 319-399-2555.

Rep. Gene Green (D), Representative from Texas, District 29

DC Office: 1024 Longworth House Office Building, Washington, DC 20515,
202-225-1688; Fax: 202-225-9903; e-mail: ggreen@hr.house.gov.

District Offices: 5502 Lawndale, Houston 77023, 713-923-9961; and
420 N. 19th St., Houston 77008, 713-880-4364.

Rep. Jim Greenwood (R), Representative from Pennsylvania, District 8

DC Office: 430 Cannon House Office Building, Washington, DC 20515,
202-225-4276; Fax: 202-225-9511.

District Offices: 69 E. Oxford Ave., Doylestown 18901, 215-348-7511; and
One Oxford Valley, Langhorne 19047, 215-752-7711.

Sen. Judd Gregg (R), Senator from New Hampshire

DC Office: 393 Russell Senate Office Building, Washington, DC 20510,
202-224-3324; Fax: 202-224-4952; e-mail: mailbox@gregg.senate.gov.

State Offices: 125 N. Main St., Concord 03301, 603-225-7115; 28 Webster St., Manchester 03104, 603-622-7979; 136 Pleasant St., Berlin 03570, 603-752-2604; and 99 Pease Blvd., Portsmouth 03801, 603-431-2171.

Rep. Steve Gunderson (R), Representative from Wisconsin, District 3

DC Office: 2185 Rayburn House Office Building, Washington, DC 20515, 202-225-5506; Fax: 202-225-6195.

District Offices: P.O. Box 247, 622 E. State Hwy. 54, Black River Falls 54615, 715-284-7431.

Rep. Luis V. Gutierrez (D), Representative from Illinois, District 4

DC Office: 408 Longworth House Office Building, Washington, DC 20515, 202-225-8203; Fax: 202-225-7810; e-mail: louisg@hr.house.gov.

District Offices: 3181 N. Elston Ave., Chicago 60618, 312-509-0999; 1751 W. 47th St., Chicago 60609, 312-247-9020; 3659 Halsted, Chicago 60609, 312-254-0797; and 2132 W. 21st St., Chicago 60608, 312-579-0886.

Rep. Gil Gutknecht (IR), Representative from Minnesota, District 1

DC Office: 425 Cannon House Office Building, Washington, DC 20515, 202-225-2472; Fax: 202-225-0051; e-mail: gil@hr.house.gov.

District Offices: 1530 Greenview Dr., Rochester 55902, 507-252-9841.

Rep. Tony P. Hall (D), Representative from Ohio, District 3

DC Office: 1432 Longworth House Office Building, Washington, DC 20515, 202-225-6465; Fax: 202-225-9272.

District Offices: 501 Fed. Bldg., 200 W. 2d St., Dayton 45402, 513-225-2843.

Rep. Ralph M. Hall (D), Representative from Texas, District 4

DC Office: 2236 Rayburn House Office Building, Washington, DC 20515, 202-225-6673; Fax: 202-225-3332.

District Offices: 104 N. San Jacinto St., Rockwall 75087, 214-771-9118; 119 N. Fed. Bldg., Sherman 75090, 214-892-1112; 211 Fed. Bldg., Tyler 75702, 214-597-3729; and Cooke Cnty. Cthse., Gainesville 76240, 819-668-6370.

Rep. Lee H. Hamilton (D), Representative from Indiana, District 9

DC Office: 2314 Rayburn House Office Building, Washington, DC 20515, 202-225-5315; Fax: 202-225-1101; e-mail: hamilton@hr.house.gov.

District Offices: 107 Fed. Ctr., 1201 E. 10th St., Jeffersonville 47130, 812-288-3999.

Rep. Mel Hancock (R), Representative from Missouri, District 7

DC Office: 438 Cannon House Office Building, Washington, DC 20515, 202-225-6536; Fax: 202-225-7700.

District Offices: 2840 E. Chestnut Expwy., Springfield 65802, 417-862-4317; and 302 Fed. Bldg., Joplin 64801, 417-781-1041.

Rep. James V. Hansen (R), Representative from Utah, District 1

DC Office: 2466 Rayburn House Office Building, Washington, DC 20515, 202-225-0453; Fax: 202-225-5857.

District Offices: 1017 Fed. Bldg., 324 25th St., Ogden 84401, 801-625-5677; and 435 E. Tabernacle, St. George 84770, 801-628-1071.

Sen. Tom Harkin (D), Senator from Iowa

DC Office: 531 Hart Senate Office Building, Washington, DC 20510, 202-224-3254; Fax: 202-224-9369; e-mail: tom_harkin@harkin.senate.gov.

State Offices: 733 Fed. Bldg., 210 Walnut St., Des Moines 50309, 515-284-4574; Fed. Bldg., Council Bluffs 51501, 712-325-0036; 150 1st Ave., NE, Cedar Rapids 52401, 319-365-4504; 131 E. 4th St., 314B Fed. Bldg., Davenport, 52801, 319-322-1338; 350 W. 6th St., Dubuque 52001, 319-588-2130; and 110 Federal Bldg., 320 6th St., Sioux City 51101, 712-252-1550.

Rep. Jane Harman (D), Representative from California, District 36

DC Office: 325 Cannon House Office Building, Washington, DC 20515, 202-225-8220; Fax: 202-225-0684; e-mail: jharman@hr.house.gov.

District Offices: 5200 W. Century Blvd., Los Angeles 90045, 310-348-8220; 3031 Torrance Blvd., Torrance 90503, 310-787-0767.

Rep. Dennis Hastert (R), Representative from Illinois, District 14

DC Office: 2453 Rayburn House Office Building, Washington, DC 20515, 202-225-2976; Fax: 202-225-0697; e-mail: dhastert@hr.house.gov.

District Offices: 27 N. River St., Batavia 60510, 708-406-1114.

Rep. Alcee L. Hastings (D), Representative from Florida, District 23

DC Office: 1039 Longworth House Office Building, Washington, DC 20515, 202-225-1313; Fax: 202-226-0690; e-mail: hastings@hr.house.gov.

District Offices: 2701 W. Oakland Park Blvd., Ft. Lauderdale 33311, 305-733-2800.

Rep. Doc Hastings (R), Representative from Washington, District 4

DC Office: 1229 Longworth House Office Building, Washington, DC 20515, 202-225-5816; Fax: 202-225-3251.

District Offices: 320 N. Johnson, Kennewick 99336, 509-783-0310; 302 E. Chestnut, Yakima 98901, 509-452-3243; and 25 N. Wenatchee Ave., Wenatchee 98801, 509-662-4294.

Sen. Orrin G. Hatch (R), Senator from Utah

DC Office: 131 Russell Senate Office Building, Washington, DC 20510, 202-224-5251; Fax: 202-224-6331.

State Offices: 8402 Fed. Bldg., Salt Lake City 84138, 801-524-4380; 109 Fed. Bldg., 51 S. University Ave., Provo 84601, 801-375-7881; 1410 Fed. Bldg., 325 25th St., Ogden 84401, 801-625-5672; and 10 N. Main, P.O. Box 99, Cedar City 84720, 801-586-8435.

Sen. Mark O. Hatfield (R), Senator from Oregon

DC Office: 711 Hart Senate Office Building, Washington, DC 20510, 202-224-3753; Fax: 202-224-0276.

State Offices: 727 Center St., NE, Salem 97301; and One World Trade Ctr., 121 SW Salmon St., Portland 97204.

Rep. James A. (Jimmy) Hayes (R), Representative from Louisiana, District 7
DC Office: 2432 Rayburn House Office Building, Washington, DC 20515, 202-225-2031; Fax: 202-225-1175.
District Offices: 100 E. Vermilion, Lafayette 70501, 318-233-4773; and 901 Lake Shore Dr., Lake Charles 70601, 318-433-1613.

Rep. J. D. Hayworth (R), Representative from Arizona, District 6
DC Office: 1023 Longworth House Office Building, Washington, DC 20515, 202-225-2190; Fax: 202-225-3263.
District Offices: 1818 E. Southern Ave., Mesa 85204, 602-926-4151; and 1300 S. Milton, Flagstaff 85001, 520-556-8760.

Rep. Joel Hefley (R), Representative from Colorado, District 5
DC Office: 2351 Rayburn House Office Building, Washington, DC 20515, 202-225-4422; Fax: 202-225-1942.
District Offices: 104 S. Cascade Ave., Colorado Springs 80903, 719-520-0055; and 9605 Maroon Cir., Englewood 80112, 303-792-3923.

Sen. Howell T. Heflin (D), Senator from Alabama
DC Office: 728 Hart Senate Office Building, Washington, DC 20510, 202-224-4124; Fax: 202-224-3149.
State Offices: B-29 Fed. Crthse., 15 Lee St., Montgomery 36104, 334-832-7287; 104 W. 5th St., P.O. Box 228, Tuscumbia 35674, 205-381-7060; 341 Fed. Bldg., 1800 5th Ave., N., Birmingham 35203, 205-731-1500; and 437 Fed. Crthse., Mobile 36602, 334-690-3167.

Rep. W. G. (Bill) Hefner (D), Representative from North Carolina, District 8
DC Office: 2470 Rayburn House Office Building, Washington, DC 20515, 202-225-3715; Fax: 202-225-4036.
District Offices: P.O. Box 385, 101 Union St. S., Concord 28025, 704-786-1612; P.O. Box 4220, 507 W. Innes St., Salisbury 28144, 704-636-0635; and P.O. Box 1503, 230 E. Franklin St., Rockingham 28379, 910-997-2070.

Rep. Fred Heineman (R), Representative from North Carolina, District 4
DC Office: 1440 Longworth House Office Building, Washington, DC 20515, 202-225-1784; Fax: 202-225-3269; e-mail: thechief@hr.house.gov.
District Offices: 16 E. Rowan St., Raleigh 27609, 919-856-4611.

Sen. Jesse A. Helms (R), Senator from North Carolina
DC Office: 403 Dirksen Senate Office Building, Washington, DC 20510, 202-224-6342; Fax: 202-224-7588.
State Offices: P.O. Box 2888, Raleigh 27602, 919-856-4630; and P.O. Box 2944, Hickory 28601, 704-322-5170.

Rep. Wally Herger (R), Representative from California, District 2
DC Office: 2433 Rayburn House Office Building, Washington, DC 20515, 202-225-3076; Fax: 202-225-3245.

District Offices: 55 Independence Cir., Chico 95926, 916-893-8363; and
410 Hemsted Dr., Redding 96002, 916-223-5898.

Rep. Van Hilleary (R), Representative from Tennessee, District 4
DC Office: 114 Cannon House Office Building, Washington, DC 20515,
202-225-6831; Fax: 202-225-3272.

District Offices: 1502 N. Main St., Crossville 38555, 615-484-1114; 400 W. Main St.,
Morristown 37814, 615-587-0396; and 300 S. Jackson St., Tullahoma 37388,
615-393-4764.

Rep. Earl F. Hilliard (D), Representative from Alabama, District 7
DC Office: 1007 Longworth House Office Building, Washington, DC 20515,
202-225-2665; Fax: 202-226-0772.

District Offices: Vance Fed. Bldg., 1800 5th Ave., Birmingham 35203, 205-328-2841;
P.O. Box 2627, Tuscaloosa 35403, 205-752-3578; Fed. Bldg., Selma 36701,
205-872-2684; and Fed. Bldg., 15 Lee St., Montgomery 36104, 334-262-4724.

Rep. Maurice D. Hinchey (D), Representative from New York, District 26
DC Office: 1524 Longworth House Office Building, Washington, DC 20515,
202-225-6335; Fax: 202-226-0774.

District Offices: 291 Wall St., Kingston 12401, 914-331-4466; 100A Fed. Bldg.,
Binghamton 13901, 607-773-2768; and 114 Prospect St., Ithaca 14850,
607-273-1388.

Rep. David L. Hobson (R), Representative from Ohio, District 7
DC Office: 1514 Longworth House Office Building, Washington, DC 20515,
202-225-4324; Fax: 202-225-1984.

District Offices: 220 P.O. Bldg., 150 N. Limestone St., Springfield 45501,
513-325-0474; and 212 S. Broad St., Lancaster 43130, 614-654-5149.

Rep. Peter Hoekstra (R), Representative from Michigan, District 2
DC Office: 1122 Longworth House Office Building, Washington, DC 20515,
202-225-4401; Fax: 202-226-0779; e-mail: tellhoek@hr.house.gov.

District Offices: 42 W. 10th St., Holland 49423, 616-395-0030; 900 Third St.,
Muskegon 49440, 616-722-8386; and 120 W. Harris St., Cadillac 49601,
616-775-0050.

Rep. Martin R. Hoke (R), Representative from Ohio, District 10
DC Office: 212 Cannon House Office Building, Washington, DC 20515,
202-225-5871; e-mail: hokemail@hr.house.gov.

District Offices: 21270 Lorraine Rd., Fairview Park 44126, 216-356-2010.

Rep. Tim Holden (D), Representative from Pennsylvania, District 6
DC Office: 1421 Longworth House Office Building, Washington, DC 20515,
202-225-5546; Fax: 202-226-0996.

District Offices: Berks Cnty. Ctr., 633 Court St., Reading 19801,610-371-9931;
Meridian Bank Bldg., 101 N. Centre St., Pottsville 17901, 717-662-4212; and
Northumberland Cnty. Cthse., Market Sq., Sunbury 17801, 717-988-1902.

Sen. Ernest F. (Fritz) Hollings (D), Senator from South Carolina

DC Office: 125 Russell Senate Office Building, Washington, DC 20510, 202-224-6121; Fax: 202-224-4293; e-mail: senator@hollings.senate.com.

State Offices: 1835 Assembly St., Columbia 29201, 803-765-5731; 112 Custom House, 200 E. Bay St., Charleston 29401, 803-727-4525; and 126 Fed. Bldg., Greenville 29304, 803-233-5366; 103 Fed. Bldg., Spartanburg 29301, 803-585-3702.

Rep. Stephen Horn (R), Representative from California, District 38

DC Office: 129 Cannon House Office Building, Washington, DC 20515, 202-225-6676; Fax: 202-225-1012.

District Offices: 4010 Watson Plaza Dr., Lakewood 90712, 310-425-1336.

Rep. John N. Hostettler (R), Representative from Indiana, District 8

DC Office: 1404 Longworth House Office Building, Washington, DC 20515, 202-225-4636; Fax: 202-225-3284; e-mail: johnhost@hr.house.gov.

District Offices: 101 M.L.K. Blvd., Evansville 47708, 812-465-6484; and 120 W. 7th St., Bloomington 47404, 812-334-1111.

Rep. Amo Houghton (R), Representative from New York, District 31

DC Office: 1110 Longworth House Office Building, Washington, DC 20515, 202-225-3161; Fax: 202-225-5574.

District Offices: 700 W. Gate Plz., W. State St., Olean 14760, 716-372-2127; 32 Denison Pkwy. W., Corning 14830, 607-937-3333; and Fed. Bldg., Prendergast & 3d Sts., Jamestown 14701, 716-484-0252.

Rep. Steny H. Hoyer (D), Representative from Maryland, District 5

DC Office: 1705 Longworth House Office Building, Washington, DC 20515, 202-225-4131; Fax: 202-225-4300.

District Offices: 6500 Cherrywood Ln., Greenbelt 20770, 301-474-0119; and 21-A Industrial Park Dr., Waldorf 20602, 301-843-1577.

Rep. Duncan Hunter (R), Representative from California, District 52

DC Office: 2265 Rayburn House Office Building, Washington, DC 20515, 202-225-5672; Fax: 202-225-0235.

District Offices: 366 S. Pierce St., El Cajon 92020, 619-579-3001; and 1101 Airport Rd., Imperial 92251, 619-353-5420.

Rep. Tim Hutchinson (R), Representative from Arkansas, District 3

DC Office: 1005 Longworth House Office Building, Washington, DC 20515, 202-225-4301.

District Offices: 30 S. 6th St., Ft. Smith 72901, 501-782-7787; 422 Fed. Bldg., 35 E. Mountain, Fayetteville 72701, 501-442-5258; and 210 Fed. Bldg., 425 N. Walnut, Harrison 72601, 501-741-6900.

Sen. Kay Bailey Hutchison (R), Senator from Texas

DC Office: 283 Russell Senate Office Building, Washington, DC 20510, 202-224-5922; Fax: 202-224-0776; e-mail: senator@hutchison.senate.gov.

State Offices: 10440 N. Central Expressway, Dallas 75231, 214-361-3500;
8023 Vantage Dr., San Antonio 78230, 210-340-2885; and 500 Chestnut St.,
Abilene 79602, 915-676-2839.

Rep. Henry J. Hyde (R), Representative from Illinois, District 6
DC Office: 2110 Rayburn House Office Building, Washington, DC 20515,
202-225-4561; Fax: 202-225-1166.
District Offices: 50 E. Oak St., Addison 60101, 312-832-5950.

Rep. Bob Inglis (R), Representative from South Carolina, District 4
DC Office: 1237 Longworth House Office Building, Washington, DC 20515,
202-225-6030; Fax: 202-226-1177.
District Offices: 201 Magnolia St., Spartanburg 29301, 803-582-6422;
300 E. Washington St., Greenville 29601, 803-232-1141; and 405 W. Main St.,
Union 29379, 803-427-2205.

Sen. James M. Inhofe (R), Senator from Oklahoma
DC Office: 453 Russell Senate Office Building, Washington, DC 20510,
202-224-4721; Fax: 202-228-0380.
State Offices: 1924 S. Utica St., Tulsa 74104, 918-748-5111; and 204 N. Robinson,
Oklahoma City 73102, 405-231-4381.

Sen. Daniel K. Inouye (D), Senator from Hawaii
DC Office: 722 Hart Senate Office Building, Washington, DC 20510, 202-224-3934;
Fax: 202-224-6747.
State Offices: 7325 Prince Kuhio Fed. Bldg., 300 Ala Moana Blvd., Honolulu 96850,
808-541-2542.

Rep. Ernest J. Istook, Jr. (R), Representative from Oklahoma, District 5
DC Office: 119 Cannon House Office Building, Washington, DC 20515,
202-225-2132; Fax: 202-226-1463; e-mail: istook@hr.house.gov.
District Offices: 5400 N. Grand Blvd., Oklahoma City 73112, 405-942-3636;
First Court Pl., Bartlesville 74003, 918-336-5546; and 5th and Grand Sts.,
Ponca City 74601, 405-762-6778.

Rep. Jesse L. Jackson, Jr. (D), Representative from Illinois, District 2
DC Office: 312 Cannon House Office Building, Washington, DC 20515,
202-225-0773; Fax: 202-225-0899.
District Offices: 11133 S. Halsted St., Chicago, IL, 312-785-1996.

Rep. Sheila Jackson Lee (D), Representative from Texas, District 18
DC Office: 1520 Longworth House Office Building, Washington, DC 20515,
202-225-3816; Fax: 202-225-3317.
District Offices: 1919 Smith St., Mickey Leland Bldg., Houston 77002,
713-655-0050.

Rep. Andy Jacobs, Jr. (D), Representative from Indiana, District 10
DC Office: 2313 Rayburn House Office Building, Washington, DC 20515,
202-225-4011; Fax: 202-226-4093.

District Offices: 441-A Fed. Bldg., 46 E. Ohio St., Indianapolis 46204, 317-226-7331.

Rep. William J. Jefferson (D), Representative from Louisiana, District 2
DC Office: 240 Cannon House Office Building, Washington, DC 20515, 202-225-6636; Fax: 202-225-1988.
District Offices: 501 Magazine St., New Orleans 70130, 504-589-2274.

Sen. James M. Jeffords (R), Senator from Vermont
DC Office: 513 Hart Senate Office Building, Washington, DC 20510, 202-224-5141; e-mail: vermont@jeffords.senate.gov.
State Offices: P.O. Box 676, 138 Main St., Montpelier 05601, 802-223-5273; 95 St. Paul St., Burlington 05401, 802-658-6001; and P.O. Box 397, 2 S. Main St., Rutland 05702, 802-773-3875.

Rep. Nancy L. Johnson (R), Representative from Connecticut, District 6
DC Office: 343 Cannon House Office Building, Washington, DC 20515, 202-225-4476; Fax: 202-225-4488.
District Offices: 480 Myrtle St., New Britain 06051, 203-223-8412.

Rep. Tim Johnson (D), Representative from South Dakota, District 1
DC Office: 2438 Rayburn House Office Building, Washington, DC 20515, 202-225-2801; Fax: 202-225-2427.
District Offices: 515 S. Dakota Ave., Sioux Falls 57102, 605-332-8896; 809 South St., Rapid City 57701, 605-341-3990; and 20 6th Ave., SW, Aberdeen 57401, 605-226-3440.

Rep. Eddie Bernice Johnson (D), Representative from Texas, District 30
DC Office: 1123 Longworth House Office Building, Washington, DC 20515, 202-225-8885; Fax: 202-226-1477.
District Offices: 2525 McKinney Ave., Dallas 75201, 214-922-8885.

Rep. Sam Johnson (R), Representative from Texas, District 3
DC Office: 1030 Longworth House Office Building, Washington, DC 20515, 202-225-4201; Fax: 202-225-1485; e-mail: samtx03@hr.house.gov.
District Offices: 9400 N. Central Expressway, Dallas 75231, 214-767-4848.

Sen. J. Bennett Johnston (D), Senator from Louisiana
DC Office: 136 Hart Senate Office Building, Washington, DC 20510, 202-224-5824; Fax: 202-224-2952; e-mail: senator@johnston.senate.gov.
State Offices: 1010 Hale Boggs Fed. Bldg., 501 Magazine St., New Orleans 70130, 504-589-2427; 300 Fannin St., Shreveport 71101, 318-676-3085; and 1 American Pl., Baton Rouge 70825, 504-389-0395.

Rep. Harry A. Johnston (D), Representative from Florida, District 19
DC Office: 2458 Rayburn House Office Building, Washington, DC 20515, 202-225-3001; Fax: 202-225-8791.
District Offices: 1501 Corporate Dr., Boynton Beach 33426, 407-732-4000.

Rep. Walter B. Jones, Jr. (R), Representative from North Carolina, District 3
DC Office: 214 Cannon House Office Building, Washington, DC 20515, 202-225-3415; Fax: 202-225-3286.
District Offices: 102-C Eastbrook Dr., Greenville 27858, 919-931-1003.

Rep. Paul E. Kanjorski (D), Representative from Pennsylvania, District 11
DC Office: 2429 Rayburn House Office Building, Washington, DC 20515, 202-225-6511; e-mail: kanjo@hr.house.gov.
District Offices: 10 E. South St., Wilkes-Barre 18701, 717-825-2200.

Rep. Marcy Kaptur (D), Representative from Ohio, District 9
DC Office: 2104 Rayburn House Office Building, Washington, DC 20515, 202-225-4146; Fax: 202-225-7711.
District Offices: Fed. Bldg., 234 Summit St., Toledo 43604, 419-259-7500.

Rep. John R. Kasich (R), Representative from Ohio, District 12
DC Office: 1131 Longworth House Office Building, Washington, DC 20515, 202-225-5355; Fax: 202-225-7695.
District Offices: 200 N. High St., Columbus 43215, 614-469-7318.

Sen. Nancy Landon Kassebaum (R), Senator from Kansas
DC Office: 302 Russell Senate Office Building, Washington, DC 20510, 202-224-4774; Fax: 202-224-3514.
State Offices: 444 S.E. Quincy, Box 51, Topeka 66683, 913-295-2888; 911 N. Main, Garden City 67846, 316-276-3423; 4200 Somerset, Prairie Village 66208, 913-648-3103; and 111 N. Market, Wichita 67202, 316-269-6251.

Rep. Sue W. Kelly (R), Representative from New York, District 19
DC Office: 1037 Longworth House Office Building, Washington, DC 20515, 202-225-5441; Fax: 202-225-3289; e-mail: dearsue@hr.house.gov.
District Offices: 21 Old Main St., Fishkill 12524, 914-897-5200.

Sen. Dirk Kempthorne (R), Senator from Idaho
DC Office: 367 Dirksen Senate Office Building, Washington, DC 20510, 202-224-6142; Fax: 202-224-5893; e-mail: dirk_kempthorne@kempthorne.senate.gov.
State Offices: 304 N. 8th St., Boise 83701, 208-334-1776; 118 N. 2d St., Coeur d'Alene 83814, 208-664-5490; 633 Main St., Lewiston 83501, 208-743-1492; 401 2d St. N., Twin Falls 83301, 208-734-2515; 250 S. 4th, Pocatello 83201, 208-236-6775; 2539 Channing Way, Idaho Falls 83404, 208-522-9779; 704 Blaine St., Caldwell 83605, 208-955-0360; and 220 E. 5th St., 208-883-9783.

Rep. Patrick J. Kennedy (D), Representative from Rhode Island, District 1
DC Office: 1505 Longworth House Office Building, Washington, DC 20515, 202-225-4911; Fax: 202-225-3290.
District Offices: 286 Main St., Pawtucket 02860, 401-729-5600; 320 Thames St., Newport 02840, 401-841-0440; also, 127 Social St., Woonsocket 02895, 401-762-2288.

Sen. Edward M. Kennedy (D), Senator from Massachusetts
DC Office: 315 Russell Senate Office Building, Washington, DC 20510,
202-224-4543; Fax: 202-224-2417; e-mail: senator@kennedy.senate.gov.
State Offices: 2400 JFK Fed. Bldg., Boston 02203, 617-565-3170.

Rep. Joseph P. Kennedy, II (D), Representative from Massachusetts, District 8
DC Office: 2242 Rayburn House Office Building, Washington, DC 20515,
202-225-5111; Fax: 202-225-9322.
District Offices: Schrafft Ctr., 529 Main St., Charlestown 02129, 617-242-0200.

Rep. Barbara B. Kennelly (D), Representative from Connecticut, District 1
DC Office: 201 Cannon House Office Building, Washington, DC 20515,
202-225-2265; Fax: 202-225-1031.
District Offices: One Corporate Ctr., Hartford 06103, 203-278-8888.

Sen. Robert Kerrey (D), Senator from Nebraska
DC Office: 303 Hart Senate Office Building, Washington, DC 20510, 202-224-6551;
Fax: 202-224-7645; e-mail: bob@kerrey.senate.gov.
State Offices: 7602 Pacific St. Omaha 68114, 402-391-3411; and
100 Centennial Mall N., Fed. Bldg, Lincoln 68508, 402-437-5246.

Sen. John F. Kerry (D), Senator from Massachusetts
DC Office: 421 Russell Senate Office Building, Washington, DC 20510,
202-224-2742; Fax: 202-224-8525: e-mail: john_kerry@kerry.senate.gov.
State Offices: One Bowdoin Sq., Boston 02114, 617-565-8519; 222 Milliken Pl.,
Fall River 02722, 508-677-0522; and 145 State St., Springfield 01103, 413-785-4619.

Rep. Dale E. Kildee (D), Representative from Michigan, District 9
DC Office: 2187 Rayburn House Office Building, Washington, DC 20515,
202-225-3611; Fax: 202-225-6393.
District Offices: 316 W. Water St., Flint 48503, 313-239-1437; and 1829 N. Perry St.,
Pontiac 48340, 313-373-9337.

Rep. Jay Kim (R), Representative from California, District 41
DC Office: 435 Cannon House Office Building, Washington, DC 20515,
202-225-3201; Fax: 202-225-1485.
District Offices: 1131 W. 6th St., Ontario 91762, 909-988-1055; and
18200 Yorba Linda Blvd., Yorba Linda 92686, 714-572-8574.

Rep. Peter T. King (R), Representative from New York, District 3
DC Office: 224 Cannon House Office Building, Washington, DC 20515,
202-225-7896; Fax: 202-226-2279.
District Office: 1003 Park Blvd., Massapequa Park 11762, 516-541-4225.

Rep. Jack Kingston (R), Representative from Georgia, District 1
DC Office: 1507 Longworth House Office Building, Washington, DC 20515,
202-225-5831; Fax: 202-226-2269.

District Offices: Enterprise Bldg., 6605 Abercorn St., Savannah 31405, 912-352-0101; Statesboro Fed. Bldg., Statesboro 30458, 912-489-8797; Thomas Henry Clarke Bldg., 208 Tebeau St., Waycross 31501, 912-287-1180; and Brunswick Fed. Bldg., 805 Gloucester St., Brunswick 31520, 912-265-9010.

Rep. Gerald D. Kleczka (D), Representative from Wisconsin, District 4
DC Office: 2301 Rayburn House Office Building, Washington, DC 20515, 202-225-4572; Fax: 202-225-8135.
District Offices: 5032 W. Forest Home Ave., Milwaukee 53219, 414-297-1140; and 414 W. Moreland Blvd., Waukesha 53188, 414-549-6360.

Rep. Ron Klink (D), Representative from Pennsylvania, District 4
DC Office: 125 Cannon House Office Building, Washington, DC 20515, 202-225-2565; Fax: 202-226-2274.
District Offices: 11279 Center Hwy., N. Huntingdon 15642, 412-864-8681; Beaver Trust Bldg., 250 Insurance St., Beaver 15009, 412-728-3005; Cranberry Municipal Bldg., 2525 Rochester Rd., Cranberry Township 16066, 412-772-6080; 2692 Leechburg Rd., Lower Burrell 15068, 412-335-4518; and 134 N. Mercer St., New Castle 16101, 412-654-9036.

Rep. Scott Klug (R), Representative from Wisconsin, District 2
DC Office: 1113 Longworth House Office Building, Washington, DC 20515, 202-225-2906; Fax: 202-225-6942; e-mail: badger02@hr.house.gov.
District Offices: 16 N. Carroll St., Madison 53703, 608-257-9200.

Rep. Joe Knollenberg (R), Representative from Michigan, District 11
DC Office: 1221 Longworth House Office Building, Washington, DC 20515, 202-225-5802; Fax: 202-226-2356.
District Offices: 30833 Northwestern Hwy., Farmington Hills 48334, 313-851-1366; and 15439 Middlebelt St., Livonia 48514, 313-425-7557.

Sen. Herb Kohl (D), Senator from Wisconsin
DC Office: 330 Hart Senate Office Building, Washington, DC 20510, 202-224-5653; Fax: 202-224-9787; e-mail: senator_kohl@kohl.senate.gov.
State Offices: 310 W. Wisconsin Ave., Milwaukee 53202, 414-297-4451; 14 W. Mifflin St., Madison 53703, 608-264-5338; 402 Graham Ave., Eau Claire 54701, 715-832-8424; and 4321 W. College Ave., Appleton 54914, 414-738-1640.

Rep. Jim Kolbe (R), Representative from Arizona, District 5
DC Office: 205 Cannon House Office Building, Washington, DC 20515, 202-225-2542; e-mail: jimkolbe@hr.house.gov.
District Offices: 1661 N. Swan Rd., Tucson 85712, 520-881-3588; and 77 Calle Portal, Sierra Vista 85635, 520-459-3115.

Sen. Jon Kyl (R), Senator from Arizona
DC Office: 702 Hart Senate Office Building, Washington, DC 20510, 202-224-4521; Fax: 202-224-2207; e-mail: info_kyl.senate.gov.
State Offices: 2200 E. Camelback, Phoenix 85016, 602-840-1891; and 7315 N. Oracle, Tucson 85704, 520-575-8633.

Rep. John J. LaFalce (D), Representative from New York, District 29

DC Office: 2310 Rayburn House Office Building, Washington, DC 20515, 202-225-3231; Fax: 202-225-8693.

District Offices: Fed. Bldg., 111 W. Huron St., Buffalo 14202, 716-846-4056; Main P.O. Bldg., 615 Main St., Niagara Falls 14302, 716-284-9976; and 409 S. Union St., Spencerport 14559, 716-352-4777.

Rep. Ray LaHood (R), Representative from Illinois, District 18

DC Office: 329 Cannon House Office Building, Washington, DC 20515, 202-225-6201; Fax: 202-225-9249.

District Offices: 100 N.E. Monroe, Peoria 61602, 309-671-7027; 3050 Montvale Dr., Springfield 62704, 217-793-0808; and 236 W. State St., Jacksonville 62650, 217-245-1431.

Rep. Tom Lantos (D), Representative from California, District 12

DC Office: 2217 Rayburn House Office Building, Washington, DC 20515, 202-225-3531; Fax: 202-225-7900; e-mail: talk2tom@hr.gov.

District Offices: 400 El Camino Real, San Mateo 94402, 415-342-0300.

Rep. Steve Largent (R), Representative from Oklahoma, District 1

DC Office: 410 Cannon House Office Building, Washington, DC 20515, 202-225-2211; Fax: 202-225-9817.

District Offices: 2424 E. 21st St., Tulsa 74114, 918-749-0014.

Rep. Tom Latham (R), Representative from Iowa, District 5

DC Office: 516 Cannon House Office Building, Washington, DC 20515, 202-225-5476; Fax: 202-225-3301.

District Offices: 123 Albany Ave., SE. Orange City 51041, 712-737-8708; 526 Pierce St., Sioux City 51101, 712-277-2114; 1411 1st Ave., S. Fort Dodge 50501, 515-573-2738; and 217 Grand Ave., Spencer 51301, 712-262-6480.

Rep. Steven C. LaTourette (R), Representative from Ohio, District 19

DC Office: 1508 Longworth House Office Building, Washington, DC 20515, 202-225-5731; Fax: 202-225-3307.

District Offices: 1 Victoria Pl., Painesville 44077, 216-352-3939.

Rep. Greg Laughlin (R), Representative from Texas, District 14

DC Office: 442 Cannon 20515, 202-225-2831; Fax: 202-225-1108.

District Offices: 312 S. Main St., Victoria 77901, 512-576-1231; and 221 E. Main St., Round Rock 78664, 512-244-3765.

Sen. Frank R. Lautenberg (D), Senator from New Jersey

DC Office: 506 Hart Senate Office Building, Washington, DC 20510, 202-224-4744; Fax: 202-224-9707; e-mail: frank_lautenberg@lautenberg.senate.gov.

State Offices: Barrington Commons, 208 Whitehorse Pk., Barrington 08007, 609-757-5353; and 1 Gateway Ctr., Newark 07102, 201-645-3030.

Rep. Rick A. Lazio (R), Representative from New York, District 2
DC Office: 314 Cannon House Office Building, Washington, DC 20515, 202-225-3335; Fax: 202-225-4669; e-mail: lazio@hr.house.gov.
District Offices: 126 W. Main St., Babylon 11702, 516-893-9010.

Rep. James A. Leach (R), Representative from Iowa, District 1
DC Office: 2186 Rayburn House Office Building, Washington, DC 20515, 202-225-6576; Fax: 202-226-1278.
District Offices: 209 W. 4th St., Davenport 52801, 319-326-1841; 102 S. Clinton, Iowa City 52240, 319-351-0789; and 309 10th St., SE, Cedar Rapids 52403, 319-363-4773.

Sen. Patrick J. Leahy (D), Senator from Vermont
DC Office: 433 Russell Senate Office Building, Washington, DC 20510, 202-224-4242; Fax: 202-224-3595; e-mail: senator_leahy@leahy.senate.gov.
State Offices: 199 Main St., Burlington 05401, 802-863-2525; and Fed. Bldg., Box 933, Montpelier 05602, 802-229-0569.

Sen. Carl Levin (D), Senator from Michigan
DC Office: 459 Russell Senate Office Building, Washington, DC 20510, 202-224-6221; Fax: 202-224-1388; e-mail: senator@levin.senate.gov.
State Offices: 1860 McNamara Bldg., 477 Michigan Ave., Detroit 48226, 313-226-6020; Fed. Bldg., 145 Water St., Alpena 49707, 517-354-5520; 623 Ludington St., Escanaba 49829, 517-789-0052; Gerald R. Ford Fed. Bldg., 110 Michigan Ave. N.W., Grand Rapids 49503, 616-456-2531; 1810 Michigan Natl. Tower, 124 Allegan St., Lansing 48933, 517-377-1508; P.O. Box 817, Saginaw 48606, 517-754-2494; 15100 Northline Rd., Southgate 48195, 313-285-8596; 24580 Cunningham, Warren 48091, 313-759-0477; and 207 Grandview Pkwy., Traverse City 49685, 616-947-9569.

Rep. Sander M. Levin (D), Representative from Michigan, District 12
DC Office: 2230 Rayburn House Office Building, Washington, DC 20515, 202-225-4961; Fax: 202-226-1033.
District Offices: 2107 E. 14 Mile Rd., Sterling Heights 48310, 810-268-4444.

Rep. Jerry Lewis (R), Representative from California, District 40
DC Office: 2112 Rayburn House Office Building, Washington, DC 20515, 202-225-5861; Fax: 202-225-6498.
District Offices: 1150 Brookside Ave., Redlands 92374, 909-862-6030.

Rep. John Lewis (D), Representative from Georgia, District 5
DC Office: 229 Cannon House Office Building, Washington, DC 20515, 202-225-3801; Fax: 202-225-0351.
District Offices:100 Peachtree St., NW, 404-659-0116.

Rep. Ron Lewis (R), Representative from Kentucky, District 2
DC Office: 412 Cannon House Office Building, Washington, DC 20515, 202-225-3501.

District Offices: 312 N. Mulberry St., Elizabethtown 42701, 502-765-4360;
B-18 Fed. Bldg., 241 W. Main St., Bowling Green 42101, 502-842-9896; and
B-17 Fed. Bldg., 423 Frederica St., Owensboro 42303, 502-688-8858.

Sen. Joseph I. Lieberman (D), Senator from Connecticut
DC Office: 316 Hart Senate Office Building, Washington, DC 20510, 202-224-4041;
Fax: 202-224-9750; e-mail: senator_lieberman@lieberman-dc.senate.gov.
State Offices: One Commercial Plz., Hartford 06103, 203-240-3566.

Rep. Jim Ross Lightfoot (R), Representative from Iowa, District 3
DC Office: 2161 Rayburn House Office Building, Washington, DC 20515,
202-225-3806; Fax: 202-225-6973.
District Offices: 501 W. Lowell, Shenandoah 51601, 712-246-1984; 413 Kellogg,
Ames 50010, 515-232-1288; 220 W. Salem, Indianola 50125, 515-961-0591;
347 E. 2d St., Ottumwa 52501, 515-683-3551; and 311 N. 3d St., Burlington 52601,
319-753-6415.

Rep. Blanche Lambert Lincoln (D), Representative from Arkansas, District 1
DC Office: 1204 Longworth House Office Building, Washington, DC 20515,
202-225-4076; Fax: 202-225-4654.
District Offices: 615 S. Main, Jonesboro 72401, 501-972-4600.

Rep. John Linder (R), Representative from Georgia, District 4
DC Office: 1318 Longworth House Office Building, Washington, DC 20515,
202-225-4272; Fax: 202-225-4696; e-mail: jlinder@hr.house.gov.
District Offices: 3003 Chamblee-Tucker Rd., Atlanta 30341, 404-936-9400.

Rep. William O. Lipinski (D), Representative from Illinois, District 3
DC Office: 1501 Longworth House Office Building, Washington, DC 20515,
202-225-5701; Fax: 202-225-1012.
District Offices: 5832 S. Archer Ave., Chicago 60638, 312-886-0481; and
12717 W. Ridgeland Ave., Palos Heights 60463, 708-371-7460.

Rep. Robert L. (Bob) Livingston (R), Representative from Louisiana, District 1
DC Office: 2406 Rayburn House Office Building, Washington, DC 20515,
202-225-3015; Fax: 202-225-0739.
District Offices: 111 Veterans Blvd., Metairie 70005, 504-589-2753.

Rep. Frank A. LoBiondo (R), Representative from New Jersey, District 2
DC Office: 513 Cannon House Office Building, Washington, DC 20515,
202-225-6572; Fax: 202-225-3318.
District Offices: 222 New Rd., Linwood 08221, 609-927-4442.

Rep. Zoe Lofgren (D), Representative from California, District 16
DC Office: 118 Cannon House Office Building, Washington, DC 20515,
202-225-3072; Fax: 202-225-3336; e-mail: zoegram@hr.house.gov.
District Offices: 635 N. 1st St., San Jose 95112, 408-271-8700.

Rep. James B. Longley, Jr. (R), Representative from Maine, District 1
DC Office: 226 Cannon House Office Building, Washington, DC 20515,
202-225-6116; Fax: 202-225-3353.
District Offices: 4 Moulton St., Portland 04101, 207-774-5019; and 168 Capitol St.,
Augusta 04330, 207-626-3608.

Sen. Trent Lott (R), Senator from Mississippi
DC Office: 487 Russell Senate Office Building, Washington, DC 20510,
202-224-6253; Fax: 202-224-2262.
State Offices: 1 Gov. Plaza, Gulfport 39501, 601-863-1988; 245 E. Capitol St.,
Jackson 39201, 601-965-4644; 3100 S. Pascagoula St., Pascagoula 39567,
601-762-5400; P.O. Box 1474, Oxford 38655, 601-234-3774; and 200 E. Washington
St., Greenwood 38930, 601-453-5681.

Rep. Nita M. Lowey (D), Representative from New York, District 18
DC Office: 2421 Rayburn House Office Building, Washington, DC 20515,
202-225-6506; Fax: 202-225-0546.
District Offices: 222 Mamaroneck Ave., White Plains 10605, 914-428-1707; and
97-45 Queens Blvd., Rego Park 11374, 718-897-3602.

Rep. Frank D. Lucas (R), Representative from Oklahoma, District 6
DC Office: 107 Cannon House Office Building, Washington, DC 20515,
202-225-5565; Fax: 202-225-8698.
District Offices: 215 Dean A. McGee, Oklahoma City 73102, 405-231-5511;
P.O. Box 3612, Enid 73701, 405-237-9224; and 1007 Main St., Woodward 73802,
405-256-5752.

Sen. Richard G. Lugar (R), Senator from Indiana
DC Office: 306 Hart Senate Office Building, Washington, DC 20510, 202-224-4814.
State Offices: 1180 Market Tower, 10 W. Market St., Indianapolis 46204,
317-226-5555; Fed. Bldg., 1300 S. Harrison St., Fort Wayne 46802, 219-422-1505;
122 Fed. Bldg., 101 NW M.L.K. Blvd., Evansville 47708, 812-465-6313; 103 Fed.
Ctr., 1201 E. 10th St., Jeffersonville 47132, 812-288-3377; and 8585 Broadway,
Merrillville 46410, 219-937-5380.

Rep. Bill Luther (DFL), Representative from Minnesota, District 6
DC Office: 1419 Longworth House Office Building, Washington, DC 20515,
202-225-2271; Fax: 202-225-3368.
District Offices: 1811 Weir Dr., Woodbury 55125, 612-730-4940.

Sen. Connie Mack III (R), Senator from Florida
DC Office: 517 Hart Senate Office Building, Washington, DC 20510, 202-224-5274;
Fax: 202-224-8022.
State Offices: 600 N. Westshore Blvd., Tampa 33609, 813-225-7483.

Rep. Carolyn B. Maloney (D), Representative from New York, District 14
DC Office: 1504 Longworth House Office Building, Washington, DC 20515,
202-225-7944; Fax: 202-225-4709.

District Offices: 110 E. 59th St., 2d Fl., New York 10022, 212-832-6531;
28-11 Astoria Blvd., Long Island City 11102, 718-932-1804; and 619 Lorimer St.,
Brooklyn 11211, 718-349-1260.

Rep. Thomas J. Manton (D), Representative from New York, District 7

DC Office: 2235 Rayburn House Office Building, Washington, DC 20515,
202-225-3965; Fax: 202-225-1909; e-mail: tmanton@hr.house.gov

District Offices: 46-12 Queens Blvd., Sunnyside 11104, 718-706-1400; and
2114 Williamsbridge Rd., Bronx 10461, 718-931-1400.

Rep. Donald Manzullo (R), Representative from Illinois, District 16

DC Office: 426 Cannon House Office Building, Washington, DC 20515,
202-225-5676; Fax: 202-225-5284.

District Offices: 415 S. Mulford Rd., Rockford 61108, 815-394-1231; and
191 Virginia Ave., Crystal Lake 60014, 815-356-9800.

Rep. Edward J. Markey (D), Representative from Massachusetts, District 7

DC Office: 2133 Rayburn House Office Building, Washington, DC 20515,
202-225-2836; Fax: 202-225-1716.

District Offices: 5 High St., Medford 02155, 617-396-2900.

Rep. Matthew G. (Marty) Martinez (D), Representative from California, District 31

DC Office: 2239 Rayburn House Office Building, Washington, DC 20515,
202-225-5464; Fax: 202-225-5467.

District Offices: 320 S. Garfield Ave., Alhambra 91801, 818-458-4524.

Rep. Bill Martini (R), Representative from New Jersey, District 8

DC Office: 1513 Longworth House Office Building, Washington, DC 20515,
202-225-5751; Fax: 202-225-3372.

District Offices: 200 Fed. Plz., Paterson 07505, 201-523-5152.

Rep. Frank R. Mascara (D), Representative from Pennsylvania, District 20

DC Office: 1531 Longworth House Office Building, Washington, DC 20515,
202-225-4665; Fax: 202-225-3377.

District Offices: 96 N. Main St., Washington 15301, 412-228-4326; 47 E. Penn St.,
Uniontown 15401, 412-437-5078; and 93 E. High St., Waynesburg 15370,
412-852-2182.

Rep. Robert T. Matsui (D), Representative from California, District 5

DC Office: 2311 Rayburn House Office Building, Washington, DC 20515,
202-225-7163; Fax: 202-225-0566.

District Offices: 8058 Fed. Bldg., 650 Capitol Mall, Sacramento 95814,
916-498-5600.

Sen. John McCain (R), Senator from Arizona

DC Office: 241 Russell Senate Office Building, Washington, DC 20510,
202-224-2235; Fax: 202-228-2862; e-mail: senator_mccain@mccain.senate.gov.

State Offices: 1839 S. Alma School Rd., Mesa 85210, 602-491-4300; 450 W. Pasco Redondo, Tucson 85701, 520-670-6334; and 2400 E. Arizona Biltmore Cir., Phoenix 85016, 602-952-2410.

Rep. Karen McCarthy (D), Representative from Missouri, District 5

DC Office: 1232 Longworth House Office Building, Washington, DC 20515, 202-225-4535; Fax: 202-225-4403.

District Offices: 811 Grand Ave., Kansas City 64106, 816-842-4545; and 301 W. Lexington, Independence 64050, 816-833-4545.

Rep. Bill McCollum (R), Representative from Florida, District 8

DC Office: 2266 Rayburn House Office Building, Washington, DC 20515, 202-225-2176; Fax: 202-225-0999.

District Offices: 605 E. Robinson Orlando 32801, 407-872-1962.

Sen. Mitch McConnell (R), Senator from Kentucky

DC Office: 120 Russell Senate Office Building, Washington, DC 20510, 202-224-2541; Fax: 202-224-2499.

State Offices: 601 W. Broadway, Louisville 40202, 502-582-6304; 1185 Dixie Hwy., Fort Wright 41011, 606-578-0188; Irvin Cobb Bldg., 602 Broadway, Paducah 42001, 502-442-4554; 1501-N S. Main St., London 40741, 606-864-2026; Fed. Bldg., 241 E. Main St., Bowling Green 42101; and 155 E. Main St., Lexington 40508, 606-252-1781.

Rep. Jim McCrery (R), Representative from Louisiana, District 5

DC Office: 225 Cannon House Office Building, Washington, DC 20515, 202-225-2777; Fax: 202-225-8039.

District Offices: 6425 Youree Dr., Shreveport 71105, 318-798-2254; and 1900 N. 18th St., Monroe 71201, 318-388-6105.

Rep. Joseph M. McDade (R), Representative from Pennsylvania, District 10

DC Office: 2107 Rayburn House Office Building, Washington, DC 20515, 202-225-3731; Fax: 202-225-9594.

District Offices: 514 Scranton Life Bldg., Scranton 18503, 717-346-3834; and 240 W. Third St., Williamsport 17701, 717-327-8161.

Rep. Jim McDermott (D), Representative from Washington, District 7

DC Office: 2349 Rayburn House Office Building, Washington, DC 20515, 202-225-3106.

District Offices: 1212 Tower Bldg., 1809 7th Ave., Seattle 98101, 206-553-7170.

Rep. Paul McHale (D), Representative from Pennsylvania, District 15

DC Office: 217 Cannon House Office Building, Washington, DC 20515, 202-225-6411; Fax: 202-225-5320; e-mail: mchale@hr.house.gov.

District Offices: 26 E. 3d St., Bethlehem 18015, 215-866-0916; Hamilton Financial Ctr., One Center Sq., Allentown 18101, 215-439-8861; and 168 Main St., Pennsburg 18073, 215-541-0614.

Rep. John M. McHugh (R), Representative from New York, District 24

DC Office: 416 Cannon House Office Building, Washington, DC 20515, 202-225-4611.

District Offices: 404 Key Bank Bldg., 200 Washington St., Watertown 13601, 315-782-3150.

Rep. Scott McInnis (R), Representative from Colorado, District 3

DC Office: 215 Cannon House Office Building, Washington, DC 20515, 202-225-4761; Fax: 202-225-0622.

District Offices: 327 N. 7th St., Grand Junction 81501, 303-245-7107; 134 W. B St., Pueblo 81003, 719-543-8200; 1060 Main Ave., Durango 81301, 303-259-2754; and 526 Pine St., Glenwood Springs 81601, 303-928-0637.

Rep. David M. McIntosh (R), Representative from Indiana, District 2

DC Office: 1208 Longworth House Office Building, Washington, DC 20515, 202-225-3021. Fax: 202-225-3382; e-mail: mcintosh@hr.house.gov.

District Offices: 2900 W. Jackson St., Muncie 47304, 317-747-5566.

Rep. Howard P. (Buck) McKeon (R), Representative from California, District 25

DC Office: 307 Cannon House Office Building, Washington, DC 20515, 202-225-1956; Fax: 202-225-0683; e-mail: tellbuck@hr.house.gov.

District Offices: 23929 W. Valencia Blvd., Santa Clarita 91355, 805-254-2111; and 1008 West Ave., Palmdale 93551, 805-948-7833.

Rep. Cynthia A. McKinney (D), Representative from Georgia, District 11

DC Office: 124 Cannon House Office Building, Washington, DC 20515, 202-225-1605.

District Offices: 1 S. DeKalb Ctr., 2853 Candler Rd., Decatur 30034, 404-244-9902; 120 Barnard St., Savannah 31401, 912-652-4118; and 505 Courthouse La., Augusta 30901, 706-722-7551.

Rep. Michael R. McNulty (D), Representative from New York, District 21

DC Office: 2442 Rayburn House Office Building, Washington, DC 20515, 202-225-5076; Fax: 202-225-5077.

District Offices: U.S. Post Office, Jay St., Schenectady 12305, 518-374-4547; O'Brien Fed. Bldg., 518-465-0700; 9 Market St., Amsterdam 12010, 518-843-3400; and 33 2d St., Troy 12180, 518-271-0822.

Rep. Martin T. (Marty) Meehan (D), Representative from Massachusetts,District 5

DC Office: 318 Cannon House Office Building, Washington, DC 20515, 202-225-3411; Fax: 202-226-0771.

District Offices: 11 Kearney Sq., Lowell 01852, 508-459-0101; Bay State Bldg., 11 Lawrence St., Lawrence 01840, 508-681-6200; and Walker Bldg., 255 Main St., Marlborough 01752, 508-460-9292.

Rep. Carrie P. Meek (D), Representative from Florida, District 17

DC Office: 404 Cannon House Office Building, Washington, DC 20515, 202-225-4506.

District Offices: 25 W. Flagler St., Miami 33130, 305-381-9541.

Rep. Robert Menendez (D), Representative from New Jersey, District 13

DC Office: 1730 Longworth House Office Building, Washington, DC 20515, 202-225-7919; Fax: 202-226-0792.

District Offices: 911 Bergen Ave., Jersey City 07306, 201-222-2828; and 654 Ave. C, Bayonne 07002, 201-823-2900.

Rep. Jack Metcalf (R), Representative from Washington, District 2

DC Office: 507 Cannon House Office Building, Washington, DC 20515, 202-225-2605; Fax: 202-225-4420.

District Offices: 2930 Wetmore Ave., Everett 98201, 206-252-3188; and 322 N. Commercial St., Bellingham 98225, 206-733-4500.

Rep. Jan Meyers (R), Representative from Kansas, District 3

DC Office: 2303 Rayburn House Office Building, Washington, DC 20515, 202-225-2865; Fax: 202-225-0554.

District Offices: 182 Fed. Bldg., Kansas City 66101, 913-621-0832; 7133 W. 95th St., Overland Park 66212, 913-383-2013; and 708 W. 9th St., Lawrence 66044, 913-842-9313.

Rep. Kweisi Mfume (D), Representative from Maryland, District 7

DC Office: 2419 Rayburn House Office Building, Washington, DC 20515, 202-225-4741; Fax: 202-225-3178.

District Offices: 3000 Druid Park Dr., Baltimore 21215, 410-367-1900; and 1825 Woodlawn Dr., Baltimore 21207, 410-298-5997.

Rep. John L. Mica (R), Representative from Florida, District 7

DC Office: 336 Cannon House Office Building, Washington, DC 20515, 202-225-4035; Fax: 202-226-0821; e-mail: mica2hr.house.gov.

District Offices: 1211 Semoran Blvd., Casselberry 32707, 407-657-8080; 840 Deltona Blvd., Deltona 32725, 407-866-1499; and 1396 Dunlawton Blvd., Port Orange 32127, 904-756-9798.

Sen. Barbara A. Mikulski (D), Senator from Maryland

DC Office: 709 Hart Senate Office Building, Washington, DC 20510, 202-224-4654; Fax: 202-224-8858; e-mail: senator@mikulski.senate.gov.

State Offices: 253 World Trade Ctr., 401 E. Pratt St., Baltimore 21202, 410-962-4510; 60 West St., Annapolis 21401, 410-263-1805; 9658 Baltimore Ave., College Park 20740, 301-345-5517; 1201 Pemberton, Salisbury 21801, 410-546-7711; and 82 W. Washington St., Hagerstown 21740, 301-797-2826.

Rep. George Miller (D), Representative from California, District 7

DC Office: 2205 Rayburn House Office Building, Washington, DC 20515, 202-225-2095; Fax: 202-225-5609; e-mail: gmiller@hr.house.gov

District Offices: 367 Civic Dr., Pleasant Hill 94523, 510-602-1880; and 3220 Blume Dr., Richmond 94806, 510-262-6500.

Rep. Dan Miller (R), Representative from Florida, District 13

DC Office: 117 Cannon House Office Building, Washington, DC 20515, 202-225-5015; Fax: 202-226-0828.

District Offices: 2424 Manatee Ave., Bradenton 34205, 813-747-9081; 1751 Mound St., Sarasota 34236, 813-951-6643.

Rep. David Minge (DFL), Representative from Minnesota, District 2

DC Office: 1415 Longworth House Office Building, Washington, DC 20515, 202-225-2331; Fax: 202-226-0836; e-mail: dminge@hr.house.gov.

District Offices: 542 1st St., Montevideo 56265, 612-269-9311; 405 E. 2nd St., Chaska 55318, 612-448-6567; and 938 4th Ave., Windom 56101, 507-831-0115.

Rep. Patsy T. Mink (D), Representative from Hawaii, District 2

DC Office: 2135 Rayburn House Office Building, Washington, DC 20515, 202-225-4906; Fax: 202-225-4987.

District Offices: 5104 Prince Kuhio Fed. Bldg., P.O. Box 50124, Honolulu 96850, 808-541-1966.

Rep. John Joseph (Joe) Moakley (D), Representative from Massachusetts, District 9

DC Office: 235 Cannon House Office Building, Washington, DC 20515, 202-225-8273; Fax: 202-225-3984; e-mail: jmoakley@hr.house.gov.

District Offices: 4 Court St., Taunton 02780, 617-824-6676; and World Trade Ctr., Boston 02210, 617-565-2920.

Rep. Susan Molinari (R), Representative from New York, District 13

DC Office: 2435 Rayburn House Office Building, Washington, DC 20515, 202-225-3371; Fax: 202-226-1272; e-mail: smolinari@hr.house.gov.

District Offices: 14 New Dorp Ln., Staten Island 10306, 718-987-8400; and 9818 4th Ave., Brooklyn 11209, 718-630-5277.

Rep. Alan B. Mollohan (D), Representative from West Virginia, District 1

DC Office: 2427 Rayburn House Office Building, Washington, DC 20515, 202-225-4172; Fax: 202-225-7564.

District Offices: 213 Fed. Bldg., Morgantown 26505, 304-292-3019; 1117 Fed. Bldg., Parkersburg 26101, 304-428-0493; 316 Fed. Bldg., Wheeling 26003, 304-232-5390; and 209 P.O. Bldg., Clarksburg 26301, 304-623-4422.

Rep. G. V. (Sonny) Montgomery (D), Representative from Mississippi, District 3

DC Office: 2184 Rayburn House Office Building, Washington, DC 20515, 202-225-5031; Fax: 202-225-3375.

District Offices: Fed. Bldg., Meridian 39301, 601-693-6681; 110-D Airport Rd., Pearl 39208, 601-932-2410; and Golden Triangle Airport, Columbus 39701, 601-327-2766.

Rep. Carlos J. Moorhead (R), Representative from California, District 27

DC Office: 2346 Rayburn House Office Building, Washington, DC 20515, 202-225-4176; Fax: 202-225-1279.

District Offices: 420 N. Brand Blvd., Glendale 91203, 818-247-8445.

Rep. James P. Moran, Jr. (D), Representative from Virginia, District 8

DC Office: 405 Cannon House Office Building, Washington, DC 20515, 202-225-4376; Fax: 202-225-0017.

District Offices: 5115 Franconia Rd., Alexandria 22310, 703-971-4700.

Rep. Constance A. Morella (R), Representative from Maryland, District 8

DC Office: 106 Cannon House Office Building, Washington, DC 20515, 202-225-5341; Fax: 202-225-1389.

District Offices: 51 Monroe St., Rockville 20850, 301-424-3501.

Sen. Carol Moseley-Braun (D), Senator from Illinois

DC Office: 320 Hart Senate Office Building, Washington, DC 20510, 202-224-2854; Fax: 202-224-1318; e-mail: senator@moseley-braun.senate.gov.

State Offices: Kluczynski Fed. Bldg., 230 S. Dearborn, Chicago 60604, 312-353-5420; 117 Fed. Bldg., 600 E. Monroe St., Springfield 62701, 217-492-4126; and Fed. Bldg., 105 S. 6th St., Mt Vernon 62864, 618-383-7920.

Sen. Daniel Patrick Moynihan (D), Senator from New York

DC Office: 464 Russell Senate Office Building, Washington, DC 20510, 202-224-4451.

State Offices: 405 Lexington Ave., New York 10174, 212-661-5150; Guaranty Bldg., 28 Church St., Buffalo 14202, 716-846-4097; and 214 Main St., Oneonta 13820, 607-433-2310.

Sen. Frank H. Murkowski (R), Senator from Alaska

DC Office: 706 Hart Senate Office Building, Washington, DC 20510, 202-224-6665; Fax: 202-224-5301.

State Offices: 222 W. 7th Ave., Box 1, Anchorage 99513, 907-271-3735; 101 12th Ave., Fairbanks 99701, 907-456-0233; Box 21647 Fed. Bldg, Juneau 99802, 907-586-7400; 130 Trading Bay Rd., Kenai 99611, 907-283-5808; and 109 Main St., Ketchikan 99901, 907-225-6880.

Sen. Patty Murray (D), Senator from Washington

DC Office: 111 Russell Senate Office Building, Washington, DC 20510, 202-224-2621; Fax: 202-224-0238; e-mail: senator_murray@murray.senate.gov.

District Offices: 2988 Jackson Fed. Bldg., 915 2nd Ave., Seattle 98174, 206-553-5545; 601 1st Ave., Spokane 99201, 509-624-9515; and 140 Fed. Bldg., 500 W. 12th St., Vancouver 98660, 206-696-7797.

Rep. John P. Murtha (D), Representative from Pennsylvania, District 12

DC Office: 2423 Rayburn House Office Building, Washington, DC 20515, 202-225-2065; Fax: 202-225-5709; e-mail: murtha@hr.house.gov.

District Offices: Vine and Walnut Sts., Centre Town Mall, Johnstown 15907, 814-535-2642.

Rep. John T. Myers (R), Representative from Indiana, District 7
DC Office: 2372 Rayburn House Office Building, Washington, DC 20515, 202-225-5805; Fax: 202-225-1649.
District Offices: 107 Fed. Bldg., Terre Haute 47808, 812-238-1619; and 107 Halleck Fed. Bldg., Lafayette 47901, 317-423-1661.

Rep. Sue Myrick (R), Representative from North Carolina, District 9
DC Office: 509 Cannon House Office Building, Washington, DC 20515, 202-225-1976; Fax: 202-225-3389; e-mail: myrick@hr.house.gov.
District Offices: 1901 Roxborough Rd., Charlotte 28211, 704-362-1060; and 224 S. New Hope Rd., Gastonia 28054, 704-861-1976.

Rep. Jerrold Nadler (D), Representative from New York, District 8
DC Office: 109 Cannon House Office Building, Washington, DC 20515, 202-225-5635; Fax: 202-225-6923.
District Offices: 1841 Broadway, New York 10023, 212-489-3530; and 2875 W. 8th St., Brooklyn 11224, 718-373-3198.

Rep. Richard E. Neal (D), Representative from Massachusetts, District 2
DC Office: 2431 Rayburn House Office Building, Washington, DC 20515, 202-225-5601; Fax: 202-225-8112.
District Offices: Fed. Office Bldg., 1550 Main St., Springfield 01103, 413-785-0325; and 4 Congress St., Milford 01757, 508-634-8198.

Rep. George R. Nethercutt, Jr. (R), Representative from Washington, District 5
DC Office: 1527 Longworth House Office Building, Washington, DC 20515, 202-225-2006; Fax: 202-225-3392; e-mail: grnwa05@hr.house.gov.
District Offices: W. 920 Riverside, Spokane 99201, 509-353-2374.

Rep. Mark W. Neumann (R), Representative from Wisconsin, District 1
DC Office: 1725 Longworth House Office Building, Washington, DC 20515, 202-225-3031; Fax: 202-225-3393; e-mail: mneumann@hr.house.gov.
District Offices: 1 Parker Pl., Janesville 53525, 608-752-4050.

Rep. Bob Ney (R), Representative from Ohio, District 18
DC Office: 1605 Longworth House Office Building, Washington, DC 20515, 202-225-6265; Fax: 202-225-3394.
District Offices: 3201 Belmont St., Bellaire 43906, 614-676-1960; 152 2nd St., NE, New Philadelphia 44663, 216-364-6380; 500 Market St., Steubenville 43952, 614-283-1915; and 225 Underwood St., Zanesville 43701, 614-452-8598.

Sen. Don Nickles (R), Senator from Oklahoma
DC Office: 133 Hart Senate Office Building, Washington, DC 20510, 202-224-5754; Fax: 202-224-6008.

State Offices: 1820 Liberty Tower, 100 N. Broadway, Oklahoma City 73102, 405-231-4941; 3310 Mid-Continent Tower, 401 S. Boston, Tulsa 74103, 918-581-7651; 1916 Lake Rd., Ponca City 74601, 405-767-1270; and American Natl. Bank Bldg., 601 D Ave., Lawton 73501, 405-357-9878.

Rep. Charlie Norwood (R), Representative from Georgia, District 10
DC Office: 1707 Longworth House Office Building, Washington, DC 20515, 202-225-4101; Fax: 202-225-3397; e-mail: ga10@hr.house.gov.
District Offices: 1056 Clausson Rd., Augusta 30807, 706-733-7066.

Sen. Sam Nunn (D), Senator from Georgia
DC Office: 303 Dirksen Senate Office Building, Washington, DC 20510, 202-224-3521; Fax: 202-224-0072.
State Offices: 75 Spring St. SW, Atlanta 30303, 404-331-4811; 915 Main St., Perry 31069, 912-987-1458; 130 Fed. Bldg., Gainesville 30501, 404-532-9976; 600 E. 1st St., Rome 30161, 404-291-5696; and 120 Barnard St., Savannah 31069, 912-944-4300.

Rep. Jim Nussle (R), Representative from Iowa, District 2
DC Office: 303 Cannon House Office Building, Washington, DC 20515, 202-225-2911; Fax: 202-225-9129.
District Offices: 2300 JFK Rd., Dubuque 52002, 319-557-7740; 3356 Kimball Ave., Waterloo 50702, 310-235-1109; 1825 4th St., SW, Mason City 50401, 515-423-0303; and 223 W. Main St., Manchester 52057, 319-927-5141.

Rep. James L. Oberstar (DFL), Representative from Minnesota, District 8
DC Office: 2366 Rayburn House Office Building, Washington, DC 20515, 202-225-6211; Fax: 202-225-0699; e-mail: oberstar@hr.house.gov.
District Offices: 231 Fed. Bldg., Duluth 55802, 218-727-7474; Chisolm City Hall, 316 Lake St., Chisholm 55719, 218-254-5761; City Hall, 13065 Orono Pkwy., Elk River 55330, 612-241-0188; and Brainerd City Hall, 501 Laurel St., Brainerd 56401, 218-828-4400.

Rep. David R. Obey (D), Representative from Wisconsin, District 7
DC Office: 2462 Rayburn House Office Building, Washington, DC 20515, 202-225-3365.
District Offices: Fed. Bldg., 317 First St., Wausau 54401, 715-842-5606.

Rep. John Olver (D), Representative from Massachusetts, District 1
DC Office: 1027 Longworth House Office Building, Washington, DC 20515, 202-225-5335; Fax: 202-226-1224.
District Offices: 78 Center St. Arterial, Pittsfield 02101, 413-442-0946; 881 Main St., Philbin Fed. Bldg., Fitchburg 01420, 508-342-8722; and 187 High St., Holyoke 01040, 413-584-8108.

Rep. Solomon P. Ortiz (D), Representative from Texas, District 27
DC Office: 2136 Rayburn House Office Building, Washington, DC 20515, 202-225-7742; Fax: 202-225-1134.

District Offices: 3649 Leopard St., Corpus Christi 78408, 512-883-5868; and 3505 Boca Chica Blvd., Brownsville 78521, 512-541-1242.

Rep. William H. Orton (D), Representative from Utah, District 3

DC Office: 440 Cannon House Office Building, Washington, DC 20515, 202-225-7751; Fax: 202-226-7683; e-mail: ortonut3@hr.house.gov.

District Offices: 51 S. University Ave., Provo 84601, 801-379-2500; and 3540 S. 40th St., West Valley City 84119, 801-964-5828.

Rep. Major R. Owens (D), Representative from New York, District 11

DC Office: 2305 Rayburn House Office Building, Washington, DC 20515, 202-225-6231; Fax: 202-226-0112.

District Offices: 289 Utica Ave., Brooklyn 11213, 718-773-3100; and 1310 Cortelyon Rd., Brooklyn 11226, 718-940-3213.

Rep. Michael G. Oxley (R), Representative from Ohio, District 4

DC Office: 2233 Rayburn House Office Building, Washington, DC 20515, 202-225-2676.

District Offices: 3121 W. Elm Plz., Lima 45805, 419-999-6455; 24 W. 3d St., Mansfield 44902, 419-522-5757; and 100 E. Main Cross St., Findlay 45840, 419-423-3210.

Rep. Ron Packard (R), Representative from California, District 48

DC Office: 2162 Rayburn House Office Building, Washington, DC 20515, 202-225-3906; Fax: 202-225-0134; e-mail: rpackard@hr.house.gov.

District Offices: 221 E. Vista Way, Vista 92084, 619-631-1364; and 629 Camino del los Mares, San Clemente 92672, 714-496-2343.

Sen. Bob Packwood (R), Senator from Oregon

DC Office: 259 Russell Senate Office Building, Washington, DC 20510, 202-224-5244; Fax: 202-228-3576; e-mail: senator_packwood@packwood.senate.gov.

State Offices: 101 SW Main St., Portland 97204-3210, 503-326-3370.

Rep. Frank Pallone, Jr. (D), Representative from New Jersey, District 6

DC Office: 420 Cannon House Office Building, Washington, DC 20515, 202-225-4671; Fax: 202-225-9665.

District Offices: IEI Airport Plz., Hazlet 07703, 908-264-9104; 67/69 Church St., New Brunswick 08901, 908-249-8892; and 540 Broadway Ave., Long Branch 07740, 201-571-1140.

Rep. Mike Parker (R), Representative from Mississippi, District 4

DC Office: 2445 Rayburn House Office Building, Washington, DC 20515, 202-225-5865; Fax: 202-225-5886.

District Offices: 245 E. Capitol, Jackson 39201, 601-352-1355; 230 S. Whitworth St., Brookhaven 39601, 601-835-0706; 118 N. Pearl St., Natchez 39120, 601-446-7250; Chancery Ct. Annex, Columbia 39429, 601-731-1622; 728 Sawmill Rd., Laurel 39440, 601-425-4999; and 176 W. Court St., Mendenhall 39114, 601-847-0873.

Rep. Ed Pastor (D), Representative from Arizona, District 2

DC Office: 223 Cannon House Office Building, Washington, DC 20515, 202-225-4065; Fax: 202-225-1655; e-mail: edpastor@hr.house.gov.

District Offices: 802 N. Third Ave., Phoenix 85003, 602-256-0551; 2432 E. Broadway, Tucson 85719, 520-624-9986; and 281 W. 24th St., Yuma 85364, 520-726-2234.

Rep. Bill Paxon (R), Representative from New York, District 27

DC Office: 2436 Rayburn House Office Building, Washington, DC 20515, 202-225-5265; Fax: 202-225-5910; e-mail: bpaxon@hr.house.gov.

District Offices: 5500 Main St., Williamsville, 14221, 716-634-2324; and 10 E. Main St., Victor 14564, 716-742-1600, 800-453-8330.

Rep. Donald M. Payne (D), Representative from New Jersey, District 10

DC Office: 2244 Rayburn House Office Building, Washington, DC 20515, 202-225-3436; Fax: 202-225-4160.

District Offices: 50 Walnut St., Newark 07102, 201-645-3213; and 333 N. Broad St., Elizabeth 07208, 908-629-0222.

Rep. L. F. Payne (D), Representative from Virginia, District 5

DC Office: 2412 Longworth House Office Building, Washington, DC 20515, 202-225-4711; Fax: 202-226-1147.

District Offices: 301 P.O. Bldg., 700 Main St., Danville 24541, 804-792-1280; Abbitt Fed. Bldg., 103 S. Main St., Farmville 23901, 804-392-8331; and 103 E. Water St., Charlottesville 22902, 804-295-6372.

Sen. Claiborne Pell (D), Senator from Rhode Island

DC Office: 335 Russell Senate Office Building, Washington, DC 20510, 202-224-4642; Fax: 202-224-4680.

State Offices: 418 Fed. Bldg., Providence 02903, 401-528-5456.

Rep. Nancy Pelosi (D), Representative from California, District 8

Rep. Douglas (Pete) Peterson (D), Representative from Florida, District 2

DC Office: 306 Cannon House Office Building, Washington, DC 20515, 202-225-5235; Fax: 202-225-1586.

District Offices: 930 Thomasville Rd., Tallahassee 32303, 904-561-3979;30 W. Government St., Panama City 32401, 904-785-0812.

Rep. Collin C. Peterson (DFL), Representative from Minnesota, District 7

DC Office: 1314 Longworth House Office Building, Washington, DC 20515, 202-225-2165; Fax: 202-225-1593; e-mail: tocollin@hr.house.gov.

District Offices: 714 Lake Ave., Detroit Lakes 56501, 218-847-5056; 110 2nd St., Waite Park 56387, 612-259-0559; and 2603 Wheat Dr., Red Lake Falls 56750, 218-253-4356.

Rep. Tom Petri (R), Representative from Wisconsin, District 6

DC Office: 2262 Rayburn House Office Building, Washington, DC 20515, 202-225-2476; Fax: 202-225-2356.

District Offices: 845 S. Main St., Fond du Lac 54935, 414-922-1180; and
115 Washington Ave., Oshkosh 54901, 414-231-6333.

Rep. Owen Pickett (D), Representative from Virginia, District 2

DC Office: 2430 Rayburn House Office Building, Washington, DC 20515,
202-225-4215; Fax: 202-225-4218; e-mail: opickett@hr.house.gov.

District Offices: 112 E. Little Creek Rd., Norfolk 23505, 804-583-5892 ;and
2710 VA Beach Blvd., Virginia Beach 23452, 804-486-3710.

Rep. Richard W. Pombo (R), Representative from California, District 11

DC Office: 1519 Longworth House Office Building, Washington, DC 20515,
202-225-1947; Fax: 202-225-0861.

District Offices: 2495 W. March La., Stockton 95207, 209-951-3091.

Rep. Earl Pomeroy (D), Representative from North Dakota, District 1

DC Office: 1533 Longworth House Office Building, Washington, DC 20515,
202-225-2611; Fax: 202-226-0893; e-mail: epomeroy@hr.house.gov.

District Offices: Fed. Bldg., 657 2nd Ave., Fargo 58102, 701-235-9760; Fed. Bldg.,
220 East Rosser Ave., Bismarck 58501, 701-224-0355.

Rep. John E. Porter (R), Representative from Illinois, District 10

DC Office: 2373 Rayburn House Office Building, Washington, DC 20515,
202-225-4835.

District Offices: 102 Wilmot Rd., Deerfield 60015, 708-940-0202; and 18 N. County
St., Waukegan 60085, 708-662-0101.

Rep. Rob Portman (R), Representative from Ohio, District 2

DC Office: 238 Cannon House Office Building, Washington, DC 20515,
202-225-3164; Fax: 202-225-1992; e-mail: portmail@hr.house.gov.

District Offices: 8010 Fed. Bldg., 550 Main St., Cincinatti 45202, 513-684-2456.

Rep. Glenn Poshard (D), Representative from Illinois, District 19

DC Office: 2334 Rayburn House Office Building, Washington, DC 20515,
202-225-5201; Fax: 202-225-1541.

District Offices: 201 E. Nolan St., W. Frankfort 62896, 618-937-6402;
New Rte. Marion 62959, 618-953-8532; 363 S. Main St., Decatur 62521,
217-362-9011; 800 Airport Rd., Mattoon 61938, 217-234-7032; 444 S. Willow St.,
Effingham 62401, 217-342-7220; and 606 N. 13th St., Lawrenceville 62439,
618-943-6036.

Sen. Larry Pressler (R), Senator from South Dakota

DC Office: 243 Russell Senate Office Building, Washington, DC 20510,
202-224-5842; e-mail: larry_pressler@pressler.senate.gov.

State Offices: 1923 6th Ave., Aberdeen 57402, 605-226-7471; 112 Rushmore Mall,
Rapid City 57701, 605-341-1185; and 309 Minnesota Ave., Sioux Falls 57102,
605-335-1990.

Rep. Deborah Pryce (R), Representative from Ohio, District 15
DC Office: 221 Cannon House Office Building, Washington, DC 20515, 202-225-2015; Fax: 202-226-0986.
District Offices: 200 N. High St., Columbus, OH 43215, 614-469-5614.

Sen. David Pryor (D), Senator from Arkansas
DC Office: 267 Russell Senate Office Building, Washington, DC 20510, 202-224-2353; Fax: 202-228-3973.
State Offices: 3030 Fed. Bldg., Little Rock 72201, 501-378-6336.

Rep. James H. (Jimmy) Quillen (R), Representative from Tennessee, District 1
DC Office: 102 Cannon House Office Building, Washington, DC 20515, 202-225-6356; Fax: 202-225-7812.
District Offices: Fed. P.O. Bldg., Kingsport 37662, 615-247-8161.

Rep. Jack Quinn (R), Representative from New York, District 30
DC Office: 331 Cannon House Office Building, Washington, DC 20515, 202-225-3306; Fax: 202-226-0347.
District Offices: 403 Main St., Buffalo 14203, 716-845-5257.

Rep. George P. Radanovich (R), Representative from California, District 19
DC Office: 313 Cannon House Office Building, Washington, DC 20515, 202-225-4540; Fax: 202-225-3402; e-mail: george@hr.house.gov.
District Offices: 2377 W. Shaw, Fresno 93711, 209-248-0800.

Rep. Nick J. Rahall (D), Representative from West Virginia, District 3
DC Office: 2269 Rayburn House Office Building, Washington, DC 20515, 202-225-3452; Fax: 202-225-9061.
District Offices: 110 Main St., Beckley 25801, 304-252-5000; 815 5th Ave., Huntington 25701, 304-522-6425; 1005 Fed. Bldg., Bluefield 24701, 304-325-6222; R.K. Bldg., 45 Washington Ave., Logan 25601, 304-752-4934; and P.O. Box 5, 101 N. Court St., Lewisburg 24901, 304-647-3228.

Rep. Jim Ramstad (IR), Representative from Minnesota, District 3
DC Office: 103 Cannon House Office Building, Washington, DC 20515, 202-225-2871; Fax: 202-225-6351; e-mail: mn03@hr.house.gov.
District Offices: 8120 Penn Ave. S., Bloomington 55431, 612-881-4600.

Rep. Charles B. Rangel (D), Representative from New York, District 15
DC Office: 2354 Rayburn House Office Building, Washington, DC 20515, 202-225-4365; Fax: 202-225-0816.
District Offices: 163 W. 125th St., New York 10027, 212-663-3900; 601 W. 181st St., New York 10033, 212-927-5333; and 2110 1st Ave., New York 10029, 212-348-9830.

Rep. Jack Reed (D), Representative from Rhode Island, District 2

DC Office: 1510 Longworth House Office Building, Washington, DC 20515, 202-225-2735; Fax: 202-225-9580.

District Offices: Garden City Ctr., 100 Midway Place, Cranston 02920, 401-943-3100.

Rep. Ralph S. Regula (R), Representative from Ohio, District 16

DC Office: 2309 Rayburn House Office Building, Washington, DC 20515, 202-225-3876; Fax: 202-225-3059.

District Offices: 4150 Belden Village St., NW, Canton 44718, 216-489-4414.

Sen. Harry Reid (D), Senator from Nevada

DC Office: 324 Hart Senate Office Building, Washington, DC 20510, 202-224-3542; Fax: 202-224-7327; e-mail: senator_reid@reid.senate.gov.

State Offices: 245 E. Liberty St., Reno 89501, 702-784-5568; 500 E. Charleston Blvd., Las Vegas 89104, 702-474-0041; and 600 E. Williams St., Carson City 89701, 702-882-7343.

Rep. Bill Richardson (D), Representative from New Mexico, District 3

DC Office: 2209 Rayburn House Office Building, Washington, DC 20515, 202-225-6190.

District Office: 1494 S. St. Francis Dr., Santa Fe 87505, 505-988-7230; Gallup City Hall, 2d & Aztec, Gallup 87301, 505-722-6522; San Miguel Cnty. Crthse., P.O. Box 1805, Las Vegas 87701, 505-425-7270; and P.O. Box 1108, Clovis 88102, 505-769-3380.

Rep. Frank D. Riggs (R), Representative from California, District 1

DC Office: 1714 Longworth House Office Building, Washington, DC 20515, 202-225-3311; Fax: 202-225-3403; e-mail: repriggs@hr.house.gov.

District Offices: 1700 2nd St., Napa 94559, 707-254-7308; and 710 E St., Eureka 95501, 707-441-8701.

Rep. Lynn N. Rivers (D), Representative from Michigan, District 13

DC Office: 1116 Longworth House Office Building, Washington, DC 20515, 202-225-6261; Fax: 202-225-3404; e-mail: lrivers@hr.house.gov.

District Offices: 106 E. Washington, Ann Arbor 48104, 313-741-4210; 3716 Newberry, Wayne 48184, 313-722-1411.

Sen. Charles S. Robb (D), Senator from Virginia

DC Office: 154 Russell Senate Office Building, Washington, DC 20510, 202-224-4024; Fax: 202-224-8689; e-mail: senator_robb@robb.senator.gov.

State Offices: 1001 E. Broad St., Richmond 23219, 804-771-2221; 310 1st St., SW, Roanoke 24011, 703-985-0103; Signet Bank Bldg., 530 Main St., Danville 24541, 804-791-0330; Dominion Towers, 999 Waterside Dr., Norfolk 23510, 804-441-3124; 8229 Boone Blvd., Vienna 22182, 703-356-2006; and First Union Bank Bldg., Main St., Clintwood 24288, 703-926-4104.

Rep. Pat Roberts (R), Representative from Kansas, District 1

DC Office: 1126 Longworth House Office Building, Washington, DC 20515, 202-225-2715; Fax: 202-225-5375; e-mail: emailpat@hr.house.gov

District Offices: P.O. Box 550, Dodge City 67801, 316-227-2244; P.O. Box 128, Norton 67654, 913-877-2454; P.O. Box 1128, Hutchinson 67502, 316-665-6138; and P.O. Box 1334, Salina 67402, 913-825-5409.

Sen. John D. (Jay) Rockefeller IV (D), Senator from West Virginia

DC Office: 109 Hart Senate Office Building, Washington, DC 20510, 202-224-6472; Fax: 202-224-7665; e-mail: senator@rockefeller.senate.gov.

State Offices: 405 Capitol St., Charleston 25301, 304-347-5372; 115 S. Kanawha St., Beckley 25801, 304-253-9704; and 200 Adams St., Fairmont 26554, 304-367-0122.

Rep. Tim Roemer (D), Representative from Indiana, District 3

DC Office: 407 Cannon House Office Building, Washington, DC 20515, 202-225-3915; Fax: 202-225-6798.

District Offices: 217 N. Main St., South Bend 46601, 219-288-3301.

Rep. Harold D. Rogers (R), Representative from Kentucky, District 5

DC Office: 2468 Rayburn House Office Building, Washington, DC 20515, 202-225-4601; Fax: 202-225-0940.

District Offices: 203 E. Mount Vernon St., Somerset 42501, 606-679-8346; 601 Main St., Hazard 41701, 606-439-0794; and 806 Hambley Blvd., Pikeville 41501, 606-432-4388.

Rep. Dana Rohrabacher (R), Representative from California, District 45

DC Office: 2338 Rayburn House Office Building, Washington, DC 20515, 202-225-2415; Fax: 202-225-0145.

District Offices: 16162 Beach Blvd., Huntington Beach 92647, 714-847-2433.

Rep. Charlie Rose (D), Representative from North Carolina, District 7

DC Office: 242 Cannon House Office Building, Washington, DC 20515, 202-225-2731; Fax: 202-225-0345; e-mail: crose@hr.house.gov.

District Offices: 208 P.O. Bldg., Wilmington 28401, 919-343-4959; and 218 Fed. Bldg., Fayetteville 28301, 919-323-0260.

Rep. Ileana Ros-Lehtinen (R), Representative from Florida, District 18

DC Office: 2440 Rayburn House Office Building, Washington, DC 20515, 202-225-3931; Fax: 202-225-5620.

District Offices: 5757 Blue Lagoon Dr., Miami 33126, 305-262-1800.

Rep. Toby Roth (R), Representative from Wisconsin, District 8

DC Office: 2234 Rayburn House Office Building, Washington, DC 20515, 202-225-5665; Fax: 202-225-0087; e-mail: roth@hr.house.gov.

District Offices: 2301 S. Oneida St., Green Bay 54304, 414-494-2800; and 126 N. Oneida St., Appleton 54911, 414-739-4167.

Sen. William V. Roth, Jr. (R), Senator from Delaware

DC Office: 104 Hart Senate Office Building, Washington, DC 20510, 202-224-2441; Fax: 202-224-0354.

State Offices: 3021 Fed. Bldg., 844 King St., Wilmington 19801, 302-573-6291; 2215 Fed. Bldg., 300 S. New St., Dover 19901, 302-674-3308; and 12 The Circle, Georgetown 19947, 302-856-7690.

Rep. Marge Roukema (R), Representative from New Jersey, District 5

DC Office: 2469 Rayburn House Office Building, Washington, DC 20515, 202-225-4465; Fax: 202-225-9048.

District Offices: 1200 E. Ridgewood Ave., Ridgewood 07450, 201-447-3900; and 1500 Rte. 517, Hackettstown 07840, 908-850-4747.

Rep. Lucille Roybal-Allard (D), Representative from California, District 33

DC Office: 324 Cannon House Office Building, Washington, DC 20515, 202-225-1766.

District Offices: Edward Roybal Fed. Bldg., 255 E. Temple St., Los Angeles 90012, 213-628-9230.

Rep. Edward R. Royce (R), Representative from California, District 39

DC Office: 1133 Longworth House Office Building, Washington, DC 20515, 202-225-4111; Fax: 202-225-0335.

District Offices: 305 N. Harbor Blvd., Fullerton 92632, 714-992-8081.

Rep. Bobby Rush (D), Representative from Illinois, District 1

DC Office: 131 Cannon House Office Building, Washington, DC 20515, 202-225-4372; Fax: 202-226-0333; e-mail: brush@hr.house.gov.

District Offices: 655 E. 79th St., Chicago 60619, 312-224-6500; and 9730 S. Western Ave., Evergreen Park 60643, 708-422-4055.

Rep. Martin Olav Sabo (DFL), Representative from Minnesota, District 5

DC Office: 2336 Rayburn House Office Building, Washington, DC 20515, 202-225-4755.

District Offices: 462 Fed. Courts Bldg., 110 S. 4th St., Minneapolis 55401, 612-348-1649.

Rep. Matt Salmon (R), Representative from Arizona, District 1

DC Office: 115 Cannon House Office Building, Washington, DC 20515, 202-225-2635; Fax: 202-225-3405.

District Offices: 401 W. Baseline Rd., Tempe 85282, 602-831-2900.

Rep. Bernard Sanders (I), Representative from Vermont, District 1

DC Office: 213 Cannon House Office Building, Washington, DC 20515, 202-225-4115; Fax: 202-225-6790; e-mail: bsanders@hr.house.gov

District Offices: 1 Church St., Burlington 05401, 802-862-0697.

Rep. Marshall (Mark) Sanford, Jr. (R), Representative from South Carolina, District 1

DC Office: 1223 Longworth House Office Building, Washington, DC 20515, 202-225-3407; e-mail: sanford@hr.house.gov.

District Offices: 640 Federal Bldg., Charleston 29043, 803-727-4175; 206 Laurel St., Conway 29526, 803-248-2660; 829-E Frost St., Georgetown 29440, 803-527-6868.

Sen. Rick Santorum (R), Senator from Pennsylvania

DC Office: 120 Russell Senate Office Building, Washington, DC 20510, 202-224-6324.

State Offices: 130 Fed. Bldg., Erie 16501, 814-454-7114; 221 Strawberry Sq., Harrisburg 17101, 717-231-7540; 2019 Industrial Dr., Bethlehem 18017, 610-865-1874; 1 S. Penn Sq, Philadelphia 19107, 215-597-9914; 1 Station Sq., Pittsburgh 15219, 412-562-0533, and 527 Linden St., Scranton 18503, 717-344-8799.

Sen. Paul S. Sarbanes (D), Senator from Maryland

DC Office: 309 Hart Senate Office Building, Washington, DC 20510, 202-224-4524; Fax: 202-224-1651: e-mail: senator@sarbanes.senate.gov.

State Offices: 100 S. Charles St., Baltimore 21201, 410-962-4436; 1110 Bonifant St., Silver Spring 20910, 301-589-0797; 111 Baptist St., Salisbury 21801, 410-860-2131; 47 S.E. Crain Hwy., Box 331, Cobb Island 20625, 301-259-2404; and 141 Baltimore St., Cumberland 21502, 301-724-4660.

Rep. Tom Sawyer (D), Representative from Ohio, District 14

DC Office: 1414 Longworth House Office Building, Washington, DC 20515, 202-225-5231; Fax: 202-225-5278.

District Offices: 411 Wolf Ledges Pkwy., Akron 44311, 216-375-5710; and 250 Chestnut St., Ravenna 44266, 216-296-9810.

Rep. H. James Saxton (R), Representative from New Jersey, District 3

DC Office: 339 Cannon House Office Building, Washington, DC 20515, 202-225-4765; Fax: 202-225-0778.

District Offices: 100 High St., Mt. Holly 08060, 609-261-5800; 1 Maine Ave., Cherry Hill 08002, 609-428-0520; and 7 Hadley Ave., Toms River 08753, 908-914-2020.

Rep. Joe Scarborough (R), Representative from Florida, District 1

DC Office: 1523 Longworth House Office Building, Washington, DC 20515, 202-225-4136; Fax: 202-225-3414.

District Offices: 4300 Bayou Blvd., Pensacola 32503, 904-479-1183; and 348 S.W. Miracle Strip Hwy., Ft. Walton Beach 32548, 904-664-1266.

Rep. Dan Schaefer (R), Representative from Colorado, District 6

DC Office: 2353 Rayburn House Office Building, Washington, DC 20515, 202-225-7882; Fax: 202-225-7885; e-mail: schaefer@hr.house.gov.

District Offices: 3615 S. Huron, Englewood 80110, 303-762-8890.

Rep. Steven H. Schiff (R), Representative from New Mexico, District 1

DC Office: 2404 Rayburn House Office Building, Washington, DC 20515, 202-225-6316; Fax: 202-225-4975.

District Offices: 625 Silver Ave. SW, Albuquerque 87102, 505-766-2538.

Rep. Patricia Schroeder (D), Representative from Colorado, District 1
DC Office: 2307 Rayburn House Office Building, Washington, DC 20515,
202-225-4431; Fax: 202-225-5842.
District Offices: 1600 Emerson St., Denver 80218, 303-866-1230.

Rep. Charles E. Schumer (D), Representative from New York, District 9
DC Office: 2211 Rayburn House Office Building, Washington, DC 20515,
202-225-6616; Fax: 202-225-4183.
District Offices: 1628 Kings Hwy., Brooklyn 11229, 718-627-9700.

Rep. Robert C. (Bobby) Scott (D), Representative from Virginia, District 3
DC Office: 501 Cannon House Office Building, Washington, DC 20515,
202-225-8351; Fax: 202-225-8354.
District Offices: 2700 Washington Ave., Newport News 23607, 804-380-1000.

Rep. Andrea Seastrand (R), Representative from California, District 22
DC Office: 320 Cannon House Office Building, Washington, DC 20515,
202-225-3601; Fax: 202-225-3426; e-mail: andrea22@hr.house.gov.
District Offices: 1525 State St., Santa Barbara 93101, 805-899-3578; and
778 Osos St., San Luis Obispo 93401, 805-541-0170.

Rep. F. James Sensenbrenner, Jr. (R), Representative from Wisconsin, District 9
DC Office: 2332 Rayburn House Office Building, Washington, DC 20515,
202-225-5101; Fax: 202-225-3190.
District Offices: 120 Bishops Way, Brookfield 53005, 414-784-1111.

Rep. Jose E. Serrano (D), Representative from New York, District 16
DC Office: 2342 Rayburn House Office Building, Washington, DC 20515,
202-225-4361; Fax: 202-225-6001; e-mail: jserrano@hr.house.gov.
District Offices: 890 Grand Concourse, Bronx 10451, 718-538-5400.

Rep. John Shadegg (R), Representative from Arizona, District 4
DC Office: 503 Cannon House Office Building, Washington, DC 20515,
202-225-3361; Fax: 202-225-3462.
District Offices: 1158 E. Missouri Ave., Phoenix 85014, 602-248-7779.

Rep. E. Clay Shaw, Jr. (R), Representative from Florida, District 22
DC Office: 2267 Rayburn House Office Building, Washington, DC 20515,
202-225-3026; Fax: 202-225-8398.
District Offices: 1512 E. Broward Blvd., Ft. Lauderdale 33301, 305-522-1800.

Rep. Christopher Shays (R), Representative from Connecticut, District 4
DC Office: 1502 Longworth House Office Building, Washington, DC 20515,
202-225-5541; Fax: 202-225-9629; e-mail: cshays@hr.house.gov.
District Offices: 10 Middle St., Bridgeport 06604, 203-579-5870;
888 Washington Blvd., Stamford 06901, 203-357-8277.

Sen. Richard C. Shelby (R), Senator from Alabama

DC Office: 110 Hart Senate Office Building, Washington, DC 20510, 202-224-5744; Fax: 202-224-3416.

State Offices: 113 St. Joseph St., 438 U.S. Crthse., Mobile 36602, 334-694-4164; 1000 Glenn Hearn Blvd., Huntsville 35824, 205-772-0460; 1800 5th Ave., N., 321 Fed. Bldg., Birmingham 35203, 205-731-1384; 15 Lee St., 828 U.S. Crthse., Montgomery 36104, 334-223-7303; and 118 Greensboro Ave., Tuscaloosa 35401, 205-759-5047.

Rep. E. G. (Bud) Shuster (R), Representative from Pennsylvania, District 9

DC Office: 2188 Rayburn House Office Building, Washington, DC 20515, 202-225-2431.

District Offices: RD 2, Box 711, Altoona 16601, 814-946-1653; and 179 E. Queen St., Chambersburg 17201, 717-264-8308; 1214 Oldtown Rd., Clearfield 16830, 814-765-9106.

Sen. Paul Simon (D), Senator from Illinois

DC Office: 462 Dirksen Senate Office Building, Washington, DC 20510, 202-224-2152; Fax: 202-224-0868; e-mail: senator@simon.senate.gov.

State Offices: Kluczynski Bldg., 230 S. Dearborn, Chicago 60604, 312-353-4952; 3 W. Old Capital Plz., Springfield 62701, 217-492-4960; and 250 W. Cherry, Carbondale 62901, 618-457-3653.

Sen. Alan K. Simpson (R), Senator from Wyoming

DC Office: 105 Dirksen Senate Office Building, Washington, DC 20510, 202-224-3424; Fax: 202-224-1315; e-mail: senator@simpson.senate.gov.

State Offices: P.O. Box 430, Cody 82414, 307-527-7121; Fed. Ctr., Casper 82601, 307-261-5172; Fed. Ctr., Cheyenne 82001, 307-772-2477; 2201 S. Douglas Hwy., P.O. Box 3155, Gillette 82716, 307-682-7091; 2020 Grand Ave., Laramie 82070, 307-745-5303; 2515 Foothills Blvd., Rock Springs 82901, 307-382-5097; and 1731 Sheridan Ave., Cody 82414, 307-527-7121.

Rep. Norman Sisisky (D), Representative from Virginia, District 4

DC Office: 2371 Rayburn House Office Building, Washington, DC 20515, 202-225-6365; Fax: 202-226-1170.

District Offices: Emporia Exec. Ctr., 425-H S. Main St., Emporia 23847, 804-634-5575; 43 Rives Rd., Petersburg 23805, 804-732-2544; and 309 County St., Portsmouth 23704, 804-393-2068.

Rep. David E. Skaggs (D), Representative from Colorado, District 2

DC Office: 1124 Longworth House Office Building, Washington, DC 20515, 202-225-2161; Fax: 202-225-7840; e-mail: skaggs@hr.house.gov.

District Offices: 9101 Harlan, Westminster 80030, 303-650-7886.

Rep. Joe Skeen (R), Representative from New Mexico, District 2

DC Office: 2367 Rayburn House Office Building, Washington, DC 20515, 202-225-2365; Fax: 202-225-9599.

District Offices: 1065 S. Main St., Las Cruces 88005, 505-527-1771; and
257 Fed. Bldg., Roswell 88201, 505-622-0055.

Rep. Ike Skelton (D), Representative from Missouri, District 4

DC Office: 2227 Rayburn House Office Building, Washington, DC 20515,
202-225-2876.

District Offices: 1616 Industrial Dr., Jefferson City 65109, 314-635-3499;
514-B N.W. 7 Hwy., Blue Springs 64014, 816-228-4242; 319 S. Lamine, Sedalia
65301, and 219 N. Adams St., Lebanon 65536, 417-532-7964.

Rep. Louise M. Slaughter (D), Representative from New York, District 28

DC Office: 2347 Rayburn House Office Building, Washington, DC 20515,
202-225-3615; Fax: 202-225-7822.

District Offices: 3120 Fed. Bldg., 100 State St., Rochester 14614, 716-232-4850.

Rep. Linda Smith (R), Representative from Washington, District 3

DC Office: 1217 Longworth House Office Building, Washington, DC 20515,
202-225-3536; Fax: 202-225-3478; e-mail: asklinda@hr.house.gov.

District Office : 1220 Main St., Vancouver 98660, 360-695-6292; and
719 Sleater-Kinney Rd., Lacey 98503, 360-923-9393.

Rep. Nick Smith (R), Representative from Michigan, District 7

DC Office: 1530 Longworth House Office Building, Washington, DC 20515,
202-225-6276; Fax: 202-225-6281; e-mail: mi107.smith@hr.house.gov.

District Offices: 121 S. Cochran Ave., Charlotte 48813, 517-543-0055; 209 E.
Washington St., Jackson 49201, 517-783-4486; 4192 W. Maple St., Adrian 49221,
517-263-5012; and 81 S. 20th St., Battle Creek 29015, 616-965-9066.

Rep. Christopher H. Smith (R), Representative from New Jersey, District 4

DC Office: 2370 Rayburn House Office Building, Washington, DC 20515,
202-225-3765; Fax: 202-225-7768.

District Offices: 1720 Greenwood, Trenton 08609, 609-890-2800; 427 High St.,
Burlington City 08016, 609-386-5534; and 100 Lacey Rd., Whiting 08759,
908-350-2300.

Sen. Bob Smith (R), Senator from New Hampshire

DC Office: 332 Dirksen Senate Office Building, Washington, DC 20510,
202-224-2841; Fax: 202-224-1353; e-mail: opinion@smith.senate.gov.

State Offices: 50 Phillippe Cote St., Manchester 03101, 603-634-5000; 46 S. Main St.,
Concord 03301, 603-228-0453; and 1 Harbour Pl., Portsmouth 03801, 603-433-1667.

Rep. Lamar S. Smith (R), Representative from Texas, District 21

DC Office: 2443 Rayburn House Office Building, Washington, DC 20515,
202-225-4236; Fax: 202-225-8628.

District Offices: 1st Federal Bldg., 1100 NE Loop 410, San Antonio 78209,
210-821-5024; 201 W. Wall St., Midland 79701, 915-687-5232; 1006 Junction Hwy.,
Kerrville 78028, 512-895-1414; 221 E. Main, Round Rock 78664, 512-218-4221; and
33 E. Twohig, San Angelo 76903, 915-653-3971.

Sen. Olympia J. Snowe (R), Senator from Maine
DC Office: 495 Russell Senate Office Building, Washington, DC 20510,
202-224-5344; Fax: 202-224-1946.
State Offices: 2 Great Falls Plz., Auburn 04210, 207-786-2451; 68 Sewall St.,
Augusta 04330, 207-622-8292; 1 Cumberland Pl., Bangor 04401, 207-945-0432;
231 Main St., Biddeford 04005, 207-282-4144; 3 Canal Plz., Portland 04112,
207-874-0833; and 169 Academy St., Presque Isle 04769, 207-764-5124.

Rep. Gerald B. H. Solomon (R), Representative from New York, District 22
DC Office: 2206 Rayburn House Office Building, Washington, DC 20515,
202-225-5614; Fax: 202-225-6234.
District Offices: Gaslight Sq., Saratoga Springs 12866, 518-587-9800;
337 Fairview Ave., Hudson 12534, 518-828-0181; and 21 Bay St.,
Glens Falls 12801, 518-792-3031.

Rep. Mark Edward Souder (R), Representative from Indiana, District 4
DC Office: 508 Cannon House Office Building, Washington, DC 20515,
202-225-4436; Fax: 202-225-3479; e-mail: souder@hr.house.gov.
District Offices: 1300 S. Harrison St., Ft. Wayne 46802, 219-424-3041.

Sen. Arlen Specter (R), Senator from Pennsylvania
DC Office: 530 Hart Senate Office Building, Washington, DC 20510, 202-224-4254;
e-mail: senator_specter@specter.senate.gov.
State Offices: 600 Arch Street, Philadelphia 19106, 215-597-7200; Fed. Bldg.,
Liberty Ave. & Grant St., Pittsburgh 15222, 412-644-3400; 1159 Fed. Bldg.,
6th & State Sts., Erie 16501, 814-453-3010; 1159 Fed. Bldg, Harrisburg 17101,
717-782-3951; Park Plaza, Scranton 18503, 717-346-2006; and P.O. Bldg.,
5th & Hamilton Sts., Allentown 18101, 610-434-1444.

Rep. Floyd D. Spence (R), Representative from South Carolina, District 2
DC Office: 2405 Rayburn House Office Building, Washington, DC 20515,
202-225-2452; Fax: 202-225-2455.
District Offices: 220 Stoneridge Dr., Columbia 29210, 803-254-5120; 1681 Chestnut
St., P.O. Box 1609, NE Orangeburg 29115, 803-536-4641; 66 E. Railroad Ave., P.O.
Box 550, Estill 29918, 803-625-3177; 807 Port Republic St., P.O. Box 1538, Beaufort
29901, 803-521-2530; 1 Town Center Ct., Hilton Head Island 29928, 803-842-7212.

Rep. John M. Spratt, Jr. (D), Representative from South Carolina, District 5
DC Office: 1536 Longworth House Office Building, Washington, DC 20515,
202-225-5501; Fax: 202-225-0464; e-mail: spratt@hr.house.gov.
District Offices: 305 Fed. Bldg., Rock Hill 29731, 803-327-1114; 39 E. Calhoun St.,
Sumter 29150, 803-773-3362; and 88 Public Sq., Darlington 29532, 803-393-3998.

Rep. Fortney H. (Pete) Stark (D), Representative from California, District 13
DC Office: 239 Cannon House Office Building, Washington, DC 20515,
202-225-5065; e-mail: petemail@hr.house.gov.
District Offices: 22320 Foothill Blvd., Hayward 94541, 510-247-1388.

Rep. Clifford B. Stearns (R), Representative from Florida, District 6

DC Office: 2352 Rayburn House Office Building, Washington, DC 20515, 202-225-5744; Fax: 202-225-3973; e-mail: cstearns@hr.house.gov.

District Offices: 115 S.E. 25th Ave., Ocala 34471, 904-351-8777; 1726 Kingsley Ave., Orange Park 32073, 904-269-3203; and 111 S. 6th St., Leesburg 34748, 904-326-8285.

Rep. Charles W. Stenholm (D), Representative from Texas, District 17

DC Office: 1211 Longworth House Office Building, Washington, DC 20515, 202-225-6605; Fax: 202-225-2234.

District Offices: 903 E. Hamilton St., Stamford 79553, 915-773-3623; 341 Pine St., Abilene 79604, 915-673-7221; and 33 E. Twohig Ave., San Angelo 76903, 915-655-7994.

Sen. Ted Stevens (R), Senator from Alaska

DC Office: 522 Hart Senate Office Building, Washington, DC 20510, 202-224-3004; Fax: 202-224-2354.

State Offices: Fed. Bldg., Box 4, 101 12th Ave., Fairbanks 99701, 907-456-0261; 222 W. 7th Ave., Anchorage 99513, 907-271-5915; Fed. Bldg., Box 020149, Juneau 99802, 907-586-7400; 120 Trading Bay Rd., Kenai 99611, 907-283-5808; and 109 Main St., Ketchikan 99901, 907-225-6880.

Rep. Steve Stockman (R), Representative from Texas, District 9

DC Office: 417 Cannon House Office Building, Washington, DC 20515, 202-225-6565; Fax: 202-225-1584.

District Offices: 2490 McFadin, Beaumont 77702, 409-838-0061; and 2102 Mechanic, Galveston 77550, 409-766-3608.

Rep. Louis Stokes (D), Representative from Ohio, District 11

DC Office: 2365 Rayburn House Office Building, Washington, DC 20515, 202-225-7032; Fax: 202-225-1339.

District Offices: 3645 Warrensville Ctr. Rd., Shaker Heights 44122, 216-522-4900.

Rep. Gerry E. Studds (D), Representative from Massachusetts, District 10

DC Office: 237 Cannon House Office Building, Washington, DC 20515, 202-225-3111; Fax: 202-225-2212.

District Offices: 1212 Hancock St., Quincy 02169, 617-770-3700; 146 Main St., Hyannis 02601, 508-771-0666; 166 Main St., Fed. Bldg., Brockton 02401, 508-584-6666; and 225 Water St., Plymouth 02360, 508-747-5500.

Rep. Bob Stump (R), Representative from Arizona, District 3

DC Office: 211 Cannon House Office Building, Washington, DC 20515, 202-225-4576; Fax: 202-225-6328.

District Offices: 230 N. First Ave., Phoenix 85025, 602-379-6923.

Rep. Bart Stupak (D), Representative from Michigan, District 1

DC Office: 317 Cannon House Office Building, Washington, DC 20515, 202-225-4735; Fax: 202-225-4744.

District Offices: 1120 E. Front St., Traverse City 49686, 616-929-4711;
111 E. Chisholm St., Alpena 49707, 517-356-0690; 1229 W. Washington St.,
Marquette 49855, 906-228-3700; 2501 14th Ave., Escanaba 49829, 906-786-4504;
and 616 Sheldon Ave., Houghton 49931, 906-482-1371.

Rep. Jim Talent (R), Representative from Missouri, District 2

DC Office: 1022 Longworth House Office Building, Washington, DC 20515,
202-225-2561; Fax: 202-225-2563; e-mail: talentmo@hr.house.gov.

District Offices: 555 N. New Balas, St. Louis 63141, 314-872-9561; and
820 S. Main St., St. Charles 63301, 314-949-6826.

Rep. John Tanner (D), Representative from Tennessee, District 8

DC Office: 1127 Longworth House Office Building, Washington, DC 20515,
202-225-4714; Fax: 202-225-1765.

District Offices: 203 W. Church St., Union City 38261, 901-885-7070; Fed. Bldg.,
Jackson 38301, 901-423-4848; and 2836 Coleman Rd., Memphis 38128,
901-382-3220.

Rep. Randy Tate (R), Representative from Washington, District 9

DC Office: 1118 Longworth House Office Building, Washington, DC 20515,
202-225-8901; Fax: 202-225-3484; e-mail: rtate@hr.house.gov.

District Offices: 33305 1st Way, S., Federal Way 98003, 206-661-1459; and
10925 Canyon Rd., Puyallup 98373, 206-539-1322.

Rep. W. J. (Billy) Tauzin (R), Representative from Louisiana, District 3

DC Office: 2183 Rayburn House Office Building, Washington, DC 20515,
202-225-4031; Fax: 202-225-0563.

District Offices: 1041 Hale Boggs Bldg., 501 Magazine St., New Orleans 70130,
504-589-6366; 107 Fed. Bldg., Houma 700360, 504-876-3033; 210 E. Main St., New
Iberia 70560, 318-367-8231; and 828 S. Irma Blvd., Gonzales 70737, 504-621-8490.

Rep. Gene Taylor (D), Representative from Mississippi, District 5

DC Office: 2447 Rayburn House Office Building, Washington, DC 20515,
202-225-5772; Fax: 202-225-7074.

District Offices: 2424 14th St., Gulfport 39501, 601-864-7670; 701 Main St.,
Hattiesburg 39401, 601-582-3246; and 706 Watts Ave., Pascagoula 39567,
601-762-1770.

Rep. Charles H. Taylor (R), Representative from North Carolina, District 11

DC Office: 231 Cannon House Office Building, Washington, DC 20515,
202-225-6401; Fax: 202-225-0519; e-mail: chtaylor@hr.house.gov.

District Offices: 22 S. Pack Sq., Asheville 28801, 704-251-1988; Cherokee Cnty.
Cthse., 201 Peachtree St., Murphy 28906, 704-837-3249; and 200 S. Lafayette St.,
Shelby 28150, 704-484-6971.

Rep. Frank M. Tejeda (D), Representative from Texas, District 28

DC Office: 323 Cannon House Office Building, Washington, DC 20515,
202-225-1640; Fax: 202-225-1641.

District Offices: 1313 SE Military Dr., San Antonio 78214, 210-924-7383; and
202 E. St. Joseph St., San Diego 78384, 512-279-3907.

Sen. Craig Thomas (R), Senator from Wyoming

DC Office: 302 Hart Senate Office Building, Washington, DC 20510, 202-224-6441;
Fax: 202-224-1724.

State Offices:2201 Fed. Bldg., Casper 82601, 307-261-5413; 2120 Capitol Ave.,
Cheyenne 82009, 307-772-2451; 2632 Foothills Blvd., Rock Springs 82901,
307-362-5012; and 325 W. Main St., Riverton 82501, 307-856-6642.

Rep. William M. Thomas (R), Representative from California, District 21

DC Office: 2208 Rayburn House Office Building, Washington, DC 20515,
202-225-2915; Fax: 202-225-2908.

District Offices: 4100 Truxtun Ave., Bakersfield 93309, 805-327-3611; and
319 W. Murray St., Visalia 93291, 209-627-6549.

Rep. Bennie G. Thompson (D), Representative from Mississippi, District 2

DC Office: 1408 Longworth House Office Building, Washington, DC 20515,
202-225-5876; Fax: 202-225-5898; e-mail: ms2nd@hr.house.gov.

District Offices: 137 Madison St., Bolton 39041, 601-859-5555.

Sen. Fred Thompson (R), Senator from Tennessee

DC Office: 523 Dirksen Senate Office Building, Washington, DC 20510,
202-224-4944; Fax: 202-228-3679.

State Office: 3322 West End Ave., Nashville 37230, 615-736-5129; 403 Fed. Bldg.,
167 N. Main St., Memphis 38103, 901-544-4224; 315 Post Office Bldg.,
501 Main St., Knoxville 37902, 615-545-4253; B-9 Fed. Bldg., 109 S. Highland St.,
Jackson 38301, 901-423-9344.

Rep. Mac Thornberry (R), Representative from Texas, District 13

DC Office: 1535 Longworth House Office Building, Washington, DC 20515,
202-225-3706; Fax: 202-225-3486.

District Offices: 724 S. Polk St., Amarillo 79101, 806-371-8844; and 811 6th St.,
Wichita Falls 76301, 817-767-0541.

Rep. Ray Thornton (D), Representative from Arkansas, District 2

DC Office: 1214 Longworth House Office Building, Washington, DC 20515,
202-225-2506; Fax: 202-225-9273.

District Offices: 1527 Fed. Bldg., 700 W. Capitol, Little Rock 72201, 501-324-5941.

Rep. Karen L. Thurman (D), Representative from Florida, District 5

DC Office: 130 Cannon House Office Building, Washington, DC 20515,
202-225-1002; Fax: 202-226-0329; e-mail: kthuman@hr.house.gov.

District Offices: 2224 Hwy. 44 W., Inverness 34453, 904-344-3044; 5700 SW 34th St.,
Gainesville 32608, 904-336-6614; and 5623 Rte. 19 S., New Port Richey 34652,
813-849-4496.

Sen. Strom Thurmond (R), Senator from South Carolina

DC Office: 217 Russell Senate Office Building, Washington, DC 20510, 202-224-5972; Fax: 202-224-1300.

State Offices: 1835 Assembly St., Columbia 29201, 803-765-5494; 334 Meeting St., Charleston 29493, 803-724-4282; 211 York St. NE, Aiken 29801, 803-649-2591; and 401 W. Evans St., Florence 29501, 803-662-8873.

Rep. Todd Tiahrt (R), Representative from Kansas, District 4

DC Office: 1319 Longworth House Office Building, Washington, DC 20515, 202-225-6216; Fax: 202-225-3489.

District Offices: 155 N. Market, Wichita 67202, 316-262-8992; and 325 N. Penn, Independence 67301, 316-331-8056.

Rep. Peter G. Torkildsen (R), Representative from Massachusetts, District 6

DC Office: 120 Cannon House Office Building, Washington, DC 20515, 202-225-8020; Fax: 202-225-8037; e-mail: torkma06@hr.house.gov.

District Offices: 70 Washington St., Salem 01970, 508-741-1600; 156 Broad St., Lynn 01901, 617-599-2424; 160 Main St., Haverhill 01830, 508-521-0111; and 61 Center St., Burlington 01803, 617-273-4900.

Rep. Esteban E. Torres (D), Representative from California, District 34

DC Office: 2368 Rayburn House Office Building, Washington, DC 20515, 202-225-5256; Fax: 202-225-9711.

District Offices: 8819 Whittier Blvd., Pico Rivera 90660, 310-695-0702.

Rep. Robert G. Torricelli (D), Representative from New Jersey, District 9

DC Office: 1026 Rayburn House Office Building, Washington, DC 20515, 202-225-5061; Fax: 202-225-0845.

District Offices: 25 Main St., Court Plz., Hackensack 07601, 201-646-1111.

Rep. Edolphus Towns (D), Representative from New York, District 10

DC Office: 2232 Rayburn House Office Building, Washington, DC 20515, 202-225-5936; Fax: 202-225-1018.

District Offices: 545 Broadway, Brooklyn 11206, 718-387-8696.

Rep. James A. Traficant, Jr. (D), Representative from Ohio, District 17

DC Office: 2446 Rayburn House Office Building, Washington, DC 20515, 202-225-5261; Fax: 202-225-3719.

District Offices: 125 Market St., Youngstown 44503, 216-743-1914; 5555 Youngstown-Warren Rd., Niles 44406, 216-652-5649; and 109 W. 3d St., E. Liverpool 43920, 216-385-5921.

Rep. Walter R. Tucker, III (D), Representative from California, District 37

DC Office: 419 Cannon House Office Building, Washington, DC 20515, 202-225-7924; Fax: 202-225-7926; e-mail: tucker96@hr.house.gov.

District Offices: 145 E. Compton Blvd., Compton 90220, 310-884-9989.

Rep. Fred Upton (R), Representative from Michigan, District 6
DC Office: 2333 Rayburn House Office Building, Washington, DC 20515,
202-225-3761; Fax: 202-225-4986.
District Offices: 421 Main St., St. Joseph 49085, 616-982-1986; and 535 S. Burdick
St., Kalamazoo 49007, 616-385-0039.

Rep. Nydia M. Velazquez (D), Representative from New York, District 12
DC Office: 132 Cannon House Office Building, Washington, DC 20515,
202-225-2361; Fax: 202-226-0327.
District Offices: 815 Broadway, Brooklyn 11906, 718 500 3660.

Rep. Bruce F. Vento (DFL), Representative from Minnesota, District 4
DC Office: 2304 Rayburn House Office Building, Washington, DC 20515,
202-225-6631; Fax: 202-225-1968; e-mail: vento@hr.house.gov.
District Offices: 175 5th St. E., Box 100, St. Paul 55101, 612-224-4503.

Rep. Peter J. Visclosky (D), Representative from Indiana, District 1
DC Office: 2464 Rayburn House Office Building, Washington, DC 20515,
202-225-2461; Fax: 202-225-2493.
District Offices: 215 W. 35th Ave., Gary 46408, 219-884-1177; City Hall,
6070 Central Ave., Portage 46368, 219-763-2904; and City Hall,
166 Lincolnway, Valparaiso 46383, 219-464-0315.

Rep. Harold L. Volkmer (D), Representative from Missouri, District 9
DC Office: 2409 Rayburn House Office Building, Washington, DC 20515,
202-225-2956; Fax: 202-225-7834.
District Offices: 370 Fed. Bldg., Hannibal 63401, 314-221-1200.

Rep. Barbara F. Vucanovich (R), Representative from Nevada, District 2
DC Office: 2202 Rayburn House Office Building, Washington, DC 20515,
202-225-6155; Fax: 202-225-2319.
District Offices: 300 Booth St., Reno 89509, 702-784-5003; 700 Idaho St., Elko
89801, 702-738-4064; and 6900 Westcliff St., Las Vegas 89128, 702-255-6470.

Rep. Enid G. Waldholtz (R), Representative from Utah, District 2
DC Office: 515 Cannon House Office Building, Washington, DC 20515,
202-225-3011; Fax: 202-225-3491; e-mail: enidutah@hr.house.gov.
District Offices: 125 S. State St., Salt Lake City 84138, 801-524-4394.

Rep. Robert S. Walker (R), Representative from Pennsylvania, District 16
DC Office: 2369 Rayburn House Office Building, Washington, DC 20515,
202-225-2411; Fax: 202-225-1116; e-mail: pa16@hr.house.gov.
District Offices: Lancaster Cnty. Crthse., 50 N. Duke St., Lancaster 17603,
717-393-0666; Exton Commons, Exton 19341, 215-363-8409.

Rep. James T. Walsh (R), Representative from New York, District 25
DC Office: 1330 Longworth House Office Building, Washington, DC 20515,
202-225-3701; Fax: 202-225-4042.

District Offices: P.O. Box 7306, Syracuse 13261, 315-423-5657; and 1 Lincoln St., Auburn 13021, 315-255-0649.

Rep. Zach Wamp (R), Representative from Tennessee, District 3
DC Office: 423 Cannon House Office Building, Washington, DC 20515, 202-225-3271; Fax: 202-225-3494.
District Offices: 6100 Eastgate Ctr., Chattanooga 37411, 615-894-7400; and 55 Jefferson Cir., Oak Ridge 37830, 615-483-3366.

Rep. Mike Ward (D), Representative from Kentucky, District 3
DC Office: 1032 Longworth House Office Building, Washington, DC 20515, 202-225-5401; Fax: 202-225-3511; e-mail: mward2@hr.house.gov.
District Offices: 216 Fed. Bldg., 600 M.L.K. Jr. Pl., Louisville 40202, 502-582-5129.

Sen. John W. Warner (R), Senator from Virginia
DC Office: 225 Russell Senate Office Building, Washington, DC 20510, 202-224-2023; Fax: 202-224-6295; e-mail: senator@warner.senate.gov.
State Offices: 600 E. Main St., Richmond 23219, 804-771-2579; 4900 World Trade Ctr., Norfolk 23510, 804-441-3079; 235 Fed. Bldg., 180 W. Main St., Abingdon 24210, 703-628-8158; and 1003 First Union Bank Bldg., 213 S. Jefferson St., Roanoke 24011, 703-857-2676.

Rep. Maxine Waters (D), Representative from California, District 35
DC Office: 330 Cannon House Office Building, Washington, DC 20515, 202-225-2201; Fax: 202-225-7854.
District Offices: 10124 S. Broadway, Los Angeles 90003, 213-757-8900.

Rep. Melvin L. Watt (D), Representative from North Carolina, District 12
DC Office: 1230 Longworth House Office Building, Washington, DC 20515, 202-225-1510; Fax: 202-225-1512; e-mail: melmail@hr.house.gov.
District Offices: 214 N. Church St., Charlotte 28202, 704-344-9950; 315 E. Chapel Hill, Durham 27702, 919-688-3004; 301 S. Greene St., Greensboro 27401, 919-375-9402.

Rep. J. C. Watts, Jr. (R), Representative from Oklahoma, District 4
DC Office: 1713 Longworth House Office Building, Washington, DC 20515, 202-225-6165; Fax: 202-225-3512.
District Offices: 2420 Springer Dr., Norman 73069, 405-329-6500; and 601 S.W. D Ave., Lawton 73501, 405-357-2131.

Rep. Henry A. Waxman (D), Representative from California, District 29
DC Office: 2408 Rayburn House Office Building, Washington, DC 20515, 202-225-3976; Fax: 202-225-4099.
District Offices: 8425 W. 3d St., Los Angeles 90048, 213-651-1040.

Rep. David J. Weldon (R), Representative from Florida, District 15
DC Office: 216 Cannon House Office Building, Washington, DC 20515, 202-225-3671; Fax: 202-225-3516; e-mail: fla15@hr.house.gov.

District Offices: 2725 St. John St., P.O. Box 410007, Melbourne 32941, 407-632-1776.

Rep. Curt Weldon (R), Representative from Pennsylvania, District 7

DC Office: 2452 Rayburn House Office Building, Washington, DC 20515, 202-225-2011; Fax: 202-225-8137; e-mail: curtpa7@hr.house.gov.

District Offices: 1554 Garrett Rd., Upper Darby 19082, 610-259-0700.

Rep. Jerry Weller (R), Representative from Illinois, District 11

DC Office: 1710 Longworth House Office Building, Washington, DC 20515, 202-225-3635.

District Offices: 51 W. Jackson St., Joliet 60432, 815-740-2028; 3331 Chicago Rd., Steger 60475, 708-754-7552; and 628 Columbus St., Ottawa 61350, 815-433-0085.

Sen. Paul D. Wellstone (DFL), Senator from Minnesota

DC Office: 717 Hart Senate Office Building, Washington, DC 20510, 202-224-5641; Fax: 202-224-8438; e-mail: senator@wellstone.senate.gov.

State Offices: 2550 University Ave., St. Paul 55114, 612-645-0323; 105 2nd Ave., S., Virginia 55792, 218-741-1074; and 417 Litchfield Ave., SW, Wilmar 56201, 612-231-0001.

Rep. Rick White (R), Representative from Washington, District 1

DC Office: 116 Cannon House Office Building, Washington, DC 20515, 202-225-6311; Fax: 202-225-3524; e-mail: repwhite@hr.house.gov.

District Offices: 21905 64th Ave., Mountlake Terrace 98043, 206-640-0233.

Rep. Edward Whitfield (R), Representative from Kentucky, District 1

DC Office: 1541 Longworth House Office Building, Washington, DC 20515, 202-225-3115; Fax: 202-225-3547; e-mail: edky01@hr.house.gov.

District Offices: 317 W. 9th St., Hopkinsville 42204, 502-885-0879; P.O. Box 717, Monroe Cnty. Courthouse, Tompkinsville 42617, 502-487-9509; 222 First St., Henderson 42420, 502-826-4180; and 100 Fountain Ave., Paducah 42001, 502-442-6901.

Rep. Roger F. Wicker (R), Representative from Mississippi, District 1

DC Office: 206 Cannon House Office Building, Washington, DC 20515, 202-225-4306; Fax: 202-225-3549; e-mail: rwicker@hr.house.gov.

District Offices: 500 W. Main St., Tupelo 38802, 601-844-5437;and 8625 Hwy. 51-N, Southaven 38671, 601-342-3942.

Rep. Pat Williams (D), Representative from Montana, District 1

DC Office: 2329 Rayburn House Office Building, Washington, DC 20515, 202-225-3211.

District Offices: 316 N. Park Ave., P.O. Box 1681, Helena 59624, 406-443-7878; 305 W. Mercury, Butte 59701, 406-723-4404; 302 W. Broadway, Missoula 59802, 406-549-5550; 2806 3rd Ave. N., Billings 59101, 406-256-1019; and 325 2nd Ave. N., Great Falls 59401, 406-771-1242.

Rep. Charles Wilson (D), Representative from Texas, District 2

DC Office: 2256 Rayburn House Office Building, Washington, DC 20515, 202-225-2401; Fax: 202-225-1764; e-mail: cwilson@hr.house.gov.

District Offices: 701 N. 1st St., Lufkin 75901, 409-637-1770.

Rep. Robert E. (Bob) Wise, Jr. (D), Representative from West Virginia, District 2

DC Office: 2434 Rayburn House Office Building, Washington, DC 20515, 202-225-2711; Fax: 202-225-7856.

District Offices: Elk Office Ctr., 4710 Chimney Dr., Charleston 25302, 304-342-7170; and 222 W. John St., Martinsburg 25401, 304-264-8810.

Rep. Frank R. Wolf (R), Representative from Virginia, District 10

DC Office: 241 Cannon House Office Building, Washington, DC 20515, 202-225-5136; Fax: 202-225-0437.

District Offices: 13873 Park Center Rd., Herndon 22075, 703-709-5800; and 110 N. Cameron St., Winchester 22601, 703-667-0990.

Rep. Lynn Woolsey (D), Representative from California, District 6

DC Office: 439 Cannon House Office Building, Washington, DC 20515, 202-225-5161; e-mail: woolsey@hr.house.gov.

District Offices: 1101 College Ave., Santa Rosa 95404, 707-542-7182; and 1050 Northgate Dr., San Rafael 94903, 415-507-9554.

Rep. Ron Wyden (D), Representative from Oregon, District 3

DC Office: 1111 Longworth House Office Building, Washington, DC 20515, 202-225-4811; Fax: 202-225-8941.

District Offices: 500 NE Multnomah, Portland 97232, 503-231-2300.

Rep. Albert R. Wynn (D), Representative from Maryland, District 4

DC Office: 418 Cannon House Office Building, Washington, DC 20515, 202-225-8699; Fax: 202-225-8714.

District Offices: 9200 Basil Ct., Landover 20785, 301-773-4094; 6009 Oxon Hill Rd., Oxon Hill 20745, 301-839-5570; and 8061 Georgia Ave., Silver Spring 20910, 301-558-7328.

Rep. Sidney R. Yates (D), Representative from Illinois, District 9

DC Office: 2109 Rayburn House Office Building, Washington, DC 20515, 202-225-2111; Fax: 202-225-3493.

District Offices: 230 S. Dearborn St., Chicago 60604, 312-353-4596; and 2100 Ridge Ave., Evanston, 60204, 708-328-2610.

Rep. Don Young (R), Representative from Alaska, District 1

DC Office: 2331 Rayburn House Office Building, Washington, DC 20515, 202-225-5765; Fax: 202-225-0425.

District Offices: 222 W. 7th Ave., Anchorage 99513, 907-271-5978; 401 Fed. Bldg., Box 1247, Juneau 99802, 907-586-7400; Fed. Bldg., Box 10, 101 12th Ave., Fairbanks 99701, 907-456-0210; and 109 Main St., Ketchikan 99901, 907-225-6880.

Rep. C. W. (Bill) Young (R), Representative from Florida, District 10

DC Office: 2407 Rayburn House Office Building, Washington, DC 20515, 202-225-5961; Fax: 202-225-9764.

District Offices: 627 Fed. Bldg., St. Petersburg 33701, 813-893-3191.

Rep. William H. Zeliff, Jr. (R), Representative from New Hampshire, District 1

DC Office: 1210 Longworth House Office Building, Washington, DC 20515, 202-225-5456; Fax: 202-225-4370; e-mail: zeliff@hr.house.gov.

District Offices: 340 Commercial St., Manchester 03101, 603-669-6330; and 601 Spaulding Tnpk., Portsmouth 03801, 603-433-1601.

Rep. Dick Zimmer (R), Representative from New Jersey, District 12

DC Office: 228 Cannon House Office Building, Washington, DC 20515, 202-225-5801; Fax: 202-225-9181; e-mail: dzimmer@hr.house.gov.

District Offices: 133 Franklin Corner Rd., Lawrenceville 08648, 609-895-1559; and 36 W. Main St., Freehold 07728, 908-303-9020.

From: "Almanac of American Politics, 1996"

Copyright (c) 1995, National Journal, Inc.

INDEX